A Quick Guide To

Meeting the Teachers' Standards

Part 1

This is a quick and handy guide to evidencing and meeting Part 1 of the Teachers' Standards. It includes:

✓ a general introduction to the Standards and how to meet them;

✓ an explanation of each strand of the Standards in easy-to-follow English;

✓ guidance on the best evidence to select and how to present it;

✓ guidance on some common evidence pitfalls;

✓ space to record your evidence as you go along.

To order, or for details of our bulk discounts, please go to our website www.criticalpublishing.com or contact our distributor, NBN International, 10 Thornbury Road, Plymouth PL6 7PP, telephone 01752 202301 or email orders@nbninternational.com.

A Quick Guide to

Meeting the Teachers' Standards

Part 1

Mike Lansdown

First published in 2018 by Critical Publishing Ltd

British Library Cataloguing in Publication Data
A CIP record for this book is available from the British Library

ISBN: 978-1-912508-52-5

Cover and table design by Out of House Limited
Text design by Greensplash
Project Management by Out of House Publishing Solutions
Printed and bound in Great Britain by 4edge, Essex

Critical Publishing
3 Connaught Road
St Albans
AL3 5RX

www.criticalpublishing.com

Paper from responsible sources

CONTENTS

About the author

Mike Lansdown is a PGCE tutor and a supervisor for the MA in education with the University of Buckingham's education department, a position he has held since retiring from his second headship in 2015. Prior to completing 18 years as a headteacher, he worked in London teaching in both the primary and secondary sectors. Before this, he taught English as a foreign language (EFL) in London and in Sweden, but started life as a teacher of geography, geology and PE in Newport, Gwent. He enjoys watching rugby, painting and writing. He has previously published a text on learning and teaching called *In the Zone*, and has self-published a historical novel, *Adam's Lock*.

Thanks and acknowledgements

I would like to thank and acknowledge the help of a number of people. First, all the trainees and mentors I have worked with as a tutor with the University of Buckingham over the past three years, especially in 2017–18 when the idea for this guide first emerged. I would also like to thank my colleagues at the university for their guidance and support, as well as Neil Brading at *Outset Education* for generously giving me his time and his opinions on the final draft. Similarly, I am extremely grateful for the guidance I received from Emma Hollis at NASBTT and Dr Elizabeth White in the School of Education at the University of Hertfordshire. Last, but not least, thanks to my family for ignoring the mess on the dining room table – we will soon be eating off it again, I promise.

Introduction

Background

This quick guide is the result of numerous discussions I have had with trainees about how to provide the strongest evidence of progress against the Teachers' Standards. It assumes that most, if not all, of the evidence will be uploaded onto an e-portfolio capable of being verified remotely – a fact that in itself makes the careful selection and presentation of the best possible evidence key to the process.

The world of education is replete with jargon and specialist words that may well mean something to teachers and school leaders but might mean something else completely (and sometimes nothing!) to the uninitiated. At the start of your teacher-training course, the unavoidable fact is that there is a good chance you will fall into this latter category. Consequently, the guide is written in the spirit of 'explicit modelling' and assumes that you, as a relatively inexperienced trainee, will need the ideas and terms that your more experienced colleagues take for granted explained to you in more detail. As a result, there is some repetition and reinforcement, but I believe this will only serve to cement your understanding over the first few weeks of the year and beyond.

An important component of your training year(s), and of the ones that follow, is the ability to reflect critically on your own practice and on how it impacts the learning and progress of the pupils you teach. To help you in this, against each strand in the guide is a space for you to reflect on what you did in your teaching and how it helped your pupils to learn.

How to use this guide

The guide is designed to be used regularly – daily even. The noting and collating of evidence should be an on-going process that avoids a last-minute rush towards the end of an already busy term, and builds up an emerging picture of improving practice.

✓ Take the guide to all meetings with your mentor, tutor and other colleagues. Refer to and add to it when you are considering particular strands of the Standards, especially when discussing how to provide strong evidence of your progress against them.

✓ Use the guide to help you focus on, and raise your own awareness of, particular areas of your professional practice. Keep it near you when you are doing academic reading, for example, so that you keep the link between the theoretical and the practical aspects firmly in mind.

✓ Keep it in your classroom so you can jot down notes against the Standards as things occur, especially where evidence may be ephemeral, eg a note of where to find a particularly successful piece of differentiated work in a pupil's book; spoken comments made by pupils that indicate progress in learning; a photo of a temporary construction or an illustration of pupils working well as a group.

A note on the layout

Each left-hand page of the guide comprises the following:

- a breakdown of the chosen Teachers' Standard strand (1a, 1b…) with a brief explanation of the key words or phrases it includes;

- a 'What kind of evidence is possible/best?' section made up of suggestions on the best sort of evidence to include and where to look for it;

- an 'Anything to avoid?' section, based on my experience of using e-portfolios over the last two years, reinforcing the points made about making the verifier's job easier (see below) and emphasising quality over quantity.

Each right-hand page of the guide comprises:

- a page (facing each strand) with a table for you to complete. The table template is also available online at www.criticalpublishing.com/free-resources. You should fill in a version of the table for each strand of the Standards. It allows you to keep on-going notes, recording anything you could use to evidence progress against the Teachers' Standard described. It will help you find the evidence you are looking for weeks, or even months, after the event. This will be important, especially towards the end of what will be a busy year! You can include reminders of where the evidence is from and where it is stored, eg Lesson observation (Year 4 science) by mentor Oct 5 2018; maths display (Year 6) Laptop folder: 'Displays'.

Note: as mentioned above, some repetition and overlap in the advice given is inevitable and preferable, I believe, to leaving gaps. It also recognises the inter-relatedness and the non-sequential nature of evidencing the Standards.

Evidencing your progress against the Teachers' Standards

Over recent years there has been increasing emphasis on trainees providing *evidence of the impact* of their teaching upon *pupil progress over time*, tracked and evidenced in *sequences of lessons* – something that is increasingly preferred to evidence relating only to *individual* teaching sessions. In Ofsted's own words:

The very recent changes to assessment are helping current trainees to make these links [between lessons] more readily. The use of 'evidence bundles', which bring together evidence of pupils' progress over time, helps trainees to recognise the positive effects of their teaching on pupils' progress over a sequence of lessons.

(Essex and Thames Primary SCITT, Ofsted, 2016)

Although the Teachers' Standards themselves have remained unchanged, the current trend is towards the use of evidence bundles (see below for description) to support a more holistic approach in evaluating a trainee's progress over the year. There appears, therefore, to be a general move away from the provision of evidence for each individual strand to the more *holistic* perspective increasingly being adopted by providers and verifiers.

This reflects and reinforces point 13 of the DfE Teachers' Standards Document (June 2013) which says:

The bullets [strands], which are an integral part of the Standards, are designed to amplify the scope of each heading. The bulleted subheadings should not be interpreted as separate Standards in their own right...

Clearly, trainees are required to meet each of the overarching Standards per se and need to provide evidence that this is the case. The provision of evidence against the strands will help them do this but it is not a requirement to provide evidence against each and every one of them.

Note: individual providers may differ in the details of how evidence is to be garnered, collated and presented, and you need to be clear on what your provider expects. Nevertheless, and whatever approach is adopted, this guide will support you in understanding the Standards and in deciding on the best sorts of evidence to present – whether stand-alone or brought together in a bundle.

What do evidence bundles look like?

The National Association of School-Based Teacher Trainers (NASBTT) says that evidence bundles could include:

- *pupil data (prior to activity to show starting point, eg. previous activity level – this needs to reflect skills, knowledge and understanding related to the intended learning outcomes);*

- *pupil progress over time;*

- *self- and peer-assessments undertaken by pupils;*

- *annotated samples of pupils' work, including homework;*

- *trainee marking and annotations to highlight impact, and how this was acted upon by pupils showing improvements;*

- *visual or electronic evidence, eg video clips of lessons or parts of lessons to show individuals at the start, middle and end of a sequence of work;*

- *completed exams and tests;*

- *comments about each pupil's progress, outcomes, behaviour and effort;*

- *weekly meeting reports and interim reviews;*

- *lesson plans, formal observations and lesson evaluations which relate to progress.*

(NASBTT: Training and Assessment Toolkit: Evidence Bundles for Tracking Progress – Supporting Guidance, December 2017)

Like a good detective or barrister, you will gradually build your case over the year, presenting evidence to support your claim that you are meeting each of the eight Standards. Naturally, your evidence should be clear, and so compelling that no reasonably-minded person could decline to verify what you have presented.

Finally…how to make your verifier's job easier!

To help you empathise with the verifier, picture *yourself* marking 30 books at the weekend, because the same things that frustrate you when you are marking (poor presentation of work; pupils missing the point and answering a different question; grammar that makes work difficult to understand; indistinct images) all have their equivalents for the struggling verifier. Imagine the verifier in their office or kitchen, possibly tired or distracted, and present them with something they cannot fail to recognise as meeting the Standard under consideration. A wise trainee aims to make their job easy!

With this firmly in mind use the following checklist.

☐ *Read carefully and fully understand the strand of the Teachers' Standards* under consideration. In effect, understand, then 'answer the question'. This guide will help you enormously in this.

☐ Wherever possible try to *link your evidence with the improved learning and progress* that you are aiming at for individual or groups of pupils. The progress you identify could be academic, behavioural, social, or some other aspect pertinent to improving outcomes for the pupil(s) concerned.

☐ *Favour quality over quantity.* The verifier does not want to spend valuable time sifting through lots of irrelevant material.

☐ Where possible, *include more than one person's view of your teaching*, eg mentor, tutor, subject lead/head of department, or other senior colleagues. This will give balance to your evidence and make it all the more compelling.

☐ *Draw upon as wide a range of teaching contexts as you can.* If you are in primary, try to avoid limiting your evidence entirely to a single teaching group, for example, just in English or maths. If you are in secondary, draw your examples of good practice from a selection of classes across the age range you teach. What opportunities are there for broadening your experience and evidencing what you can do more widely?

☐ *Ensure* that your final selection of *evidence* for a particular Standard *spans a decent range of time* to show that it reflects an embedded, consistent behaviour, rather than a one-off. Obviously, this will become easier as the year progresses and stronger evidence is likely to emerge as time goes by.

Note: this will be especially important when you move on to evidencing 'good' or 'outstanding' practice, as many of the Standards include words such as consistently, much of the time, systematically, maintains, sustains, *and* over time. *Evidence collected 'over time' will certainly better support your claims against the higher-level descriptors.*

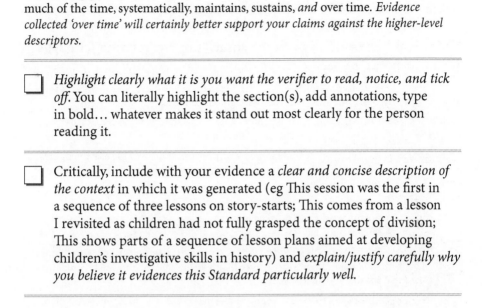

Highlight clearly what it is you want the verifier to read, notice, and tick off. You can literally highlight the section(s), add annotations, type in bold… whatever makes it stand out most clearly for the person reading it.

Critically, include with your evidence a *clear and concise description of the context* in which it was generated (eg This session was the first in a sequence of three lessons on story-starts; This comes from a lesson I revisited as children had not fully grasped the concept of division; This shows parts of a sequence of lesson plans aimed at developing children's investigative skills in history) and *explain/justify carefully why you believe it evidences this Standard particularly well.*

You also need to recognise that some parts of the Standards are easier to evidence than others. Many lend themselves to the uploading of documentation and reports, whereas others (eg 8a: 'is able to make a positive contribution to the… ethos of the school') might rely more on comments by a range of people, which are not so easily available and in this case you may need to request supporting evidence from a colleague or other professional, for instance an email or thank you note from your mentor or head teacher.

Finally, remember that 'meeting' the Standards is just the first step of a longer journey. The NASBTT Training and Assessment Toolkit makes it clear that 'Partnerships should work with trainees… to realise the trainees' potential *in becoming good and outstanding teachers* [my italics] as seen through the lens of the progress that pupils make'. A lot of trainees achieve the higher levels, so this can and should be your ambition too!

Teachers' Standard 1: set high expectations which inspire, motivate and challenge pupils

TS 1a: 'is able to establish a safe and stimulating environment for pupils rooted in mutual respect'

Key words	Understanding the Standard: guidance notes
a safe... environment	Primarily, this is a health and safety consideration. Is the place (classroom, hall, gym, playground, field, lab...) a *safe place to be*?
	Are there any health and safety concerns with the way the environment is set up – bags on the floor, dangerous/faulty equipment, lack of guidance or instruction, dangerous behaviours?
	Or is the environment tidy and well-ordered, and are you aware of potential risks and proactive in keeping learners safe? Is the room the right temperature, has it enough airflow, and can children see the board/IWB?
	In addition, this strand could refer to the climate for learning. Do children feel safe from bullying and are they able to share their ideas and opinions without fear of ridicule?
a stimulating environment	This relates to the environment as a place *conducive to learning*. Are there resources (including displays) which would excite and inspire children of this age to learn and make progress?
	Is the learning environment reflective of the children who learn there and can they relate to the displays, and is their work or that of their peers in evidence?
rooted in mutual respect	Do the students behave in a manner that suggests they respect each other's right to learn?
	Do you model this behaviour by showing and expecting mutual respect from the group?
Is able to establish	This implies that you are an *active participant* in the process and do what you can to ensure the environment is safe and conducive to learning.

In relation to pupils' learning and progress, what kind of evidence is possible/best?

✓ Photographs of classroom displays including a copy of the agreed classroom rules/charter.

✓ Lesson observations by mentor/tutor/senior colleagues that make direct reference to the quality of the environment, and/or positive behaviour of learners towards each other and the teacher, and/or the role of the teacher in establishing and cultivating a positive climate for learning.

✓ Lesson planning that shows that you have considered the effect of the environment on your pupils' learning.

✓ Health and safety audits, safety checklists... especially relating to higher-risk activities and subjects (eg PE; design and technology; science; learning outdoors).

Anything to avoid?

✗ A copy of the school health and safety policy, or similar, which says nothing about your own professional practice.

Source of evidence, eg: • my own reflective notes • lesson observations by mentor, tutor, HOD, subject leader • meeting notes with other colleagues, parents, specialist professionals • lesson plans, schemes of work	Date of evidence source	Any notes you may want to add, particularly those relating to pupil progress, learning and other outcomes.

Note here what you have learned and how your practice has improved as a result of addressing this Standard.

TS 1b: 'is able to set targets that stretch and challenge pupils of all backgrounds, abilities, and dispositions'

Key words	Understanding the Standard: guidance notes
set targets	Show that you write down and share targets (academic, behavioural, effort-based…) with pupils, colleagues or parents. Show that they are/will be referred to, and pupils' progress checked against them at an agreed later date.
	Remember, a target without an end date is a wish or a hope or a dream.
stretch and challenge	Targets are only useful if they lead to a positive change, ie progress of some sort.
	They must be seen as at least 'quite hard or hard' by the learners.
backgrounds	This is about socio-economic and cultural backgrounds.
	Are you inclusive and expect that children from all groups will work hard and make good progress?
abilities	This is about stretch and challenge for all ability groups – including the least *and* the most able.
dispositions	This is about looking to challenge *all* pupils.
	It includes those that are highly able and desperate to go beyond what may be normally on offer in the classroom. Conversely, it also includes those pupils who may not be naturally disposed (inclined) to work hard at their studies.
	Can you find ways to engage, motivate and challenge these pupils too?

In relation to pupils' learning and progress, what kind of evidence is possible/best?

✓ Examples of targets (whenever possible – SMART – Specific/Measurable/Attainable/Relevant/Time-related) set down and used to encourage/monitor/record a pupil's progress. Ensure that you include a range of types (two or three at least). For example:

- SEND support plan (complete/part completed where possible);
- behavioural support plan (complete/part completed where possible);
- academic target plan where the target and the progress against it are clearly indicated.

Note: use the commentary box (or similar) to give any background information that might help the assessor understand the context more clearly. This could include, for example, that the child was gifted but had emotional issues, that the pupil came from a traveller community, that the child had been excluded by their previous school, and so on.

Anything to avoid?

✗ A target that is essentially a 'wish' or a 'hope', with nothing to show how it will be attained.

✗ A target that lacks evidence that you monitor progress against it and that you use the information gleaned.

Source of evidence, eg: • my own reflective notes • lesson observations by mentor, tutor, HOD, subject leader • meeting notes with other colleagues, parents, specialist professionals • lesson plans, schemes of work	Date of evidence source	Any notes you may want to add, particularly those relating to pupil progress, learning and other outcomes.

Note here what you have learned and how your practice has improved as a result of addressing this Standard.

TS 1c: 'is able to demonstrate consistently the positive attitudes, values and behaviour which are expected of pupils'

Key words	Understanding the Standard: guidance notes
demonstrate consistently	The interesting word here is *consistently*, a word that appears much more frequently in the descriptors for Good and Outstanding. Do you show the target behaviours day in, day out? If so, how are these modelled and how are your expectations of pupils communicated?
positive attitudes, values and behaviour	Your *positive attitudes and values* will come over to pupils in what you say and do when you are teaching, ie through your behaviours. The list of possible attitudes and values is endless but would include, for example, tolerance, patience, regard for equality, helpfulness, perseverance and resilience, honesty, enthusiasm, optimism and ambition, trust in others… Which of these do you transmit to pupils, and how can you show this to others?
expected of pupils	This suggests that you need to act as a role model for pupils and is a question of 'do as I do, not as I say'.

In relation to pupils' learning and progress, what kind of evidence is possible/best?

✓ Comments in lesson observations that make reference to your positive, upbeat approach to teaching. These might comment on your welcoming style, your use of praise, the easy relationship you have with pupils, and their willingness and eagerness to discuss their learning or concerns with you.

✓ Similarly, comments that mention the fact that you insist on children behaving respectfully towards you and each other, and that this is modelled by you in the way that you, personally, deal with your pupils.

✓ The way in which you handle more difficult issues (eg low-level disruptive behaviour, disputes between children, a pupil's inability to grasp a learning point, a pupil in distress) can, if captured, illustrate these deeper beliefs well. Has a more senior colleague made written comments on how you have coped in such circumstances?

Anything to avoid?

✗ Unsubstantiated claims in your commentary such as 'I always try to be positive with children as I believe this is the best way to treat learners'. Here especially, you need to show not tell.

Source of evidence, eg: • my own reflective notes • lesson observations by mentor, tutor, HOD, subject leader • meeting notes with other colleagues, parents, specialist professionals • lesson plans, schemes of work	Date of evidence source	Any notes you may want to add, particularly those relating to pupil progress, learning and other outcomes.

Note here what you have learned and how your practice has improved as a result of addressing this Standard.

Teacher's Standard 2: promote good progress and outcomes by pupils

TS 2a: 'is able to take accountability for pupils' attainment, progress and outcomes'

Key words	Understanding the Standard: guidance notes
to take accountability	I take this to mean that you accept a large measure of responsibility for improving your pupils' attainment, progress and outcomes.
	The evidence for this will come through the things you actually *do* which show that you take a responsible and professional approach to supporting your pupils.
attainment	A measure of the level of learning.
	In simple terms, a mark or a grade, for example.
progress	A measurement of the distance that a pupil has made in their learning.
	In other words, the difference your teaching has made to the learning of this pupil. What do they know or understand, or are able to do now that they could not do before?
outcomes	This is a trickier term to pin down exactly. It includes the acquired knowledge and skills implied above, but would also imply elements such as attendance, attitudes and behaviour, learning habits and so on.
	These are important for all children, but for particularly vulnerable groups (eg Traveller children, Looked After children and children with EAL) they might be especially pertinent.

In relation to pupils' learning and progress, what kind of evidence is possible/best?

✓ Planning, annotated and/or adapted, which shows you have taken into account the varying progress of individuals and groups in your class(es). Include a commentary to explain what the planning sheets show, what you did to adjust your teaching, and why.

✓ Examples of tracking sheets with a commentary explaining what they show and how you use the information they contain.

✓ Any targets – curriculum or behavioural – you have set pupils and how you monitor them. Again, a commentary explaining simply the context in which the targets were set would be useful.

✓ Notes of meetings with the SENCO, SLT or others in which you have shared concerns and decided on any actions needed.

✓ Examples of changes to teaching input following marking. Did you, for example, repeat material or change the level of challenge as a result?

Anything to avoid?

✗ Unsubstantiated claims that you take these responsibilities seriously.

Source of evidence, eg: • my own reflective notes • lesson observations by mentor, tutor, HOD, subject leader • meeting notes with other colleagues, parents, specialist professionals • lesson plans, schemes of work	Date of evidence source	Any notes you may want to add, particularly those relating to pupil progress, learning and other outcomes.

Note here what you have learned and how your practice has improved as a result of addressing this Standard.

TS 2b: 'is aware of pupils' capabilities and their prior knowledge and plans to build on these'

Key words	Understanding the Standard: guidance notes
Is aware of	You know, and *can show that you know.*
pupils' capabilities	What pupils (the class in general, groups or individuals) are capable of doing/understanding.
	What is their potential for learning? Are they considered to be a particularly able group? Is there a high proportion of early stage EAL learners? Have some, or no, pupils got very specific learning needs – including SEND, HA (higher ability)?
prior knowledge	What children already know and understand.
	You will know this from a range of sources, including: assessment data (both hard and soft); your own reflections/notes on what has been successfully covered; teachers who have taken the class previously; schemes of work/syllabuses.
	This is a critical element in demonstrating that pupils have made progress over time (eg a sequence of lessons) as it indicates a starting point in their learning.
plans to build on	Can you demonstrate that you take pupils' capabilities and prior knowledge into account when you are planning lessons?
	Have you got examples of plans which explicitly mention prior knowledge and/or capabilities?
	Essentially this is about *challenge, next-steps learning* and *promoting good progress.*

In relation to pupils' learning and progress, what kind of evidence is possible/best?

✓ Planning sheets which explicitly refer to prior knowledge (eg 'last lesson all/most/some pupils understood/could do... so that next lesson I need to teach').

✓ Evidence that you are using assessments (informal/tests/marking...) to inform your plans for future teaching and learning. This could include tweaks to plans, re-teaching something, a decision to group children differently, and so on.

Anything to avoid?

✗ Records of pupils' capabilities and prior knowledge accompanied by planning which suggests/indicates little or no progress (eg unnecessary repetition of content; learning tasks which appear to be offering little extra challenge).

✗ Records of pupils' capabilities and prior knowledge with no indication of how they will be/ were used to inform future learning.

Source of evidence, eg: • my own reflective notes • lesson observations by mentor, tutor, HOD, subject leader • meeting notes with other colleagues, parents, specialist professionals • lesson plans, schemes of work	Date of evidence source	Any notes you may want to add, particularly those relating to pupil progress, learning and other outcomes.

Note here what you have learned and how your practice has improved as a result of addressing this Standard.

TS 2c: 'plans suitably differentiated assessment opportunities that measure progress for pupils with a range of learning needs'

Key words	Understanding the Standard: guidance notes
Plans... assessment opportunities	This implies that you have *actively prepared* activities in order to assess pupils' progress.
	These could include pieces of work (later marked), formal tests (eg at the start, middle and end of a unit of work), 'planned-for' oral questions used in lessons, a summative-type project, and so on.
suitably differentiated	The assessment opportunities selected should *show* that you have taken into consideration the different needs and range of ability within your teaching group. As a result of the differentiated approach, *all pupils should be able to access the assessment at their level.*
measure progress	Normally, progress will refer to learning (a change in understanding, knowledge, ability to do...) *measurable over a period of time.*
	This is most often a series of lessons, a few weeks, a unit of work... so that the most useful examples show attainment before and after the learning input, eg pre-unit and post-unit tests, or pieces of written work demonstrating that pupils' understanding or knowledge about a topic has improved as a result of your teaching input.
pupils with a range of learning needs	Obviously, this is heavily dependent upon the make-up of the teaching group. It is highly likely to include higher, middle and lower abilities, but could also include EAL and/or SEND among others. Whatever the make-up of the class, it is important that the assessment approaches *acknowledge* and then *cater for/take into account* these differences.

In relation to pupils' learning and progress, what kind of evidence is possible/best?

✓ Lesson observations by mentor/tutor/senior colleagues that refer specifically to good use of assessment. For example, they may refer to differentiated teacher questioning, to a teacher's observation and recording of individual pupils' or group responses, to well-designed tests, or to pieces of written work used to assess progress.

✓ Examples of teacher notes/observations relating to pupils' work on assessment tasks including an indication of how the results of the assessment were/will be used to inform future teaching and learning.

✓ Examples of actual differentiated assessment activities including notes/commentary about how the results were/will be used to inform future teaching and learning.

Anything to avoid?

✗ A copy of a mark-book lacking a commentary to explain what the marks refer to and how they were/will be used to change teaching approaches or improve pupils' learning.

✗ Testing/other assessments which are clearly undifferentiated, 'one-size-fits-all' affairs.

Source of evidence, eg: • my own reflective notes • lesson observations by mentor, tutor, HOD, subject leader • meeting notes with other colleagues, parents, specialist professionals • lesson plans, schemes of work	Date of evidence source	Any notes you may want to add, particularly those relating to pupil progress, learning and other outcomes.

Note here what you have learned and how your practice has improved as a result of addressing this Standard.

TS 2d: 'is able to guide pupils so that some reflect on the progress they have made and their emerging needs'

Key words	Understanding the Standard: guidance notes
guide pupils	This is about suggesting, showing to and supporting pupils so that they become more aware of what helps or hinders their understanding. It is about developing their metacognition and their understanding of the role they have in their own learning.
some reflect	Generally, the more children are aware of and consider how they are getting on in school, the better. How do you help them to do this, and do you give them the space and time necessary to do it well?
progress	Progress will mainly refer to academic work, but for some children there may be particular concerns around behaviour, attitudes to learning, confidence and social issues. In all cases, *progress* deals with the differences between where children are now compared with where they were some time ago.
emerging needs	This is about helping children recognise, early in the process, that there may be particular challenges around the corner. Your interventions may help pupils prepare for what comes next and empower them to seek help so that the needs that emerge are kept to manageable proportions.

In relation to pupils' learning and progress, what kind of evidence is possible/best?

✓ Examples of formative assessments in which pupils have evaluated their own progress and identified appropriate targets for themselves.

✓ Examples of feedback to pupils (beyond simple 'right or wrong' marking) that causes them to think about their work and respond in some way. This may be captured in next-steps type marking, formal pupil conferences, or in the comments of those observing your interactions with individuals.

✓ Examples of clear success criteria shared with pupils and their evaluations of how well they have met them.

Anything to avoid?

✗ Marking which fails to show how pupils have responded or moved on in their learning.

Source of evidence, eg: • my own reflective notes • lesson observations by mentor, tutor, HOD, subject leader • meeting notes with other colleagues, parents, specialist professionals • lesson plans, schemes of work	Date of evidence source	Any notes you may want to add, particularly those relating to pupil progress, learning and other outcomes.

Note here what you have learned and how your practice has improved as a result of addressing this Standard.

TS 2e: 'is able to demonstrate knowledge and understanding of how pupils learn and how this impacts on teaching'

Key words	Understanding the Standard: guidance notes
demonstrate knowledge and understanding of how pupils learn	For this part of the descriptor you need to show that you understand the theory about how children learn.
	What have you learned about this as part of your university studies and whatever in-service training you have attended? What evidence can you use to show that you have understood what you have been told?
how this impacts on teaching	Critically, whatever you have understood of the theory needs to be used in the classroom.
	Here you should show the link between the theory and your classroom practice.
	How have you used your knowledge and understanding of how pupils learn to improve your teaching, their learning, and their progress?

In relation to pupils' learning and progress, what kind of evidence is possible/best?

✓ For the first part of the descriptor, you could use comments from colleagues (including your academic tutor at university) to show that you have a good grasp of the various theories underpinning what we think we understand about how children learn.

✓ In addition, you could list some of the in-service sessions or courses you have attended that focus on this aspect of teaching and learning, noting the main points of what you personally took away from the sessions.

✓ In the second part, you need to link the theory to some aspect of teaching. For example, following training, did you change your approach to teaching a child with additional needs? Or, based on your university reading, did you alter the groupings in your class (from ability to mixed, or vice versa, for example) and how did this impact upon pupils' learning? Can you demonstrate improved learning and progress?

✓ In your commentary be sure to highlight the link between the two parts, evaluating the success (*or otherwise*, as not everything you do will be successful) of whatever changes you instigated.

Anything to avoid?

✗ Presenting evidence for just one side (eg the theoretical aspects) without indicating the impact on teaching and learning.

Source of evidence, eg: • my own reflective notes • lesson observations by mentor, tutor, HOD, subject leader • meeting notes with other colleagues, parents, specialist professionals • lesson plans, schemes of work	Date of evidence source	Any notes you may want to add, particularly those relating to pupil progress, learning and other outcomes.

Note here what you have learned and how your practice has improved as a result of addressing this Standard.

TS 2f: 'is normally able to encourage most pupils to demonstrate a responsible and conscientious attitude to their own work'

Key words	Understanding the Standard: guidance notes
encourage	The word *encourage* suggests positive ways of persuading and supporting children in their efforts.
	How do you convince learners, especially when things are difficult or they are disinclined to work, that they should apply themselves in class?
a responsible and conscientious attitude	This aspect is about helping children to take responsibility for, and ownership of, their own work.
	It includes a broad array of expectations you may have. For example:
	• pupils need to look after their own equipment and books;
	• they should try to complete their work, and do it neatly so that others can understand it;
	• they should do work to the best of their ability;
	• at times, they should be able to take the lead in their own learning;
	• they should do as they are being asked to do and not disturb others' learning;
	• at times, they should be able to work independently of you or others while at other times they should learn co-operatively with their peers.

In relation to pupils' learning and progress, what kind of evidence is possible/best?

✓ Comments in lesson observations that refer to the way children are able to work independently of you or other adult supervision, using resources well and letting others get on with what they are learning.

✓ Comments in lesson observations remarking on pupils' ability to work with others well, avoiding the temptation to go off-task or waste learning time.

✓ Similarly, comments in observations, which attest to the fact that pupils take care with their learning (including looking after books and equipment, doing their work neatly, being careful with spellings and handwriting and so on).

✓ Examples of the ways in which you have put things into practice to support and reward positive attitudes to work, eg class charts rewarding effort and responsible behaviour; individual targets or plans to encourage particular children who may find this aspect more challenging.

✓ In your commentary, explain why you introduced any charts, individual plans and so on, making a comment(s) about their effectiveness.

Anything to avoid?

✗ Charts and plans without evaluative comments.

Source of evidence, eg: • my own reflective notes • lesson observations by mentor, tutor, HOD, subject leader • meeting notes with other colleagues, parents, specialist professionals • lesson plans, schemes of work	Date of evidence source	Any notes you may want to add, particularly those relating to pupil progress, learning and other outcomes.

Note here what you have learned and how your practice has improved as a result of addressing this Standard.

Teachers' Standard 3: demonstrate good subject and curriculum knowledge

TS 3a: 'has a secure knowledge of the relevant subject(s) and curriculum areas, fosters and maintains pupils' interests in the subject, and addresses misunderstandings'

Key words	Understanding the Standard: guidance notes
secure knowledge of	In your planning and in your practice, can you show that you have a firm understanding of what it is you are trying to teach others?
	This would include the factual information-based knowledge you require as well as the understanding of which methods and approaches best transmit this to learners.
	Note: in practical subjects, such as PE and DT, the way a person teaches particular aspects safely and effectively would have as great a bearing on an evaluation of their subject knowledge as their theoretical understanding of their area of expertise.
relevant subject(s) and curriculum areas	This will depend on what phase you are in but is essentially any subject you are required to teach.
fosters and maintains pupils' interests	Can you demonstrate that you are able to get pupils to be interested in what you want them to learn?
	And once you have 'hooked them in', can you demonstrate that this interest is sustained, leading to improved learning and progress?
addresses misunderstandings	Misunderstanding (which reveals itself in 'wrong' answers, errors and mistakes) is an essential and natural part of learning.
	What is your attitude to error? Can you show how the way you address misunderstandings actually supports pupils' learning in a positive and constructive manner?

In relation to pupils' learning and progress, what kind of evidence is possible/best?

✓ *Secure knowledge* is best evidenced by lesson observation comments made by colleagues with more experience/expertise in the areas you are teaching. So, head of department, subject leader, senior leader and tutor comments are normally solid evidence here. Look for comments which refer specifically to subject knowledge (which in EYFS and Key Stage 1 would include 'the EY curriculum' and its elements, and 'phonics').

✓ In order to demonstrate that you *foster and maintain pupils' interests*, include anything written in observations that refer to this. You may also want to include example(s) of particularly imaginative planning where you have attempted to make a relatively mundane area of study more appealing. Positive comments made by pupils, especially in 'pupil voice' style feedback, would also be good evidence here.

✓ Again, favourable comments in lesson observations which show that you *address misunderstandings* positively and constructively are ones to evidence this element of the Standard. Do you turn the misunderstanding into an opportunity for the pupil(s) to move forward in their learning? You may also have evidence from marking that demonstrates a similarly constructive approach – effective next-steps marking, for example. Alternatively, perhaps you have a classroom display where mistakes are explored, explained or 'celebrated'?

Anything to avoid?

✗ Any statement along the lines of 'I always plan my lessons to captivate my pupils' type, with no hard evidence to substantiate it.

Source of evidence, eg: • my own reflective notes • lesson observations by mentor, tutor, HOD, subject leader • meeting notes with other colleagues, parents, specialist professionals • lesson plans, schemes of work	Date of evidence source	Any notes you may want to add, particularly those relating to pupil progress, learning and other outcomes.

Note here what you have learned and how your practice has improved as a result of addressing this Standard.

TS 3b: 'is able to demonstrate a critical understanding of developments in the subject and curriculum areas and the value of scholarship'

Key words	Understanding the Standard: guidance notes
demonstrate a critical understanding	The word *critical* here means that you are able to take an evaluative view of 'developments', in which you weigh up and articulate what you think of them.
	In teaching and learning, things are rarely black and white and it is important to show that you have thought about the various arguments and come to a personal view about what you believe.
developments	Generally, things develop quite slowly in education and today's practice is still heavily influenced by some decades-old theories and ideas.
	Consequently, you should be able to show your understanding of the main well-established ideas about teaching and learning covered by your university studies.
	However, it is also important to keep up with current developments, especially in a world increasingly influenced by computer technology and improved understanding of how the brain works, for example.
scholarship	The OED defines scholarship as *'academic achievement; learning of a high level (and) the methods and Standards characteristic of a good scholar (ie a learned person)'*.
	Are you able to demonstrate that *you* value learning and help to promote the love of learning in your pupils? Do you model tackling something that you yourself find difficult to learn? Can you also demonstrate that you take the learning of *how to teach* (pedagogy) seriously through, for instance, your application of educational theories to classroom practice? For example, experimenting with different approaches to classroom groupings (ability, mixed-ability, gender).

In relation to pupils' learning and progress, what kind of evidence is possible/best?

✓ Extracts taken from meetings with your mentor and others that show you can articulate a view on different approaches to teaching and learning, explaining your reasons for your beliefs. This could come through others' comments about your ability to reflect, or could be evident from what you yourself have written.

✓ Your own reflections on how lessons went that include reference to relevant theory (eg social constructivism; growth mindsets).

✓ Extracts from written work that you have done as part of your studies. *(Note: different establishments may have different rules on, for example, including parts of essays as evidence. Please check with your own institution on this one.)*

✓ Anything which demonstrates that you encourage pupils to go the extra mile in their studies, eg asking children to find additional information about a topic at home, using books, the internet, adult friends or relatives.

✓ Evidence that you encourage children who may be of a more academic bent to challenge themselves further, praising them for their efforts and hard work.

Anything to avoid?

✗ Simple statements outlining the university work you have done on various pedagogies.

Source of evidence, eg: • my own reflective notes • lesson observations by mentor, tutor, HOD, subject leader • meeting notes with other colleagues, parents, specialist professionals • lesson plans, schemes of work	Date of evidence source	Any notes you may want to add, particularly those relating to pupil progress, learning and other outcomes.

Note here what you have learned and how your practice has improved as a result of addressing this Standard.

TS 3c: 'is able to demonstrate an understanding of and take responsibility for promoting high standards of literacy, articulacy and the correct use of Standard English, whatever the teacher's specialist subject'

Key words	Understanding the Standard: guidance notes
demonstrate an understanding of	In teaching, this will be apparent by the way that you yourself speak and write. It will also come through the choices you make to correct, or not, pupils' use of English.
	Not *every* mistake needs to be corrected, but some errors (repeated use of the incorrect past tense of a common verb, perhaps) do need addressing.
take responsibility for promoting	This refers to your role in encouraging your pupils to speak and write in ways that will be comprehensible to others.
	If what they say or write is unintelligible, they are unlikely to do well in the education system as it stands, and will be vulnerable to underachievement.
	Things are rarely straightforward, however – for example, children recently arrived in the country for whom the production of any English phrases, incorrect or not, could be considered an achievement in itself.
literacy (and) articulacy	*Literacy* refers to the ability to read and write.
	Articulacy is the ability to speak clearly and fluently.
Standard English	There is no one definition of this but *'The English language in its most widely accepted form, as written and spoken by educated people in both formal and informal contexts, having universal currency while incorporating regional differences'* seems to me to cover most angles.
whatever the teacher's specialist subject	Essentially, this is reinforcing the idea that every teacher is a teacher of English.

In relation to pupils' learning and progress, what kind of evidence is possible/best?

✓ Comments in lesson observations that make direct reference to the way you promote the correct use of English in your pupils. This could, for example, include the ways you model spoken and written target language (eg the language of discussion or debate), the ways you handle pupils' errors, or the methods you employ to increase and improve pupils' vocabulary choices.

✓ Snapshots of work you have marked focusing on the use of Standard English (eg word-order or verb tenses; irregular plural nouns; formal versus informal language in letter writing). Explain in your commentary what it was you were teaching children to understand.

✓ Examples of planning or pupils' work where you have focused on the teaching and learning of specialist subject-related language, eg a vocabulary focus in science, geography or art.

Anything to avoid?

✗ 'Run of the mill' English lesson plans that fail to bring out the focus on the promotion of high standards and the correct use of Standard English.

Source of evidence, eg: • my own reflective notes • lesson observations by mentor, tutor, HOD, subject leader • meeting notes with other colleagues, parents, specialist professionals • lesson plans, schemes of work	Date of evidence source	Any notes you may want to add, particularly those relating to pupil progress, learning and other outcomes.

Note here what you have learned and how your practice has improved as a result of addressing this Standard.

TS 3d: 'is able to, if teaching early reading, demonstrate a clear understanding of systematic synthetic phonics'

Key words	Understanding the Standard: guidance notes
if teaching early reading	The teaching of *early reading* normally refers to that which happens in EYFS and Key Stage 1. However, there may be children in Key Stage 2, or even beyond, for whom these early reading teaching approaches are effective and entirely appropriate.
	If you are in a primary school and are *not* teaching in these classes, the advice given is at the very least to spend some time (two or three sessions?) observing good practice and recording your observations as part of your own professional development portfolio.
	Note: we are living in an increasingly diverse society however, and one in which reading is not, perhaps, given the status it once had at home. As a result, older children may for all practical purposes still be at the 'early reading' stage of development and, as 'every teacher is an English teacher', expertise in the teaching of these skills is important whatever the age group in question.
demonstrate a clear understanding of systematic synthetic phonics	If you *are* teaching lower down the school, the best demonstration of this understanding is in how you, as the practitioner, apply it to real lessons.
	How do you adapt your approaches so that the youngest learners can access what it is you want them to be able to know, do or understand? How do you take into account their early stage of development, while still extending your more able learners who may be several months or years ahead of their peers?
	If you are *not* teaching these age groups, what do you notice about how the teacher adapts their methods for very young pupils? Is there something for you to take back to your own class, to support children with additional needs, or EAL, maybe?

In relation to pupils' learning and progress, what kind of evidence is possible/best?

✓ Lesson observation comments that highlight your ability to teach systematic synthetic phonics. These are likely to include reference to the way in which you make this fun and appealing to children, how you have built children's knowledge and understanding over time, and the accuracy with which you teach sounds and how they are represented on paper.

✓ Lesson plans and/or materials with a clear commentary on how and why they were used with the pupils in question, ie the stage they were at and any contextual information about the make-up of the class itself.

✓ Records, including any certificates you may have gained, of attendance at phonics training.

✓ Your own observations of colleagues teaching phonics and your reflective comments relating to what you have seen.

Anything to avoid?

✗ Examples of lesson plans or materials without clear contextual commentary.

Source of evidence, eg: • my own reflective notes • lesson observations by mentor, tutor, HOD, subject leader • meeting notes with other colleagues, parents, specialist professionals • lesson plans, schemes of work	Date of evidence source	Any notes you may want to add, particularly those relating to pupil progress, learning and other outcomes.

Note here what you have learned and how your practice has improved as a result of addressing this Standard.

TS 3e: 'is able to, if teaching early mathematics, demonstrate a clear understanding of appropriate teaching strategies'

Key words	Understanding the Standard: guidance notes
if teaching early mathematics	The teaching of *early mathematics* normally refers to that which happens in EYFS and Key Stage 1. However, there may be children in Key Stage 2, or even beyond, for whom these early mathematics teaching approaches are effective and entirely appropriate.
	If you are in a primary school and *are not* teaching in these classes, the advice given is to at least spend some time (perhaps two or three sessions) observing good practice and include your observations as part of your own professional development portfolio.
demonstrate a clear understanding of appropriate teaching strategies	If you *are* teaching lower down the school, the best demonstration of this understanding is in how you, as the practitioner, apply it to real lessons. How do you adapt your approaches so that the youngest learners can access what it is you want them to be able to know, do or understand? How do you take into account their early stage of development, while still extending your more able learners who may be several months or even years ahead of their peers?
	If you *are not* teaching these age groups, what do you notice about how the teacher adapts their methods for very young pupils? Is there something for you to take back to your own class, to support children with additional needs, perhaps?

In relation to pupils' learning and progress, what kind of evidence is possible/best?

✓ Lesson observation comments that highlight your ability to teach early mathematics. These are likely to include reference to the way in which you use familiar, everyday materials and contexts to teach abstract concepts in clear practical situations. There may be references to hands-on learning, investigative approaches, the use of the outdoors, links with English and other areas of learning, focused teaching groups and teacher modelling, support for correct numeral formation etc.

✓ Photographs or other images that show how you teach early maths effectively, eg children practising number work in a sand tray; pupils counting objects outdoors; simple games you have devised. Remember to include a rationale for what you have chosen to show, explaining how your strategies support mathematical understanding in young children.

✓ Lesson plans and/or materials with a clear commentary on how and why they were used with the pupils in question, ie the stage they were at and any contextual information about the make-up of the class itself.

✓ Your own observations of colleagues teaching early mathematics and your reflective comments relating to what you have seen.

Anything to avoid?

✗ Examples of lesson plans or materials without clear contextual commentary.

Source of evidence, eg: • my own reflective notes • lesson observations by mentor, tutor, HOD, subject leader • meeting notes with other colleagues, parents, specialist professionals • lesson plans, schemes of work	Date of evidence source	Any notes you may want to add, particularly those relating to pupil progress, learning and other outcomes.

Note here what you have learned and how your practice has improved as a result of addressing this Standard.

Teachers' Standard 4: plan and teach well-structured lessons

TS 4a: 'plans sequences of lessons that are appropriately structured to support pupils in developing their knowledge, skills, understanding, interests and positive attitudes'

Key words	Understanding the Standard: guidance notes
plans sequences of lessons	A sequence of lessons is a string of lessons (at least three I would say) which could be over a week, a half term or even longer. For it to be a 'sequence' you will need to *ensure that something links the lessons to each other*, eg a theme or a topic, or the development of a skill. To give a sense of progression in learning, show how the different aspects build from lesson to lesson.
appropriately structured	This refers to the structure of the *sequences* rather than the individual lessons. So you should try to show how/why Lesson 2 builds on what was done in Lesson 1, how Lesson 3 builds on Lesson 2 and so on.
to support pupils in developing	The key word here is *developing* – how the series of lessons helps to build the pupils' learning, step by step, week by week.
knowledge	Have you identified and included in your planning the key bits of factual information pupils need to learn this subject or topic?
skills	What did you teach pupils *to do* as part of their learning?
understanding	Have you identified the key elements of understanding that pupils need to learn? Are these key elements highlighted/emphasised in the plans/work you do with your pupils?
interests	How have you tried to make the lessons as interesting to pupils as you can? Are they pitched appropriately? Have you tapped into something that you know engages your pupils, eg a particular topic or way of working?
positive attitudes	Linked to all of the above, how do you help maintain the positivity of the class?

In relation to pupils' learning and progress, what kind of evidence is possible/best?

✓ Planning documents that clearly show the sequential and linked nature of a number of lessons. This should include a commentary that points the reviewer towards the features of planning upon which you want to focus attention, eg the step-by-step building of essential pupil knowledge or the development of particular skills over time.

✓ Lesson observation comments that highlight pupils using prior knowledge or the teacher contextualising the learning (referring to the last lesson and/or the lesson to come) will give a sense of *supporting pupils in developing…* as seen in the strand.

✓ Similarly, pupils' interests and positive attitudes will be best evidenced in lesson observation comments and/or comments made by pupils themselves if these have been recorded appropriately (eg as part of a pupil voice survey; sticky notes displayed on a working wall).

Anything to avoid?

✗ A collection of lesson plans, even if taught one after the other, which does not indicate a 'sequence' as described above.

Note: TS 4a is a very wide and disparate part of TS4 and at the 'meeting' level you may not be able to show every single element. What is important is to show a sequence *of lessons planned to develop children's learning over time. Evidence of the five elements (knowledge, skills, understanding, interests, positive attitudes) will come out in lesson observation comments and through other sources, such as demonstrably improved learning over time (eg the quality of work at the end of the sequence compared with at the start).*

Source of evidence, eg: <ul><li>my own reflective notes</li><li>lesson observations by mentor, tutor, HOD, subject leader</li><li>meeting notes with other colleagues, parents, specialist professionals</li><li>lesson plans, schemes of work</li></ul>	Date of evidence source	Any notes you may want to add, particularly those relating to pupil progress, learning and other outcomes.
Note here what you have learned and how your practice has improved as a result of addressing this Standard.		

TS 4b: 'is able to impart knowledge and develop understanding through the effective use of lesson time'

Key words	Understanding the Standard: guidance notes
impart knowledge	This is about how you transfer factual knowledge – bits of content as well as the skills of how to do things – to your pupils. There are many ways to do this, including simply telling them, modelling and scaffolding, all the way through to devising ways in which they research and find it all out by themselves. None are right or wrong in themselves, but should be chosen as the most appropriate and effective method according to the particular context of learning.
develop understanding	This is a more complex aspect of teaching and involves you, as the teacher, making sure that pupils comprehend the elements of knowledge imparted to them. Included in this is how you build upon previous knowledge, use well-thought-out questioning to check that they understand, and revisit/revise materials according to their current levels of comprehension.
effective use of lesson time	This part refers to the way in which you use the teaching and learning time available to you. Is the pitch and pace of the lesson right for the teaching group? Do the sessions run smoothly with little time lost to routines such as the giving out of materials and transitions from tables to carpet and back again? Think about well-judged teacher talk and the good use of talk partners to prime children for learning. *Note: diverting from a lesson plan that is not working is often a good indicator of making effective use of lesson time, so don't be afraid to do this if the circumstances demand it.*

In relation to pupils' learning and progress, what kind of evidence is possible/best?

✓ Comments made in lesson observations referring directly to the effective use of lesson time. Observers might also remark on the speed with which pupils respond to your requests, how familiar they are with the well-established routines, and how every element of the lesson seems to be helping children in their understanding and their progress towards meeting the learning objective(s).

✓ Planning which shows that you have used assessments/evaluations of previous learning to plan subsequent lessons. Make sure you highlight and explain to the reader what it is you want them to notice.

✓ Observations referring to good explanations and your use of resources to support children's understanding, especially of more challenging concepts which could otherwise stall the pace of learning.

Anything to avoid?

✗ A copy of lesson plans with clear timings but no comment/indication of how effective the division of the time was in supporting learning.

Source of evidence, eg: • my own reflective notes • lesson observations by mentor, tutor, HOD, subject leader • meeting notes with other colleagues, parents, specialist professionals • lesson plans, schemes of work	Date of evidence source	Any notes you may want to add, particularly those relating to pupil progress, learning and other outcomes.

Note here what you have learned and how your practice has improved as a result of addressing this Standard.

TS 4c: 'is able to promote a love of learning and children's intellectual curiosity'

Key words	Understanding the Standard: guidance notes
promote	Essentially this means encouraging and supporting pupils' learning. Sometimes you may be the instigator of this by introducing new topics and ideas or, perhaps, you recognise and capitalise on something your pupils already have an interest in.
a love of learning	Learning can be hard work, and generally people don't like working hard! So, what is it that you do to make learning attractive, to tempt pupils in and make learning irresistible?
children's intellectual curiosity	Children are naturally curious, 'why?' being a favourite word among the very young. What do you do to develop this natural curiosity and help maintain it in the face of the pressure to cover lots of material and 'to get things done'?

Note: this might be one of the shortest of all Standards but it is absolutely central and key to the job of a teacher.

In relation to pupils' learning and progress, what kind of evidence is possible/best?

✓ Lesson observation comments highlighting the way in which you encourage children to ask questions, discuss things they find fascinating, and research answers for themselves – either in class or at home.

✓ Similarly, observation comments in which children's engagement and enjoyment of what they are doing is highlighted. This may also be expressed in phrases like 'absorbed in their learning', 'highly motivated', 'keen to find out more', and so on.

✓ Planning which shows that you involve children in making decisions about what and how they learn, allowing them a degree of freedom to follow their own noses and to research things that really interest them.

✓ Any comments by pupils or parents that attest to the fact that children really enjoy their learning with you. Pupil or parent voice surveys might include a question about this that you could use as evidence.

Anything to avoid?

✗ Any unsubstantiated claims that you promote pupils' love of learning, eg 'I always try to make my lessons really interesting'.

Source of evidence, eg: • my own reflective notes • lesson observations by mentor, tutor, HOD, subject leader • meeting notes with other colleagues, parents, specialist professionals • lesson plans, schemes of work	Date of evidence source	Any notes you may want to add, particularly those relating to pupil progress, learning and other outcomes.

Note here what you have learned and how your practice has improved as a result of addressing this Standard.

TS 4d: 'is able to set homework and plan other out-of-class activities to consolidate and extend the knowledge and understanding pupils have acquired'

Key words	Understanding the Standard: guidance notes
homework	This means the work (reading, writing, maths, research, learning of facts, collection of materials etc) you ask children to do after the school day, when they are no longer under your responsibility.
other out-of-class activities	This would include anything that you plan or organise to support children's learning about things studied in class, eg visits to the local area, activity centres, theatre, museum or sports trips. This might also include involvement in an after school club.
consolidate and extend the knowledge and understanding pupils have acquired	In other words, the extra activities should reinforce or develop further whatever learning pupils have already covered with you in their class lessons.

In relation to pupils' learning and progress, what kind of evidence is possible/best?

✓ Examples of pupils' responses to consolidation and extension tasks that you have set as homework, including contextual information on what had been learned in class.

✓ Descriptions of other out-of-class activities you have been involved in or responsible for planning and what pupils did to extend their learning.

Anything to avoid?

✗ Homework titles or lists of visits with no explanation of how they added value to pupils' knowledge and understanding of what they have learned in class.

Source of evidence, eg: <ul><li>my own reflective notes</li><li>lesson observations by mentor, tutor, HOD, subject leader</li><li>meeting notes with other colleagues, parents, specialist professionals</li><li>lesson plans, schemes of work</li></ul>	Date of evidence source	Any notes you may want to add, particularly those relating to pupil progress, learning and other outcomes.

Note here what you have learned and how your practice has improved as a result of addressing this Standard.

TS 4e: 'is able to reflect systematically on the effectiveness of lessons and approaches to teaching'

Key words	Understanding the Standard: guidance notes
to reflect systematically	*To reflect* means to think about how the lesson went, evaluate it – often against criteria/development targets agreed beforehand with your mentor – and come to some sort of overall balanced view on what went well, and what you could do differently next time. *Systematically* implies that there is a structure to your reflection (eg using a standard format) and that it is done on a regular basis (eg weekly, at least).
effectiveness of lessons and approaches to teaching	The effectiveness of a lesson, or the approach you take with pupils, is measured by how well they learn. As *learning* is the key concept here, make sure you make reference to pupils' learning in your evidence. *Approaches to teaching* I understand to mean the decisions you make and the methods you use to teach a particular lesson (ie pedagogical considerations). For example, in science: you could opt to do whole-class observation of the teacher modelling an experiment, or small, mixed-ability groups investigating the same question, or ability groups investigating different but closely related questions. Demonstrate that you think about (and can justify) the decisions you make in teaching various lessons and try to show that you are flexible in your approach.

In relation to pupils' learning and progress, what kind of evidence is possible/best?

✓ Meeting notes with mentor or similar in which you have reflected on a lesson(s). Show that you are able to recognise both the strengths and areas for development in your own teaching. Analyse what happened and try to explain why things went as they did. Remember to include reference to pupils' learning and, if possible, identify which pupils or groups did better than others did, and why.

✓ Summary reports by your mentor or tutor in which your ability to reflect on your practice is highlighted.

✓ Snapshots of planning sheets, annotated with your own 'scribbles', illustrating your reflections following a lesson/sequence of lessons. In your commentary, include any explanations necessary to help the verifier understand what it is they are looking at.

Anything to avoid?

✗ Notes from entire meetings with your mentor where the 'reflection' part is not clearly highlighted.

Source of evidence, eg: • my own reflective notes • lesson observations by mentor, tutor, HOD, subject leader • meeting notes with other colleagues, parents, specialist professionals • lesson plans, schemes of work	Date of evidence source	Any notes you may want to add, particularly those relating to pupil progress, learning and other outcomes.

Note here what you have learned and how your practice has improved as a result of addressing this Standard.

TS 4f: 'is able to contribute to the design and provision of an engaging curriculum within the relevant subject area(s)'

Key words	Understanding the Standard: guidance notes
contribute to the design and provision	I believe this includes, but goes beyond, the planning of interesting lessons for your own particular pupils. The wording implies that you are part of a bigger team (year group; key stage; curriculum planning group…) and contribute your ideas and/or materials.
	This could mean, for example, you doing all the planning in either English or maths for you and your year-group colleague(s), or that you are part of a subject-planning group charged with the responsibility of updating a scheme of work. It could also indicate your involvement in action research into a selected aspect of teaching and learning in which you have to feed back to colleague(s). In relation to outdoor learning, for example in the EYFS, it could mean redesigning and then changing the outdoor provision, while higher up the school it could entail involvement in developing the wider use of the school grounds.
an engaging curriculum	This is self-explanatory but vitally important.
	How does the curriculum you have helped design draw in, then hook, your learners? What makes the learning 'irresistible' so that they want to learn more?
relevant subject area(s)	Essentially, any subjects you are responsible for teaching as part of your daily job.

In relation to pupils' learning and progress, what kind of evidence is possible/best?

✓ Comments by senior members of staff acknowledging and highlighting your contribution(s) to the wider curriculum team.

✓ Examples of the sort of changes/additions you have introduced to make the curriculum more engaging. This might include part of a new scheme of work or year-group plans in which you highlight your contribution. It could also include images to illustrate improved provision (equipment, pupil materials, learning areas etc). Remember to explain/justify what you did and how it increased pupil engagement.

Anything to avoid?

✗ (Unless you have never contributed more widely) over-concentration on your own personal lesson planning. *Note: this is likely to be rare, but if it is the case, you should request the opportunity to work as part of a curriculum planning team.*

Source of evidence, eg: • my own reflective notes • lesson observations by mentor, tutor, HOD, subject leader • meeting notes with other colleagues, parents, specialist professionals • lesson plans, schemes of work	Date of evidence source	Any notes you may want to add, particularly those relating to pupil progress, learning and other outcomes.
Note here what you have learned and how your practice has improved as a result of addressing this Standard.		

Teachers' Standard 5: adapt teaching to respond to the strength and needs of all pupils

TS 5a: 'knows when and how to differentiate appropriately, using approaches which enable pupils to be taught effectively'

Key words	Understanding the Standard: guidance notes
knows when [to differentiate appropriately]	In the real world, not everything can, or needs to be, differentiated. You need to show that you can identify those points in a lesson when, *in order to make learning accessible to all pupils*, work will need to be presented in different ways and/or particular pupils given additional support.
and how to differentiate appropriately	Essentially, this is about showing that you can use a range of methods to make your teaching and pupils' learning accessible to all the pupils you teach. To do this as effectively as possible, you need to show that you know your pupils' backgrounds and capabilities well and that you can adapt the teaching/learning tasks accordingly. For example, a text for a child with visual impairment might simply need enlargement, whereas, if both pupils are going to benefit from what it contains, the same text for a child with EAL might require simplifying.
to be taught effectively	This element stresses the link between the input (teaching) and the learning (implied by the word *effectively*). Can you show that the differentiation you have planned and used has *made a difference to the learning and progress* of the child(ren) in question?

In relation to pupils' learning and progress, what kind of evidence is possible/best?

✓ Lesson planning which identifies children of differing needs and abilities and how the lesson is going to be adapted to cater for these differences. This could include, for example, pre-planned differentiated questioning during whole-class input, clear reference to different tasks for different groupings, teaching assistant support linked to particular individuals…

✓ Examples of work set for different pupils with differing needs or abilities. Where this is accompanied by the actual work done and any follow-up marking/comments, so much the better.

✓ Planning for children with very specific or more acute needs, eg a separate plan of work to help a teaching assistant teach a child with SpLD (specific learning difficulty) or a group of pupils with EAL.

✓ Lesson observation comments (or similar comments from a specialist, such as a SENCO or a speech and language therapist) that highlight the positive approaches you have taken to support a child or children with additional needs. Any indication of the impact that your differentiated approach has had (eg 'Asha is now confident to swim a length herself. Thank you!' 'David is now able to choose his own book and read a whole story by himself for the first time!'; or a significant improvement in test marks following the intervention described by you) would also be strong evidence.

Anything to avoid?

✗ Sheets of planning or worksheets (even when differentiated) with little or no contextual information, especially when unaccompanied by an indication of how effective this was in terms of pupils' learning and progress.

Source of evidence, eg: • my own reflective notes • lesson observations by mentor, tutor, HOD, subject leader • meeting notes with other colleagues, parents, specialist professionals • lesson plans, schemes of work	Date of evidence source	Any notes you may want to add, particularly those relating to pupil progress, learning and other outcomes.

Note here what you have learned and how your practice has improved as a result of addressing this Standard.

TS 5b: 'has a secure understanding of how a range of factors can inhibit pupils' ability to learn, and how best to overcome these'

Key words	Understanding the Standard: guidance notes
a range of factors	This implies the need to address the different reasons for a pupil's learning being slower than we would expect or hope for. These include a variety of medical/neurological issues (ADHD, ASD, dyslexia and so on); mother-tongue language issues; physical disabilities, such as deafness, poor eyesight or mobility issues; home background/social factors (eg parental illiteracy; poverty; parental mental health); behavioural/emotional issues. *Note: this is not a definitive list and the issues listed are not mutually exclusive. Additionally, caution should always be exercised in 'diagnosing' and then labelling children in this way.*
inhibit pupils' ability to learn	All children learn at different rates and some, as we know, can be so-called 'late-starters'. However, we do have certain expectations of children's attainment and progress at various points in their life (variously described as 'expected', 'typical', 'normal' – in the sense of being close to 'the norm' – and so on). Sometimes the reason for a child's apparent lack of progress is easy to ascertain (eg a diagnosis of glue ear leading to loss of hearing), while other problems can go undiagnosed for years.
overcome these	Part of a teacher's job is to find ways in which children, with whatever issues they present, can be helped to learn. This is often expressed as 'helping the child fulfil their potential'. While we will never be successful in totally overcoming these problems, we can help lessen the impact on individual learners' progress and attainment.

In relation to pupils' learning and progress, what kind of evidence is possible/best?

✓ Meeting notes with your SENCO or other colleagues, especially those specialising in different sorts of learning difficulties, which show you are engaging with them to address your pupils' learning and progress.

✓ Evidence of attendance at training that focuses on additional learning needs.

✓ Individual pupil plans (eg IEPs) which you have helped formulate and which you monitor and evaluate, possibly with more experienced others.

✓ Planning which indicates clearly that you have identified particular learning needs and are taking appropriate actions to help address them (eg differentiated teaching resources; use of support staff).

✓ Extracts from university work relating to SEND which show your understanding of the issues. *(Note: different establishments may have their own rules on including parts of essays, for example, as evidence. Please check with your own institution on this one.)*

Anything to avoid?

✗ Listing the types of issues you may have heard of, or have in your class, without indicating what you understand or can do to help overcome them.

Source of evidence, eg: • my own reflective notes • lesson observations by mentor, tutor, HOD, subject leader • meeting notes with other colleagues, parents, specialist professionals • lesson plans, schemes of work	Date of evidence source	Any notes you may want to add, particularly those relating to pupil progress, learning and other outcomes.

Note here what you have learned and how your practice has improved as a result of addressing this Standard.

TS 5c: 'is able to demonstrate an awareness of the physical, social and intellectual development of children, and knows how to adapt teaching to support pupils' education at different stages of development'

Key words	Understanding the Standard: guidance notes
demonstrate an awareness of the physical, social and intellectual development of children	Essentially, can you present evidence that shows you are aware of the fact that children have different teaching and learning needs as they progress through the educational system? These needs are part biological, part social/emotional and part intellectual.
adapt teaching to support pupils' education at different stages of development	Can you show that you take these differences into account when teaching children who are at different ages or, perhaps, different levels of ability?

For example, you may teach two groups from the same class, one of which is regarded as highly able, the other with significant learning needs. How do you adapt your teaching with this in mind? |

In relation to pupils' learning and progress, what kind of evidence is possible/best?

✓ The best evidence will simply show that you can adapt your teaching to suit the needs of the children in front of you. If you teach across a wide age range, for example in both lower Key Stage 1 and upper Key Stage 2, does your planning show that you adopt different approaches in these groups? *(Note: these groups could be selected from both your home school and your placement school, if this applies.)* Highlight those aspects of your teaching which indicate your awareness and how you use this to inform your teaching; for example, shorter periods during which infants need to sit and listen; more opportunity to learn through play, or move around the learning space.

✓ Similarly, if you teach children of the same age but different abilities, does your differentiated planning show how you have taken this fact into account?

✓ In both cases, explain clearly what you have done and why. For example: 'as this group is young and generally rather immature for their age I decided to...'

Anything to avoid?

✗ Simple statements which say that you understand the differences but fail to show how you have used this understanding to impact upon the teaching approaches you adopt.

Source of evidence, eg: • my own reflective notes • lesson observations by mentor, tutor, HOD, subject leader • meeting notes with other colleagues, parents, specialist professionals • lesson plans, schemes of work	Date of evidence source	Any notes you may want to add, particularly those relating to pupil progress, learning and other outcomes.

Note here what you have learned and how your practice has improved as a result of addressing this Standard.

TS 5d: 'has a clear understanding of the needs of all pupils, including those with special educational needs; those of high ability; those with English as an additional language; those with disabilities; and is able to use and evaluate distinctive teaching approaches to engage and support them'

Key words	Understanding the Standard: guidance notes
Has a clear understanding of the needs of all pupils	Although the descriptor says *all pupils*, the rest of the sentence suggests your focus here should be on pupils taken from the list of groups which follows, ie those who may face barriers to learning and have particular needs different from 'the norm'. It may be difficult/impossible to draw your examples from every category, but aim for at least two, three if at all possible.
	Your understanding of their needs, as in TS 5c, will come out in the way you respond and adapt your teaching accordingly.
is able to use and evaluate distinctive teaching approaches	This is about showing that (a) you can adapt your teaching and use different approaches for different pupils, and (b) that you are reflective and can evaluate how effective the *distinctive teaching approaches* turned out to be. Your evidence (including your commentary) should show both (a) and (b).
to engage and support them	All good teaching should do this but there may be particularly strong evidence that children who were disengaged or struggling prior to your teaching are now turned on to learning and making better progress.
	If you have evidence of this, certainly use it!

In relation to pupils' learning and progress, what kind of evidence is possible/best?

✓ Lesson observation comments which highlight the engagement, enthusiasm for learning, progress, and/or attainment of pupils in any of the groups mentioned, together with a clear link made to the provision you have made for their learning, eg small teaching focus groups; differentiated teaching/learning materials; clear targets and support plans. If you have good examples of 'before and after' work, use these to illustrate the impact of your interventions.

✓ Extracts from university work that show you have an understanding of pupils' needs, eg assignments or your summaries of academic articles relating to differing pupil needs. (See note in TS 5b on using extracts from essays.)

✓ Examples showing that you having evaluated pupil progress and subsequently taken the decision to adapt your approaches to cater for their particular needs, eg *Assess-Plan-Do-Review*. Include any pupil case studies if you have them here. Your approach need not always have been successful, but you do need to show that you have evaluated how it went and made meaningful decisions based on what you concluded.

Anything to avoid?

✗ Statements saying you understand pupils' needs with little or no evidence to show that this actually is the case, ie you need to present evidence that you adapt your teaching to match your pupils' needs.

Source of evidence, eg: • my own reflective notes • lesson observations by mentor, tutor, HOD, subject leader • meeting notes with other colleagues, parents, specialist professionals • lesson plans, schemes of work	Date of evidence source	Any notes you may want to add, particularly those relating to pupil progress, learning and other outcomes.

Note here what you have learned and how your practice has improved as a result of addressing this Standard.

Teachers' Standard 6: make accurate and productive use of assessment

TS 6a: 'know and understand how to assess the relevant subject and curriculum areas including statutory requirements'

Key words	Understanding the Standard: guidance notes
how to assess	A broad interpretation of this would include being able to use continuous, formative assessment (AfL) as well as more formal, summative approaches such as tests and exams.
	The understanding and use of formative assessment is, of course, a key skill and one you need to develop from day one of your training.
relevant subject and curriculum areas	This will depend on your personal circumstances and whether you are primary or secondary, a generalist or specialist, teacher. However, at secondary level it would include, as a minimum, your specialism, and at primary level all the currently 'reportable' elements of English and maths. Good practice would suggest that you should be able to use the national curriculum descriptors to assess and report (to SLT or parents, for example) pupils' achievements in any of the subject areas you teach.
	Note: different schools will have different interpretations of the word 'relevant', so for clarity's sake you would need to check this with your school leaders.
statutory requirements	This refers currently to end of key stage reporting requirements at the end of EYFS, Key Stage 1, Key Stage 2 and Key Stage 4 (in England).

In relation to pupils' learning and progress, what kind of evidence is possible/best?

✓ Examples of marking which demonstrate your sound teacher subject knowledge and your use of accurate feedback to pupils (including constructive comments and next-steps approaches).

✓ Assessment which relates to national (eg end of key stage) expectations. You may, for example, be involved in cluster or local authority moderation-type activities.

✓ Examples of completed targeted assessment sheets (including, for example, periodic tests) with an indication of how you interpreted and then used the results and/or pupil responses.

Anything to avoid?

✗ Copies of school policies, pro formas, or assessment sheets and data unsupported by a clear indication of what they are and how they were used.

Source of evidence, eg: • my own reflective notes • lesson observations by mentor, tutor, HOD, subject leader • meeting notes with other colleagues, parents, specialist professionals • lesson plans, schemes of work	Date of evidence source	Any notes you may want to add, particularly those relating to pupil progress, learning and other outcomes.

Note here what you have learned and how your practice has improved as a result of addressing this Standard.

TS 6b: 'is able to make use of formative and summative assessment to secure pupils' progress'

Key words	Understanding the Standard: guidance notes
make use of formative assessment	Are you able to use ongoing assessment (eg responding to pupils' responses in classroom discussions, regular marking of work, records of your observations of pupils' working, pupil conference notes) to inform subsequent teaching and learning?
	Typically, this type of assessment happens on a frequent (eg daily) basis and can lead to 'on-the-hoof', sometimes immediate, changes in the direction of a lesson or of subsequent planning.
make use of... summative assessment	Are you able to use tests, examinations and other end-of-unit type assessments to inform subsequent teaching and learning? *Note: this type of assessment typically happens at the end of units or blocks of work, eg half-termly, termly, annually.*
to secure pupils' progress	This is key to the statement.
	How have you *used* the assessment information to ensure that pupils have not stayed still or become stuck in their learning?

In relation to pupils' learning and progress, what kind of evidence is possible/best?

✓ Examples of the use of formative assessment including lesson observation comments referring refer to the positive use of formative assessment (including teacher questioning) to inform next steps in teaching and learning; examples of marked work illustrating next-steps marking and learners' responses; lesson plans annotated to show that you have reflected on the learning and have used this information to make changes to subsequent teaching sessions (which you could also show).

✓ Examples of the use of summative assessment could include: tables of test/exam results annotated to show how you used/intend to use the information they contain; examples of completed test/exam papers marked and annotated to show how you used/intend to use the information they contain; a series of such documents showing an improvement in pupils' marks over time; and comments highlighting how this improvement was achieved.

✓ In both cases, you need to show what you did as a result of having this information. For example, did you decide to repeat a piece of teaching and learning? Did you take a group of learners and explain the work again, differently? Did you decide to increase the challenge as the class showed they were more advanced in their learning than you thought? Do lesson observation notes indicate that you actively respond to the answers given to you by pupils by, for instance, exploring their comprehension further and explaining things again? Have you used assessment information (eg from last year) to inform the pitch and pace of your lessons?

Anything to avoid?

✗ Solely focusing on just one of the two broad types of assessment. Include both!

✗ Any assessment (eg tables of results, test sheets, snapshots of marking) which does not indicate clearly what it shows and how you used the information positively to effect changes in your teaching and in your pupils' learning.

Source of evidence, eg: • my own reflective notes • lesson observations by mentor, tutor, HOD, subject leader • meeting notes with other colleagues, parents, specialist professionals • lesson plans, schemes of work	Date of evidence source	Any notes you may want to add, particularly those relating to pupil progress, learning and other outcomes.

Note here what you have learned and how your practice has improved as a result of addressing this Standard.

TS 6c: 'is able to use relevant data to monitor progress, set targets, and plan subsequent lessons'

Key words	Understanding the Standard: guidance notes
data	*Data* normally refers to numerical, statistical information such as percentages of pupils at certain levels or grades. However, it can be more broadly thought of as any information you might hold on your learners, especially with regard to their attainment or progress.
to monitor progress	This implies using data on a reasonably regular basis to ensure that children are making at least expected, but preferably, good or better, progress.

What processes and procedures do you employ to make sure that any data you hold is put to effective use? For example, periodic monitoring by you, maybe in conjunction with year-group colleagues or assessment lead. |
| *set targets* | This could refer to individual or group/class targets set, based on your analysis of the data you have collected. The target could, for example, be a percentage of children you aim to be at or beyond expected levels by a certain date or could, in contrast, be a very specific curricular target for a particular child, eg the number of CVC (consonant-vowel-consonant) words they can recognise by half term. |
| *plan subsequent lessons* | The idea here is that you *use* whatever information you have gleaned from the data to inform your lesson planning. How have you altered or adapted your lesson plans in response to what you now know about the progress and attainment of your learners? For example, have you decided to repeat some or all of what the class have already covered? Alternatively, will you perhaps *not* teach the lesson you had planned as you now realise that your pupils already have a good enough grasp of the content? |

In relation to pupils' learning and progress, what kind of evidence is possible/best?

✓ Examples of the kind of data you collect with a clear explanation of what it shows and how you have used it to monitor progress, set targets or plan subsequent lessons. This could be snapshots of data sheets (anonymised if sensitive) with a commentary on how they are used. If the data is more of the 'soft' variety (eg reports written on a pupil's progress by the SENCO or educational psychologist), you could show how the curriculum or behavioural targets you set the pupil support the advice of the specialist. Examples of the targets or *subsequent lesson* plans would also make the link between the data and its use clearer for the reader.

Anything to avoid?

✗ Any of the above lacking a clear explanation of how the data is used to impact upon pupils' learning.

Source of evidence, eg:	Date of evidence source	Any notes you may want to add, particularly those relating to pupil progress, learning and other outcomes.
• my own reflective notes		
• lesson observations by mentor, tutor, HOD, subject leader		
• meeting notes with other colleagues, parents, specialist professionals		
• lesson plans, schemes of work		

Note here what you have learned and how your practice has improved as a result of addressing this Standard.

TS 6d: 'is able to give pupils regular feedback, both orally and through accurate marking, and encourages pupils to respond to the feedback'

Key words	Understanding the Standard: guidance notes
give pupils regular feedback	Feedback is 'the breakfast of champions' and you will be the main person to provide this to your pupils. In order to be effective, this exchange needs to be woven into the fabric of your teaching and should be a feature of your daily practice. Note that it does not mean simply saying things are right or wrong, or giving pupils your opinions or ideas, but will include you asking searching questions to help them reflect on and evaluate their own work.
orally	This means 'spoken'.
accurate marking	*Marking* implies responding to pupils' work in a more systematic, formal way, eg by writing comments or giving marks or grades. The *accuracy* aspect means both getting your own facts right (the teacher's subject knowledge) and being selective in what you do, or do not, choose to correct or highlight. Which things need to be focused upon, and which can be ignored?
encourages pupils to respond to the feedback	To me, *encourages* implies two things: (a) that you are positive, supportive and directive, and (b) that you actually *give time* for pupils to make their responses. The first without the second is unlikely to have much impact on pupils' learning.

In relation to pupils' learning and progress, what kind of evidence is possible/best?

✓ Lesson observation comments that highlight your evaluation of, and response to, pupils' efforts to learn. This could, for example, come through as part of a classroom discussion where you question and guide pupils (using hints and clues, for instance) towards a better understanding of a concept they are finding difficult to grasp.

✓ Snapshots of written responses to children's work in which the marking goes beyond simply identifying things that are 'right' or 'wrong'. The best marking focuses on things of importance, draws the child's attention to them, then expects and allows the child to make some sort of improvement. *Note: if your school uses a system of various pen colours to distinguish between teachers' and pupils' writing, explain this so that the verifier understands what they are looking at.*

✓ Snapshots of pupils' responses to your marking. Highlight the fact that they have been given time to make their responses and explain how you build this time into your weekly planning. This, plus examples over time, will help satisfy the *regular* part of the descriptor.

Anything to avoid?

✗ Simple right or wrong marking where pupils' responses are unclear or absent.

Source of evidence, eg: • my own reflective notes • lesson observations by mentor, tutor, HOD, subject leader • meeting notes with other colleagues, parents, specialist professionals • lesson plans, schemes of work	Date of evidence source	Any notes you may want to add, particularly those relating to pupil progress, learning and other outcomes.

Note here what you have learned and how your practice has improved as a result of addressing this Standard.

Teachers' Standard 7: manage behaviour effectively to ensure a good and safe learning environment

TS 7a: 'has clear rules and routines for behaviour in classrooms, and takes responsibility for promoting good and courteous behaviour in classrooms and around the school, in accordance with the school's behaviour policy'

Key words	Understanding the Standard: guidance notes
clear rules and routines	These are the rules and routines that pupils associate with you when you are teaching or supervising them. Are your expectations clear and consistent so that pupils know how they should conduct themselves when you are around?
takes responsibility for	It is your responsibility to manage children's behaviour when they are in your care. Are you able to shoulder this responsibility confidently with the pupils you teach?
promoting good and courteous behaviour	Behavioural management is more than mere 'control'. It involves modelling and encouraging the sort of social interactions you want from your pupils.
in accordance with the school's behaviour policy	These are the behavioural rules and routines you apply should be in line with the school policy.

In relation to pupils' learning and progress, what kind of evidence is possible/best?

✓ Lesson observation comments that refer to the clear use of rules and routines, helping children understand how it is they should behave in class and beyond. It would be even better if the comments make additional reference to the school's behaviour policy.

✓ A photograph of a classroom charter or similar, signed by children, in which you have agreed the rules or guidelines for the year.

✓ Observation comments or similar that highlight the polite behaviour of pupils (towards you, each other, or visitors) and your role in encouraging them to behave in this way, eg reminding children to say please, thank you, and excuse me, and praising them when they do so.

Anything to avoid?

✗ Copies of school/classroom rules with no reference to your own involvement or contribution.

✗ A simple description/copy of the school's behaviour policy.

Source of evidence, eg: • my own reflective notes • lesson observations by mentor, tutor, HOD, subject leader • meeting notes with other colleagues, parents, specialist professionals • lesson plans, schemes of work	Date of evidence source	Any notes you may want to add, particularly those relating to pupil progress, learning and other outcomes.

Note here what you have learned and how your practice has improved as a result of addressing this Standard.

TS 7b: 'has high expectations of behaviour and establishes a framework for discipline, with a range of strategies using praise, sanctions and rewards consistently and fairly'

Key words	Understanding the Standard: guidance notes
high expectations of behaviour	Self-explanatory maybe, but how do you *communicate* this to your pupils?
establishes a framework for discipline	This is about you laying down markers that you stick to from lesson to lesson, week to week. Examples include your classroom rules, how you expect pupils to talk to you and each other, and making it clear if/when they are allowed to leave their seat, take a drink, or use the toilet without seeking permission.
range of strategies	Good teachers need to be able to respond flexibly to the myriad situations that arise in school life. What works with one pupil may not work with another; what works well on a Monday morning may not on a Friday afternoon!
using praise, sanctions and rewards	Praise generally means the informal positive remarks you say or write about pupil(s). Sanctions and rewards tend to be more formal and in line with agreed school policy.
consistently and fairly	This is extremely important in practice – especially in the eyes of pupils and their parents/carers. *Consistently* refers to even-handedness over time and between children. Inconsistency confuses children and may even suggest favouritism or bias in how you are treating individuals. *Fairly* refers more to the level of sanction or reward and needs to be seen as just by all concerned.

In relation to pupils' learning and progress, what kind of evidence is possible/best?

✓ Lesson observation comments referring to the good behaviour of the children and your contribution to it; for example, praising your good classroom management, equitable use of praise, sanctions and rewards, adherence to the school's behaviour policy, and so on.

✓ Similar to above, but anything which refers to the confident handling of particularly difficult situations or challenging pupils, enabling learning to proceed smoothly, would be powerful evidence to include.

✓ A photograph of a classroom charter or similar, signed by children, in which you have agreed the rules or guidelines for the year.

Anything to avoid?

✗ Copies of school/classroom rules with no reference to your own contribution.

✗ A simple description of the school's rewards and sanctions, or copy of the behaviour policy.

Source of evidence, eg: • my own reflective notes • lesson observations by mentor, tutor, HOD, subject leader • meeting notes with other colleagues, parents, specialist professionals • lesson plans, schemes of work	Date of evidence source	Any notes you may want to add, particularly those relating to pupil progress, learning and other outcomes.

Note here what you have learned and how your practice has improved as a result of addressing this Standard.

TS 7c: 'is able to manage classes effectively, using approaches which are appropriate to pupils' needs in order to involve and motivate them'

Key words	Understanding the Standard: guidance notes
manage classes effectively	This is about maintaining good order so that children are able to learn well during the time you are teaching them.
approaches... appropriate to pupils' needs	For a variety of reasons, different classes need different approaches to classroom management. Age is an obvious factor (for instance, Reception vs Year 6, Year 7 vs Year 11? for instance) but so too is the distinctive make-up and nature of any particular group of children and how outside influences might affect them over time. Part of the skill of teaching is to know your children well enough to alter your approaches according to their needs at any particular time, eg Friday afternoon, during 'wet play', following an incident in the playground.
involve and motivate them	How do your approaches to classroom management encourage a feeling of inclusion? Do your pupils feel part of the learning process, actively contribute to the daily life of the class and show an eagerness to learn?

In relation to pupils' learning and progress, what kind of evidence is possible/best?

✓ Lesson observation comments that make specific reference to the way you skilfully manage your class in order for them to be able to learn. This might also include, for example, reference to how you dealt with a specific difficult situation so that learning could continue unimpeded.

✓ Any records of discussion (eg with your mentor) which indicate that you reflect upon your approaches to classroom and behavioural management and then make changes to subsequent teaching plans (eg by trying a different approach with a particular child or with the class as a whole; changing the timing or nature of particular activities or lessons in the light of your experience thus far).

✓ Comments made by observers about the level of pupil engagement and enthusiasm for learning. Similarly, you may have pupil voice style (or parental) feedback that indicates high levels of enjoyment and motivation to learn.

Anything to avoid?

✗ Copies of school/classroom rules with no reference to how you use them to establish and maintain good order.

Source of evidence, eg: • my own reflective notes • lesson observations by mentor, tutor, HOD, subject leader • meeting notes with other colleagues, parents, specialist professionals • lesson plans, schemes of work	Date of evidence source	Any notes you may want to add, particularly those relating to pupil progress, learning and other outcomes.

Note here what you have learned and how your practice has improved as a result of addressing this Standard.

TS 7d: 'is able to maintain good relationships with pupils, exercising appropriate authority and acts decisively when necessary'

Key words	Understanding the Standard: guidance notes
maintain good relationships with pupils	Here, *good* means 'professional'. It is worth quoting in full the first bullet point in Part 2: '*Treating pupils with dignity, building relationships rooted in mutual respect and at all times observing proper boundaries appropriate to a teacher's professional position*'. These are the types of characteristics you will need to evidence.
exercising appropriate authority	Children have to know that you are in charge so you need to demonstrate 'presence' in the classroom. This does not in any way rule out the encouragement of democratic principles, or negate pupil voice – but ultimately, and legally, you are in charge.
acts decisively when necessary	There are times when you will need to impose your will on a child or children. This is especially true when there are possible concerns about health and safety or about a worrying lack of order in the group. At times like these, you will need to show that you are able to make a decision that helps to rectify the situation swiftly.

In relation to pupils' learning and progress, what kind of evidence is possible/best?

✓ Lesson observation comments referring to the positive (professional) relationships in your class, the mutual respect you engender, your use of humour, praise and so on, to sustain relationships. Similarly, reports by others that comment upon this positively.

✓ Comments by your mentor and others that demonstrate you know when and how to be firm and decisive if necessary. This could be a reference to a particular incident or occurrence when swift action prevented things escalating, evidencing the fact that you know your pupils and how best to handle more difficult situations.

✓ Anonymised behavioural records and notes showing how you dealt with an issue (eg alleged bullying) and brought matters to a satisfactory conclusion (which ultimately may have meant having to pass it on to a higher authority). This could include, for example, anonymised emails from parents acknowledging your efforts and thanking you for tackling the issue.

Anything to avoid?

✗ Personal statements expressing your beliefs but otherwise giving no evidence, eg 'I believe in respecting each and every child'. Good evidence should aim to 'show not tell'.

Source of evidence, eg: • my own reflective notes • lesson observations by mentor, tutor, HOD, subject leader • meeting notes with other colleagues, parents, specialist professionals • lesson plans, schemes of work	Date of evidence source	Any notes you may want to add, particularly those relating to pupil progress, learning and other outcomes.

Note here what you have learned and how your practice has improved as a result of addressing this Standard.

Teachers' Standard 8: fulfil wider professional responsibilities

TS 8a: 'is able to make a positive contribution to the wider life and ethos of the school'

Key words	Understanding the Standard: guidance notes
positive contribution	This is self-explanatory really: how does what you do help to make a difference to the life of the school and its community?
wider life	This refers to those things that happen beyond the confines of your own classroom. It may include working alongside other adults in their bid to provide the best overall education for the school's children, so being part of the PTA, helping to run a club, taking a sports team, or volunteering to be part of a lesson-study group would all count in this respect.
ethos	The *ethos* of a school describes its fundamental beliefs and approaches to education. Although the ethos of many schools will share common elements (eg respect for each other; valuing honesty and hard work), there is still variation between different schools. For example, one school might emphasise religious, cultural or more 'traditional' values such as discipline, obedience and loyalty whereas another might place particular importance on friendship, team-work and the rights of the child. How do you contribute to the distinctive core of *your* school's life?

In relation to pupils' learning and progress, what kind of evidence is possible/best?

✓ Reports/messages from a range of people (SLT, PTA, governors, parents) recognising and thanking you for your contribution.

✓ Photographs or other evidence showing that you contribute to after-school clubs, sports teams or the like.

✓ Evidencing your contribution specifically to the ethos of the school is more difficult but could include support for particular cultural activities (eg dance, language groups, religious observance) or helping pupils contribute to the local community. Similarly, statements attesting to the fact that you have 'fitted in well' to the school and its way of life might be helpful here.

Anything to avoid?

✗ Anything which fails to illustrate your own contribution, eg a simple list of clubs or societies that the school runs.

Source of evidence, eg: • my own reflective notes • lesson observations by mentor, tutor, HOD, subject leader • meeting notes with other colleagues, parents, specialist professionals • lesson plans, schemes of work	Date of evidence source	Any notes you may want to add, particularly those relating to pupil progress, learning and other outcomes.

Note here what you have learned and how your practice has improved as a result of addressing this Standard.

TS 8b: 'is able to develop effective professional relationships with colleagues, knowing how and when to draw on advice and specialist support'

Key words	Understanding the Standard: guidance notes
effective professional relationships with colleagues	This part of the Standard is concerned with the role you play as part of a professional team.
	Colleagues includes anyone employed at your own school, but also teachers employed at other schools with which the school has formal contacts (eg partner academies or parts of an assessment cluster). Additionally, external specialists such as speech and language therapists or behavioural advisers would be included here.
	Effective implies that the relationships have a positive impact upon your teaching and your pupils' learning.
how and when to draw on advice and specialist support	All teachers (and especially ones early in their careers) need help from time to time.
	As a trainee, you will be expected to look for advice and support when you are unsure what to do. It is far better to seek help than wait until things go terribly wrong, but at the same time, you need to be conscious and respectful of others' time commitments.
	The main sources of support are likely to be your mentor, year-group colleagues, the SENCO, subject leaders or specialists (eg music, MFL or PE) and tutor.

In relation to pupils' learning and progress, what kind of evidence is possible/best?

✓ Meeting notes that record the fact that you have sought support or advice from a colleague. This could relate to the general curriculum, or be pedagogical in nature, or could be with reference to a particular child(ren) with more complex needs, for example.

✓ Written comments made by colleagues that attest to the fact that you seek *and then act upon* advice that you have been given.

Anything to avoid?

✗ Statements which tell the reader that you hold regular meetings with colleagues or are a member of a team (eg year-group planning team) without evidencing that your relationships are effective and that you are able to take on board what is suggested for your professional development.

Source of evidence, eg: • my own reflective notes • lesson observations by mentor, tutor, HOD, subject leader • meeting notes with other colleagues, parents, specialist professionals • lesson plans, schemes of work	Date of evidence source	Any notes you may want to add, particularly those relating to pupil progress, learning and other outcomes.

Note here what you have learned and how your practice has improved as a result of addressing this Standard.

TS 8c: 'is able to deploy support staff effectively'

Key words	Understanding the Standard: guidance notes
support staff	Ideally, this refers to a teaching/learning-support assistant assigned to you on a regular basis.
	If you don't have a regular TA or LSA, for the purposes of this strand I take this to mean any additional adults you have at your disposal, eg do you have a parent or someone on work experience or similar you can use? Additionally, if you have a TA for only part of the week, request that at least some of your observations at least include these lessons so that observers can make meaningful comments. And don't forget that the class at your placement school, if you have one, may have a support assistant – so find out beforehand if you can.
deploy... effectively	*Effectively* is a key word as it is not good enough merely to have an extra pair of hands in the room.
	How well do you utilise this useful (and relatively expensive) resource? Do you include them in planning? Are they well prepared when the lesson starts? Do you deploy them for general support, or do they work mainly with an individual pupil, a group of more/less able pupils, or a combination?
	Critically, whatever the level or frequency of support, you need to evaluate the *impact* of this on children's learning and progress.

In relation to pupils' learning and progress, what kind of evidence is possible/best?

✓ Comments in lesson observations that make specific reference to your deployment of support staff. This should include something about the decisions/rationale behind the way they are used, eg to support a child with significant learning needs... to provide additional challenges to a group of high ability learners, or enabling a pupil with ADHD to stay on task.'

✓ Similarly, anything which comments favourably on your inclusion of the support staff in the preparation and teaching of the lesson – do you have any meeting time with TAs (eg informally at the start of the day; five minutes before lessons; weekly, after school)? Do you actively include them in class discussions or 'team teach' parts of the lessons where they may have better knowledge or expertise? Do you discuss (then record) with support staff how their target pupils/groups have learned?

✓ Attainment and progress information that indicates the effectiveness of support for individual pupils or groups of pupils.

Anything to avoid?

✗ A timetable or similar which describes when you have a TA and who they work with, devoid of any evaluation of the effectiveness of their support.

Source of evidence, eg: • my own reflective notes • lesson observations by mentor, tutor, HOD, subject leader • meeting notes with other colleagues, parents, specialist professionals • lesson plans, schemes of work	Date of evidence source	Any notes you may want to add, particularly those relating to pupil progress, learning and other outcomes.

Note here what you have learned and how your practice has improved as a result of addressing this Standard.

TS 8d: 'is able to take responsibility for improving teaching through appropriate professional development responding to advice and feedback from colleagues'

Key words	Understanding the Standard: guidance notes
take responsibility for improving teaching	The focus of this strand is on the practicalities of improving your classroom practice, and what you do about it.
appropriate professional development	This is a broad dimension that would include in-service training, year group and staff meetings, curriculum group meetings, external courses, working with other schools, lesson observation and team teaching. *Note: the final element, below, suggests this Standard focuses more on the feedback from colleagues than it does, say, on private reading or university studies.*
responding to advice and feedback from colleagues	Colleagues would include anybody working in the same school as you, as well as other teachers, advisers and specialists with whom you collaborate professionally. The important thing here is that you can show, as a result of working and listening to others, that you have made positive changes to your practice.

In relation to pupils' learning and progress, what kind of evidence is possible/best?

✓ Comments in reports (eg by mentor, tutor or SLT) which refer to the fact that you are reflective and will make changes to your practice as a result of discussions with more experienced colleagues.

✓ Comments and descriptions written by yourself that show you have made such changes, eg self-reflective notes with examples of planning or pupil targets you have amended following discussions.

✓ Examples of a change made in response to in-service training held at school or elsewhere.

Anything to avoid?

✗ Lists of in-service or other types of development courses attended with no link to changes in classroom practice.

Source of evidence, eg: • my own reflective notes • lesson observations by mentor, tutor, HOD, subject leader • meeting notes with other colleagues, parents, specialist professionals • lesson plans, schemes of work	Date of evidence source	Any notes you may want to add, particularly those relating to pupil progress, learning and other outcomes.

Note here what you have learned and how your practice has improved as a result of addressing this Standard.

TS 8e: 'is able to communicate effectively with parents with regard to pupils' achievements and well-being'

Key words	Understanding the Standard: guidance notes
communicate effectively	When you contact parents/carers, whether by email, written reports, or in face-to-face meetings, are you able to give them clear information which allows them to understand how their child is progressing and if they are happy and well at school?
pupils' achievements and well-being	*Achievements* means academic accomplishments as well as a wide range of others including sporting, musical, dramatic and cultural.
	Well-being refers to pupils' emotional health at school – are they happy and confident at school, do they have friends, and do they feel safe from bullying?

In relation to pupils' learning and progress, what kind of evidence is possible/best?

Note: in my experience, it can be a little tricky to show you have met this Standard. In the absence of other evidence, you may need a more senior colleague to write a comment specifically about how you relate to and communicate with parents.

✓ Anonymised examples of meeting notes, with additional contextual details, can help illustrate this Standard, eg notes from a short series of meetings with a parent in which a learning or behavioural issue was discussed and resolved to the parent's satisfaction.

✓ Any communication from a parent thanking you for your clear communication, eg response to a termly report or parents' evening meeting.

✓ In your commentary give a general overview of how and when you meet parents, eg daily, at the classroom door; half-termly, in a 'meet the teacher' session; termly, at parents' evenings.

✓ As suggested above, a comment that highlights your effective communication with parents, written by a senior member of staff who knows your practice, can be very illuminating.

Anything to avoid?

✗ Timetables of parents' evenings or similar with no external evaluation of how effective your communication with parents was.

Source of evidence, eg: • my own reflective notes • lesson observations by mentor, tutor, HOD, subject leader • meeting notes with other colleagues, parents, specialist professionals • lesson plans, schemes of work	Date of evidence source	Any notes you may want to add, particularly those relating to pupil progress, learning and other outcomes.

Note here what you have learned and how your practice has improved as a result of addressing this Standard.

Top ten checklist ☑

The following is not meant to be a definitive or even 'essential-in-all-cases' list of considerations, but is included to help you reflect on the quality of your evidence and your reasons for selecting it.

Before uploading or otherwise presenting a piece of evidence, ask yourself the following questions.

1 Does the material I have selected *match precisely* the wording of the Standard/strand in question?

2 Does it evidence *my impact on pupils' progress* (eg academic, behavioural, social)?

3 Does it evidence *embedded practice over time* (eg in a sequence of lessons) – or is it simply a one-off? If it is a one-off, be prepared to add further evidence at a later date.

4 Does it *illustrate clearly* exactly what I want the verifier to look at?

5 Have I *highlighted the key features* so that they stand out from the background information?

6 Have I *explained the context for learning*, simply and clearly?

7 Have I *explained and justified* my reasons for selecting the evidence, simply and clearly?

And, considering your selection of evidence overall:

8 Does it draw on *a range of contexts* for learning, eg different age groups; different classes/schools; different subjects; different ability groups?

9 Does it include a *range of professional (or other) opinions*, eg mentor; tutor; head of year/department; speech therapist; educational psychologist; pupil or parent voice?

10 Does it constitute/contribute to a *more holistic, evidence bundle*-style array of evidence?

Stakes In The Ground

VOL. 2

DR. CLARK ANTHONY D. MINORS

Copyright

Acknowledgments

I am very grateful to Almighty God for enabling and gracing me to publish this work. I had no idea in April, 2020, when I joined the Zoom Room family, that this publication would happen. God did though, and that is the amazing thing about this whole journey. His ways are truly "past finding out" (Rom.11: 33)! This would not have been happened had I resisted the urging of the Holy Spirit that October, 2020 morning. Thank you Father!

Bishop Ishmael & 'First Lady' Patricia Charles, godly visionaries with a passion for God and a heart for people – "thank you" for giving me the honor of expressing and using the gift God has given me to serve in the Zoom Room with you. It was Bishop Charles's apostolic urging that prompted me to ponder and muse upon the possibilities of this work. I am so grateful that he encouraged me to put this gift from God into book form, and for believing before I did that this can and will happen. He and Lady Charles are notable servants of God, and I, along with Beverley and our children, honor, highly respect, and love them dearly.

Sis. Darlene Baptiste, "thank you" for being so patient with me – waiting in the early hours of the morning each day to send you what God downloaded for the Zoom Room; and for formatting the Declarations with such precision and professionalism. I commend you for demonstrating nothing but excellence with the gift God has given you.

When Rev. Dr. Lois Burgess said "yes" to editing the numerous pages of typing this manuscript yielded with eagerness and excitement, I felt a heavy weight lift off me. I am very thankful for Dr. Burgess's intellectual prowess as she edited the manuscript without changing its meaning and message. I have to confess that the many red ink markings were amusing when I read them (my use of the English language had a proper workover by her); yet, they proved very helpful. "Thank you" Dr. Burgess for encouraging me during this journey. I honor her as a literary icon, an eminent scholar, and an admired Kingdom Woman of God.

Thanks are also extended to Mrs. Letitia Washington of WordWorld Publishing for agreeing to publish this work, and for ensuring a wonderful finished article.

Finally, I acknowledge and thank the Caribbean/International Prayer Movement Family. Thank you for the numerous acts of love, prayers for me, and words of encouragement to me as I prepared this work. You are a wonderful family of saints in the global village that I am immensely proud to be a part of! "Stakes In The Ground" is dedicated to every one of you.

Shalom!

Special Acknowledgements

To my wife Beverley, and our fruit Chloe and Calon.

Thanks Bev for being extremely patient with me, and giving me the space to commit to this work. Thanks for being my greatest and loudest cheerleader, and valued asset in the ministry to which God has called us. Thanks for the first class cover design for this project – your artistic creativity is phenomenal. Thank you for loving me unconditionally during our journey together. I love you darling.

Thanks Chloe for the invaluable assistance, consistent encouragement, and keen sensitivity to your "Daddy". I am so proud of the steady and strong woman of God you have become.

Thanks Calon, "Champ", for giving me the honor of sharing your work featured as Day 365 of this book, and for representing the battalion of Men of God who will impact their generation and the world for Jesus. You WIN!

Foreword

Can a man know the thoughts of God? In the true environment of the Trinity, God creates a perfect plan through fellowship, relationships, and in His Word.

Bishop Clark Minors has followed and amalgamated the mind of God in this book; and every relationship requires discipline to achieve its goal, so its disciplined work.

These thought-provoking Declarations, "Stakes in the Ground", have been truly effective and infectious. They will move you to have a deeper trust in God as you peruse and muse upon them daily.

As we look at the present pandemic, who can dispute God's sovereignty? We are having a difficult time in life. The world is in crisis, and God knows that amidst every crisis, we need a voice of faith to help us through this time of hysteria.

Come now and hear the Spirit of God as you indulge in these current and sobering thoughts! They will not dismiss your sufferings, but will help you develop and strengthen your faith in God to face the mountains.

Bishop Minors has now summoned us to a higher view, beyond the suffering of this present time. These Declarations will give us an unobstructed view beyond all we are facing today. He is simply saying to us that God's supply of grace and faith declared from the authority of His Word will always meet the demands of our crises.

Bishop Ishmael P. Charles

Church of God Caribbean Field Director,

Caribbean/International Prayer Movement Founder/Visionary

Introduction

Saturday 24 October, 2020 is etched in stone in the corridors of my memory. Having become a member of the Caribbean/International Prayer Movement family in the third week of its inception in April of that year, I became addicted to the atmosphere and aura of the Zoom Room, and the permeating power of prayer among the saints scattered, yet gathered, on the virtual platform as the world grappled with the effects of the ravaging corona virus COVID-19 pandemic. Its impact and influence upon my life is no trite thing. I am certain that my wife Beverley shares these sentiments as well, having joined the family the following day.

On that brisk, cool October morning, the Minors family from Miracle Temple, Bermuda was assigned to lead the day's Zoom Room proceedings. Each of us – my wife Beverley, our children Chloe and Calon, and other young people who are endeared to our hearts, had a part in the meeting.

I was assigned as the Moderator, and as I began to welcome people to the Zoom Room feast of the Lord, I felt a prompting in my spirit like a powerful, surging river overflowing its banks. The Holy Spirit made utterances through me that reverberated through the room like a tsunami. Needless to say, the surge of the Spirit I felt that day, and the spontaneous declarations that came forth, were the beginnings to what you now have in your hands. Day #1 of "Stakes In The Ground" is what I can recall of the October 24, 2020 utterances, as I made scribbled notes after the fact of what I declared in the Zoom Room that initial day.

These Declarations are based upon Job 22:28: "Thou shalt also decree a thing, and it shall be established unto thee: and the light shall shine upon thy ways" (KJV).

According to Persian customs, when a king made a decree, it was binding, enforceable, supreme, and irrevocable. As Solomon wrote, "Where the word of a king is, there is power: and who may say unto him, What doest thou?" (Eccl. 8: 4). It was perilous to attempt revoke what the king decreed.

You and I are not known as "royals", like the members of royal families in the earth today. However, according to the Scriptures, we "are a royal priesthood" (1 Pet. 2: 9); and, having "washed us from our sins in His own blood", Jesus Christ has "made us kings and priests unto God" (Rev. 1: 5, 6) . Therefore, based upon the truth of the Scriptures, you and I have the spiritual legal authority to decree and declare a thing in our lives.

I have no doubt that, as you make application of the Scriptures in your daily living; meditate, memorize, and muse upon "Stakes in the Ground", either in the privacy of your daily devotions, or in the fellowship of others during Bible study or a social Christian gathering, the Holy Spirit will help you to discover and unlock the power of the Bible in your life.

You will note that the Declarations are formatted as an official herald would read a decree. The repeated use of "Forasmuch"; "Whereas"; "I decree and declare"; and, "Be it therefore resolved" are intended to evoke reinforcement in God's 'royals' that there is life and quickening power in His inspired, spoken Word (Jn. 6: 63; 2 Tim. 3: 16), and in the words you speak (Prov. 18: 21). The Word of God is your greatest weapon against the insidious assaults of the enemy against your life, so wield it boldly and bravely.

You will also note that the Declarations become more and more meaty as the days progress. The Holy Spirit began to pour copious inspiration into me for the day to the Zoom Room, and the content, substance and weight of each day is the obvious result. Some are dedicated to young people; some to senior saints; and some highlight the birth of Jesus during the Christmas Season.

I encourage you to be intentional and prayerful over these daily declarations. And do not keep the blessings to yourself. Share them with your family, friends, work colleagues, and any other person(s) you make contact with. This work is the result of numerous hours of waiting before the Lord, and writing what the Holy Spirit said to me.

Congratulations! You have made an invaluable investment in your walk with Christ. For the next 365 days, I pray that you will enjoy the open portals of Heaven's boundless benedictions and blessings as you "**drive these decrees, declarations, and resolutions as "Stakes in the Ground!"**

Shalom!

Dr. Clark Minors

Biblical Abbreviations
OLD TESTAMENT

1. Genesis – Gen.
2. Exodus – Ex.
3. Leviticus – Lev.
4. Numbers – Num.
5. Deuteronomy – Deut.
6. Joshua – Josh.
7. Judges – Judg.
8. Ruth – Ruth
9. 1 & 2 Samuel – 1 & 2 Sam.
10. 1 & 2 Kings – 1 & 2 Kin.
11. 1 & 2 Chronicles – 1 & 2 Chron.
12. Ezra – Ezra
13. Nehemiah – Neh.
14. Esther – Est.
15. Job – Job
16. Psalms – Psa.
17. Proverbs – Prov.
18. Ecclesiastes – Eccl.
19. Song of Solomon – SoS.

20. Isaiah – Isa.
21. Jeremiah – Jer.
22. Lamentations – Lam.
23. Ezekiel – Ezek.
24. Daniel – Dan.
25. Hosea – Hos.
26. Joel – Joel
27. Amos – Amos
28. Obadiah – Oba.
29. Jonah – Jon.
30. Micah – Mic.
31. Nahum – Nah.
32. Habakkuk – Hab.
33. Zephaniah – Zeph.
34. Haggai – Hag.
35. Zechariah – Zech.
36. Malachi – Mal.

Biblical Abbreviations

NEW TESTAMENT

1. Matthew – Matt.
2. Mark – Mark
3. Luke – Lu.
4. John - Jn
5. The Acts - Acts
6. Romans – Rom.
7. 1 & 2 Corinthians – 1 & 2 Cor.
8. Galatians – Gal.
9. Ephesians – Eph.
10. Philippians - Phil
11. Colossians – Col.
12. 1 & 2 Thessalonians – 1 & 2 Thess.
13. 1 & 2 Timothy – 1 & 2 Tim.
14. Titus – Tit.
15. Philemon – Phm.
16. Hebrews – Heb.
17. James – Jam.
18. 1 & 2 Peter – 1 & 2 Pet.

19. 1,2,3 John – 1,2,3 Jn.
20. Jude - Jude
21. Revelation – Rev.

Day 121

FORASMUCH as God has, by His grace, lovingkindness, and mercy, watched over me throughout the night, and He has breathed His breath into me to arise to see the light of another day; and

WHEREAS, I rise today with anticipation and expectation for my personal manna from Heaven, and moments of meditation and worship to the Father floods my soul; and

WHEREAS, God has manifested His excellent greatness in my life, and I can testify of breakthrough, deliverance, freedom, and victory in Jesus from bondages that will only be reversed by His might and power; and

WHEREAS, I refuse to be shut down, shut out, or silenced by difficulties that I encounter; instead, I give God high praise and worship, will proclaim His honor in the earth by Holy Ghost anointing and power; and

WHEREAS, the COVID-19 impact in the earth has mobilized, motivated and moved the Church of the Lord Jesus Christ to realigning, reawakening, repositioning, and revival: God Almighty in my midst has radicalized and revolutionized me into a spiritual force to be reckoned with

I DECREE AND DECLARE this Day 121 that

- I am in the earth as a called, chosen and commissioned representative of the Kingdom of God agenda, and I exercise my God-ordained authority by the Holy Ghost to take territory for Jesus

- I have the ear of God to hear me; the hand of God to manifest for me; the heart of God to love through me, and the favor of God to bless me to be a blessing

- I give no place to the devil (Eph. 4: 27); I hold fast what I have, that no man takes my crown (Rev. 3: 11), and I speak death and doom to principalities, powers and strongholds of the wicked one who is against me

- I am anointed by God to have incredible influence for Him in the global village, and those I connect with are beneficiaries of God's bestowments of grace and goodness

- I am kept by the power of God (1 Pet. 1: 5); I have the mind of Christ (1 Cor. 2: 16), and I am strengthened with might by His Spirit in the inner man (Eph. 3: 16)

BE IT THEREFORE RESOLVED by me this day that

- I take repose and rest in the safe haven of God in the midst of troublesome and turbulent times

- I make the deliberate choice to shine as a light for Jesus in a dark and dismal world that is spiraling out of control into chaos and confusion

AS A KING AND PRIEST UNTO GOD MY FATHER (Rev. 1: 6), I DRIVE THESE DECREES, DECLARATIONS, AND RESOLUTIONS AS STAKES IN THE GROUND; they are established and settled in the earth by the words that I speak; they have the legal assent of the courts of Heaven; the ways and works of Satan against them are negated and nullified, and I am confident that the light shall shine upon my ways (Job 22: 28).

In the name of the Father, the Son, and the Holy Ghost! It is the WILL, the WORK, and the WITNESS of the Triune God!

AND IT IS SO!

Day 122

*"Praise waiteth for thee, O God, in Sion: and unto thee shall the
vow be performed"*
Psa. 65: 1

FORASMUCH as the goodness and grace of Almighty God
has been extended to me today to be alive; in Him I live, and
move, and have my being (Acts 17: 28); and

WHEREAS, the Lord's grace and mercy is continually
extended to me for spiritual refreshing and refueling for my walk
of faith with Him, and today is another opportunity and
privilege to remain connected in fellowship with Him; and

WHEREAS, the hand of God is mightily upon me, and His
presence prompts and provokes me to desire and yearn more of
Him; and

WHEREAS, God's power and presence in my life saturates and
stirs me; I have an insatiable desire for more of Him (Phil. 3: 10-

12), and this yearning sets the tone for a great day walking with Him in the power of His might; and

WHEREAS, I acknowledge my need for consistent spiritual shaping and sharpening, and personal moments of intimacy with God provide me with the divine supply and sustenance I require daily for my journey of faith.

I DECREE AND DECLARE this Day 122 that

- I am under the complete authority and rulership of my Sovereign Father; all the other gods of this earth are less than nothing (Isa. 41: 24)

- the peace of God keeps my heart and mind through Christ Jesus (Phil. 4: 7); I am in nothing terrified by my adversaries (Phil. 1: 28), and I have strength in quietness and confidence in Him (Isa. 30: 15)

- despite the troublesome and turbulent times around me, I am guilty for having a firm, fixed and focused faith in the All-Sufficiency of God

- I rebuke, refuse and reject all seeds of doubt the enemy tries to sow into my heart, and I distance and isolate my spirit from the bondage of fear, self-condemnation and timidity that originates from the Devil, the father of lies (Jn. 8: 44)

- nothing, no one, no circumstance, or situation, will alter or change who God is in my life, and my position and standing in Christ is without doubt and question: I am "more than a conqueror through Him" (Rom. 8: 37).

BE IT THEREFORE RESOLVED by me this day that

- I place great value and worth in my position of redemption and righteousness that I have with God through Christ (Phil. 3: 9)

- I remain undaunted and undeterred in my quest to proclaim the good news of the Gospel of salvation through Jesus Christ (Acts 4: 12)

AS A KING AND PRIEST UNTO GOD (Rev. 1: 6), AND WITH AUTHORITY AND BOLDNESS, I DRIVE THESE DECREES, DECLARATIONS, AND RESOLUTIONS AS STAKES IN THE GROUND; they are established in the earth by the fruit of my mouth; Heaven fully backs and blesses them; Satan's designs and devices against them fall flatly to the ground without effect upon them, and I am confident that the light shall shine upon my ways (Job 22: 28).

In the name of the Father – it is His WILL, the Son – it is His WORK, and the Holy Ghost – He is the WITNESS!

AND IT IS SO!

Day 123

"How amiable are thy tabernacles, O Lord of hosts! My soul longeth, yea, even fainteth for the courts of the Lord: my heart and my flesh crieth out for the living God. Blessed are they that dwell in thy house: they will still be praising thee. Selah. Blessed is the man whose strength is in thee, in whose heart are the ways of them. Who passing through the valley of Baca make it a well; the rain also filleth the pools. They go from strength to strength, every one of them in Zion appeareth before God"
- Psa. 84: 1, 2, 4, 5-7

FORASMUCH as I can breathe, feel, taste, touch, see, smell, and walk – I am a beneficiary of the grace of God. I am alive because of Him, who has extended mercy to me another day; and

WHEREAS, I lift my holy hands, heart and head to the Eternal God, Creator of the heaven and the earth, whose name is higher than anything or anyone (1 Chron. 29: 11); and

WHEREAS, I am honored and humbled to serve in the Kingdom for such a time as this; even though troublesome times are affecting the world, God has raised me up as member of His army of believers in the earth who march valiantly to the drumbeat of the Holy Ghost; and

WHEREAS, I take time to petition, pray, and intercede to God for those afflicted by bodily illness and disease, and for those affected adversely by trial, tribulation, trouble, and turmoil.

I DECREE AND DECLARE this Day 123 that

- I hold on tenaciously and tightly to the altar with fervent intercession, persistent prayer and supplication, and strong groaning and tears, knowing that the hand of God will interpose and intervene in matters that are beyond my control

- God sends a strong wind of His power into the lives of those beset by difficult circumstances, and He reverses the effect and impact of them upon those for whom I pray to redound to His glory, honor and praise

- I seek no retaliation, retribution or revenge upon those whom the devil uses to harm, haunt or hurt me; rather, I pray God's extended compassion, grace, and mercy upon them

- my intense and strong prayers are as arrows and daggers that annihilate, bulldoze, consume and destroy every argument, lofty opinion, presumption and pretension of evil that exalts itself against the knowledge of God, and I take captive every thought, and demand that they obey Christ (2 Cor. 10: 5)

- God fights for me, pushes back the darkness, lights up His Kingdom that cannot be shaken, and defeats every enemy in Jesus' All-Conquering name (Darlene Zschech)

BE IT THEREFORE RESOLVED by me this day that

- I remain prostrate before God in humble contrition, expecting that He will move in and for me as I offer prayers to Him

- I remain pliable in His hand of grace and mercy, and keep the upward look unto the hills, where my help comes from (Psa. 121: 1)

AS A KING AND PRIEST UNTO GOD MY FATHER (Rev. 1: 6), I BOLDLY AND COURAGEOUSLY DRIVE THESE DECREES, DECLARATIONS, AND RESOLUTIONS AS STAKES IN THE GROUND; they are established and settled in the earth by the words I speak; Heaven grants them its high and holy approval; Satan's plots and ploys against them will not taint or touch them, and I have confidence that the light shall shine upon my ways (Job 22: 28).

In the name of the Father – it is His WILL, the Son – it is His WORK, and the Holy Ghost – He is the WITNESS to it!

AND IT IS SO!

Day 124
HONORING SENIOR SAINTS

"I will go in the strength of the Lord God: I will make mention of thy righteousness, even of thine only. O God, thou hast taught me from my youth: and hitherto have I declared thy wondrous works. Now also when I am old and grey-headed, O God, forsake me not; until I have shewed thy strength unto this generation, and thy power to everyone that is to come"
- Psa. 71: 16-18

FORASMUCH as a new day has dawned, and I am alive in my right mind, I give praise and honor to my Sovereign Creator and Heavenly Father; and

WHEREAS, I make a public acknowledgement and proclamation of the excellence, greatness and majesty of God Almighty; and

WHEREAS, on this beautiful day, I honor those who are deemed esteemed elders, seasoned saints, or seniors; and

WHEREAS, I applaud them for their longevity, commend them for their godly example and unselfish service in the Kingdom, and appreciate them while they can see and smell their flowers.

I DECREE AND DECLARE this Day 124 that

- in their advanced years, the aged have blessed hands, and will still produce fruit (Psa. 92: 14), and they remain viable, vital and victorious assets in the global village

- the strength of the Lord is upon them; they are legacy-leavers and difference-makers, and they emanate the aroma, fragrance and grace that becomes an elder who lives for, and loves the Lord

- they are favored by God with physical strength and mental agility, and divine angelic escorts safely lead them into goodly places and to a goodly heritage (Psa.16: 6)

- I rebuke, refuse and reject the assumption and presumption that, because they are aged, they have no place to function and be effective in the Father's Kingdom; rather, they have value and worth, and they impact and influence those who are privileged to follow and be mentored by them

- they are steadfast in their faith, strong in fidelity, secure in their identity, and are fueled daily by the fire of the Holy Ghost, who dwells in them

BE IT THEREFORE RESOLVED by me this day that

- I will highly esteem and regard the aged saints, and I celebrate and commemorate their life and legacy in the earth

- I will intreat elders as fathers, and elder women as mothers, and highly regard them for their fervent prayers and supplications

AS A KING AND PRIEST UNTO MY GOD AND FATHER (Rev. 1: 6), I DRIVE THESE DECREES, DECLARATIONS, AND RESOLUTIONS AS STAKES IN THE GROUND; they are established in the earth by the words I speak; Heaven grants them holy assent; Satan's threats and menaces against them recoil and fall to the ground in swift destruction, and I am confident that the light shall shine upon their ways (Job 22: 28).

In the name of the Father, the Son, and the Holy Ghost! It is the WILL, the WORK, and the WITNESS of the Triune God!

AND IT IS SO!

Day 125

"O Lord, thou art my God; I will exalt thee, I will praise thy name; for thou hast done wonderful things; thy counsels of old are faithfulness and truth."
- Isa. 25: 1

FORASMUCH as my faithful and loving Father has breathed breath into me another day, blessing me to be alive today with strength and vitality because of Him; and

WHEREAS, this is a day of exaltation and jubilation toward the high and holy name of the Lord who continues to abide and dwell in me; and

WHEREAS, I rejoice that God Almighty has, by His Spirit, held me firm and fixed when panic, paranoia and pessimism abound in the lives of so many in the earth; and

WHEREAS, I praise the Living God who secures, shields, and shelters me from harm, hostile enemy fire, and hurt; this is His promise to the faithful in the earth (Psa. 91: 4-10); and

WHEREAS, as the Psalmist said, "Blessed are the people that know the joyful sound: they shall walk, O Lord, in the light of thy countenance" (Psa. 89: 15), and I am one of His people.

I DECREE AND DECLARE this Day 125 that

- my intense praises unto God permeate and pierce the atmosphere around me; they penetrate the dark domain of the devil, and they plunder and pulverize every high and ungodly thing that exalts itself against the knowledge God (2 Cor. 10: 5)

- the prince of this world has nothing in me (Jn. 14: 30); his tactics and tricks are stripped of effect, and when I speak, the power of the Holy Ghost in me causes chaos, a commotion, and utter confusion of all his designs and devices

- the DNA of God is in me; the blood of Jesus avails for me, and prevails against the works of darkness; the intelligence of the Holy Ghost is a witness to me, and the Word of God is hidden in me, and is a two-edged sword in my mouth

- I am graced with wisdom from above (Jam. 3: 17), and God downloads surprising and wonderful ideas and insights to me that cause awe and astonishment to critics and cynics

- my spiritual heritage and legacy will not be cancelled or cut off; instead, I firmly embrace the mantle and continue the mandate and mission of the Kingdom in the earth.

BE IT THEREFORE RESOLVED by me this day that

- I will ardently follow the order and protocol of Heaven's assignments to me in the global village without favor or fear

- I will obediently walk the narrow way of godliness every day, warring, witnessing, working and winning as I "GO" (Matt. 28: 19, 20).

AS A KING AND PRIEST UNTO MY GOD AND FATHER (Rev. 1: 6), I AUDACIOUSLY DRIVE THESE DECREES, DECLARATIONS, AND RESOLUTIONS AS STAKES IN THE GROUND; I am convinced and persuaded by them, and they are established and settled in my life; the open portals of Heaven fully back and bless them; Satan's hostile hounds against them are mortally wasted and wounded, and I am confident that the light shall shine on my ways (Job 22: 28).

In the name of the Triune Godhead: it is the WILL of the Father, the WORK of the Son, and the WITNESS of the Holy Ghost!

AND IT IS SO!

Day 126

We give you all the glory,
We worship you, our Lord,
You are worthy to be praised.
(Israel & New Breed)

FORASMUCH as my kind and loving Father has breathed life into me to see the dawn of a brand new day with our souls anchored in Him, and the full activity of mind and body; and

WHEREAS, I acknowledge the faithfulness and sustaining grace of Almighty God for preserving and protecting me during my journey of faith with Him; and

WHEREAS, I am deeply grateful to God that I can praise Him joyfully and jubilantly without condemnation (Rom. 8: 1), and to worship Him intensely and intentionally for the marvelous and miraculous works of His hands upon me is my absolute joy; and

WHEREAS, I sing like Moses and the children of Israel: "Who is like unto thee, O Lord, among the gods? who is like thee, glorious in holiness, fearful in praises, doing wonders?" (Ex. 15: 11); and

WHEREAS, there is no God like Jehovah!

I DECREE AND DECLARE this Day 126 that

- God graces me with the character, credibility and courage to walk steadfastly and surely in a crooked and perverse world, and I shine for Him as a light in the darkness around me (Phil. 2: 15)

- I have the strength to fight the good fight of faith, and the stamina to lay hold on eternal life (1 Tim. 6: 12), and nothing will come my way that will cause me to back down or back up, bend or bow over, or break up

- with Christ in my vessel, I will smile at every storm, wave my hands to the One I love the best, and ride on with King Jesus - no man will hinder me

- I walk free from the condemnation and guilt of the past (Rom. 8: 1), I faithfully serve Him today, and I commit and trust my tomorrow into His safe and secure hands (Prov. 3: 5, 6)

- my hands are clean, my head lifted up, my heart is pure, my body is under subjection to the Holy Ghost, and God enables me to live undisturbed, unmoved, and unperturbed by contrary winds and hostile enemy fire that comes my way.

BE IT THEREFORE RESOLVED by me this day that

- I remain strengthened, sustained, and supported by the preserving power of God; my eyes are upon Him (2 Chron. 20: 12), and I remain still to see His salvation (2 Chron. 20: 16).

BY THE AUTHORITY OF THE HOLY GHOST, AND BY VIRTUE OF MY KINGLY AND PRIESTLY POSITION IN GOD (Rev. 1: 6), I DRIVE THESE DECREES, DECLARATIONS, AND RESOLUTIONS AS STAKES IN THE GROUND; they are firmly established and settled in the earth by the words I speak; they have the acceptance and affirmation of Heaven; Satan's ways and works against them are crumbled and crushed by the weight of God's glory, and I am confident that the light shall shine upon my ways (Job 22: 28).

In the name of the Father – it is His WILL, the Son – it is His WORK, and the Holy Ghost – He is the WITNESS of it all!

AND IT IS SO!

Day 127

We bring the sacrifice of praise into the house of the Lord (2x);
And we offer unto you the sacrifices of thanksgiving;
And we offer unto you the sacrifices of praise.
(Kirk Dearman)

FORASMUCH as my good and gracious Father has touched me to arise to see the light of another day; and

WHEREAS, I honor and give a high note of praise for the wonderful works of God's Almighty hand upon me; and

WHEREAS, I can testify about the manifold, marvelous, and miraculous acts of God Omnipotent in my life, and I confirm that everything good in my life is orchestrated and ordered by God Himself; they are not the works of man (Psa. 118: 23); and

WHEREAS, like Isaiah said, "thou hast been a strength to the poor, a strength to the needy in his distress, a refuge from the storm", and "a shadow from the heat" (25: 4).

I DECREE AND DECLARE this Day 127 that

- as I wait on the Lord, He will swallow up the threats and menaces of the devil by the Word of His power, and I am confident that He will bring me out and into a large room of triumph and victory

- as I journey by faith in the earth, I do so with God's favor and fruitfulness, and He crowns my life with prosperity and productivity (Deut. 8: 18; Josh. 1: 8)

- I speak deliverance, emancipation, freedom and liberty from the claims and clutches of the Devil over my unsaved loved ones, and by the Holy Ghost, I sow precious seed in their lives, and reap an unprecedented harvest for the Kingdom

- my prayers for spiritual effectiveness go before me, and I anticipate unparalleled success because of the good hand of God upon my life

- I have the anointing and the grace of God to live influentially among all men; the sharp Sword of the Spirit within me manifests through me, and nothing I do, experience, or say will be wasted, or fall to the ground.

BE IT THEREFORE RESOLVED by me this day that

- I remain an ardent follower and imitator of Jesus Christ in the global visit, letting His light shine through me for His glory

- I remain activated and available for His use in His Kingdom, and will always abound in the work of the Lord

AS A KING AND PRIEST UNTO GOD MY FATHER (Rev. 1: 6), I BOLDLY DRIVE THESE DECREES, DECLARATIONS, AND RESOLUTIONS AS STAKES IN THE GROUND; they are established and settled in the earth by the words I speak; Heaven sanctions and seals them;

Satan's hateful hostility against them is as a puff of wind, and I am assured that the light shall shine upon my ways (Job 22: 28).

In the name of the Father – it is His WILL, the Son - He WORKS it, and the Holy Ghost – He is the WITNESS to it all!

AND IT IS SO!

Day 128

What a mighty God we serve (x2);
Angels bow before Him, Heaven and earth adore Him;
What a mighty God we serve!
(Donn Thomas)

FORASMUCH as the loving hand of God has touched me to arise from rest last night to see the dawn of this new day; and

WHEREAS, I praise Almighty God for His excellence greatness and wonderful works toward me during my journey of faith in the earth; and

WHEREAS, I am deeply and immensely affected and impacted by the grace of God in my life, and only eternity will reveal and testify of the true effect of the Lord upon my life; and

WHEREAS, God Almighty is mobilizing, motivating and moving me to engage fields of opportunity for the proclamation of the Gospel of Jesus Christ in the global village, a message of the hope the Savior gives, who can change anything, save anyone, at any time, and anywhere.

I DECREE AND DECLARE this Day 128 that

- I hoist and hold up the blood-stained banner of the love of Jesus Christ everywhere I go; the Anointed One is my example

- I hide myself under the cover of Jesus' precious blood, which avails for me, and which prevails against the enemy of my souls

- I block every potential access spot where Satan may try to intrude in my life, and I barricade my blind spots from his pernicious and predatory ways

- I confidently engage others with the gospel, grace, and love of Jesus, showing by my own living and testimony that He changes lives, and sets the redeemed on the straight and narrow path (Matt. 7: 13, 14)

- when storms come my way, I will be courageous and keep driving, and remind myself that no storm is too severe, no storm can separate me from the love of God, and that no storm can stay forever in my life.

BE IT THEREFORE RESOLVED by me this day that

- I remain anchored and harbored safely in the freedoms, protections and rights of a citizen of the Kingdom

- I remain available to the Father as His workmanship for His use in the earth, harnessed and helped by the enabling power of the Holy Spirit

AS A KING AND PRIEST UNTO GOD MY FATHER, (Rev. 1: 6), AND BY THE AUDACIOUS ANOINTING OF THE HOLY GHOST, I DRIVE THESE DECREES, DECLARATIONS, AND RESOLUTIONS AS STAKES

IN THE GROUND; by the fruit of my lips (Prov. 13: 2), they are established and settled in my life; they are sealed and stamped as legally authorized by the holy courts of Heaven; Satan's hostile fire against them is smothered and suffocated, and the light shall shine upon my ways (Job 22 28).

In the name of the Father, the Son, and the Holy Ghost! It is the WILL, the WORK, and the WITNESS of the Triune God!

AND IT IS SO!

Day 129

"And the Lord said, Behold, there is a place by me, and thou shalt stand upon a rock: And it shall come to pass, while my glory passeth by, that I will put thee in a clift of the rock, and will cover thee with my hand while I pass by" -
- Ex. 33: 21, 22

FORASMUCH as my kind and loving Heavenly Father has breathed His breath into my body, and He caused blood to course warmly through my veins so that can live for another day; and

WHEREAS, I acknowledge and declare the excellence and greatness of my Sovereign God for His unending faithfulness toward me as I live in the earth; and

WHEREAS, I am an excited Christian; I have found a place of joy, jubilation, praise, prayer, and worship of God Omnipotent, and the sheer gladness I have of sharing such a personal and intimate relationship with Him is beyond description; and

WHEREAS, God has miraculously healed me; chains of bondage in my life have been burst asunder and broken; He has reconciled and made me whole, and the darkness of evil against me has been arrested; all the work of the Lord (Psa. 118: 23).

I DECREE AND DECLARE this Day 129 that

- a tsunami of God's supernatural glory and power will sweep over the world, and every work of the natural man will bow in complete and humble submission to His Sovereignty and All-Supremacy

- the fire and force of God's Holy Spirit will engulf me continually, and embers of His fire will torch and touch countless lives through me, and such an awakening will be noised abroad to the far reaches of the earth

- all classes of people in the global village will be affected and impacted by this surge of Holy Ghost power in me, and I prophesy beauty for ashes, the oil of joy for mourning, and the garment of praise for the spirit of heaviness in abundant measure, that He might be glorified (Isa. 61: 3)

- fueled by an internal love and passion for God, intense and intentional praise and thanksgiving to Him erupts from my mouth; and, like volcanic lava, the glory, hallelujahs, and honor I give to God cascades into my circles of association that will cause conviction for sins, repentance of sins, and the conversion of the lost into the Kingdom of light

- I refuse, reject, and repel the acclaim and applause of man for the service I give for the Kingdom; God gets ALL the credit and glory for the marvelous manifestations of His power through my life.

BE IT THEREFORE RESOLVED by me this day that

- I choose to represent the Kingdom of God in the earth with credibility, fidelity and excellence, not wavering or wilting under the weight of opposition or oppression

- I remain at rest and repose in the safe haven of God, not fearing the tyranny or wrath of man

AS A KING AND PRIEST UNTO GOD MY FATHER (Rev. 1: 6), I DRIVE THESE DECREES, DECLARATIONS, AND RESOLUTIONS AS STAKES IN THE GROUND; they are established and settled by the words that I speak; Heaven fully embraces and endorses them; the ways and works of the Devil are devoid of impact or influence upon them, and the light shall shine upon my ways (Job 22: 28).

In the name of the Father, the Son, and the Holy Ghost. The Triune God WILLS, WORKS, and WITNESSES it!

AND IT IS SO!

Day 130

"The smallest grain of faith is a deathless and incorruptible germ which will yet plant the heavens and cover the earth with harvests of imperishable glory"
(A.B. Simpson)

FORASMUCH as God has shown His steadfast faithfulness and love to awaken me to see another day with my bodily faculties and strength in tact; and

WHEREAS, my heart is full of gratitude and thanksgiving, and I rejoice in the Lord with unspeakable joy for salvation and freedom in the Holy Ghost, and victory in Jesus my Savior; and

WHEREAS, considering the Bible account of Jesus healing the man with palsy in Mark 2, and that this is faith-building day, as long as "He (Jesus) is in the house", faith puts Christ between itself and circumstances so that they (circumstances) are not seen; and

WHEREAS, as Hannah Smith said, "Sight is not faith, and hearing is not faith, neither is feeling faith, but believing when we can neither see, hear, nor feel, is faith"; and

WHEREAS, the four who carried the sick man were faith FULL, and their radical faith prompted them to act when common sense suggested otherwise; so, they tore the roof off and broke it up to get the man to Jesus!

I DECREE AND DECLARE this Day 130 that

- because I have a torrent of desire for more of Jesus, His Word, and the benefits that pursuing Him yield in my life, I tear off logic, rationale, reasoning, and all that appears to make sense, and break up the barriers to win Christ

- so that my faith in God for our earthly pilgrimage grows and matures correctly, I refuse and reject the instant, quick-and-easy, one-size-fits-all, microwave-like Christian experience that neglects a proven, tried-and-tested, genuine faith in Him

- I will back, build and buttress my faith with God's ways, will and Word, and not my weak, whimsical, worn-out waywardness

- like the ingredients that make concrete, I mix my faith with the water (the Word - Heb. 4: 2) and good works (Jam. 4: 17), and allow the Holy Spirit to build me into a solid and strong spiritual habitation (Eph. 2: 22)

- because my faith in God is radical, reckless and right, despite the storm-tossed seas, I step out of the boat today - my aim is to get to Jesus!

BE IT THEREFORE RESOLVED by me this day that

- I remain fixed in my faith in the Father; His faithfulness does not fail

- I remain strong in faith, the belief that behaves right; it confirms and testifies who Christ is in me, the hope of glory (Col. 1: 27)

WITH A BOLD AND BRAVE FAITH, I DRIVE THESE PROPHETIC DECREES, DECLARATIONS, AND RESOLUTIONS AS PILLARS AND STAKES IN THE GROUND; they have their establishment in the earth because life is in the power of my tongue (Prov. 18: 21); Heaven guarantees their fulfillment; Satan's agenda and agents against them are devoid of effect or impact, and Jesus the Light shines upon my ways (Job 22: 28).

In the name of the Father - He WILLS it, the Son - He WORKS it, and Holy Ghost - He WITNESSES it!

AND IT IS SO!

Day 131

FORASMUCH as my kind and loving Father has breathed upon me to arise to see another day; "in Him I live and move, and have my being...I am also His offspring" (Acts 17: 28); and

WHEREAS, I exalt and extol the mighty name of the Lord for His excellent greatness, and the marvelous manifestations of His power in my life; and

WHEREAS, I live under the open portals of Heaven to experience the mighty outpouring of the presence of God in my life; and

WHEREAS, winds of Pentecostal fire, glory, power, refreshing and revival are blowing with CAT. 5 hurricane-like intensity in my life, and I validate and verify the impact of Holy Ghost power moving in and through me; and

WHEREAS, I function only by supernatural means; this is not by might, nor by power, but by the Spirit (Zech. 4: 6), and this Heavenly impact is astonishing and awe-inspiring as I champion the causes of Christ in the global village with boldness and confidence.

I DECREE AND DECLARE this Day 131 that

- the drive and dynamism of the Holy Ghost prompts and propels me into exploits of staggering proportions in the global village

- the audacity and authority of the Holy Ghost makes me irresistible and unstoppable like Stephen, full of faith and power, who did great wonders and miracles among the people (Acts 6: 8, 10)

- the anointing of David rests upon me, so that when hostile Philistine-like encroachments challenge the living God who lives in me, they will be met by the unconventional weapons of my warfare (like the sling and a stone) that smite and silence the enemy (1 Sam. 17: 48-54)

- the anointing of the Spirit graces me during this end-time move of righteousness in the earth; the voice of the bold prophet sounds like the fanfare of the trumpet; the stirring of the evangelist is activated with fresh unction from Heaven, and the watch-care, grace and sensitivity of the shepherd pastor/teacher drapes God's chosen ones - all for the perfecting of the saints, the work of the ministry, and the edifying of the body of Christ (Eph. 4: 11, 12)

- I tread triumphantly in the earth, I am effectual, impactful and influential, and, as God's soldier, I march with confidence and courage that the world will be turned upside down (Acts 17: 6) with the message of Jesus - the way, the truth, and the life (Jn. 14: 6).

BE IT THEREFORE RESOLVED by me this day that

- I will remain ready at all times with an Eph. 6: 10 mind-set: "strong in the Lord, and in the power of His might"

- I will repeatedly consult my Sovereign Father through intercession, prayer and supplication for governance and guidance with the affairs of His kingdom in the earth.

BY THE AUTHORITY OF THE HOLY GHOST, I PILE-DRIVE THESE DECREES, DECLARATIONS, AND RESOLUTIONS AS STAKES IN THE GROUND; I speak their establishment in the earth by the fruit of my lips (Prov. 18: 21); they have the full backing and blessing of Heaven's holy court; the designs and devices of evil against them are dead, done, and dusted, and I am confident that the light shines upon my ways (Job 22: 28).

In the powerful, precious, and pre-eminent name of the Triune Godhead, three-in-One, blessed Trinity!

AND IT IS SO!

Day 132

"If the Son therefore shall make you free, ye shall be free indeed"
- Jn. 8: 36

FORASMUCH as my kind and loving Father has caused death to behave throughout the night, and breathed His breath into my body to be alive another day; and

WHEREAS, His lovingkindness is better than life (Psa. 63: 3); therefore, I bless, exalt, honor and praise His most excellent and great name: He is higher than the highest, greater than the greatest, and has the rightful claim to my glory and worship; and

WHEREAS, I am unspeakably joyful and thankful today that God has ordained and predestinated me to be His child in the earth (Rom. 8: 30); and

WHEREAS, I am eternally grateful that there are some things about me God does not remember: my "sins and iniquities" (Heb. 8: 12), into which I was born (Psa. 51: 5) before I repented (Acts 3: 19); and

WHEREAS, living in Pentecostal Power, I have a deep sense of anticipation and expectation of what the Lord has planned and purposed for me; and

WHEREAS, I live free from the enslavement of sin, liberated from the perversion, power and punishment of sin by the stainless blood of Jesus Christ to live in Pentecostal power.

I DECREE AND DECLARE this Day 132 that

- I will not walk in self-condemnation, defeat, or guilt over my past; instead, because I have traded my sin for salvation in Jesus, I hold my head high, and boldly announce my freedom from the grip and guilt of sin and unrighteousness to live in Pentecostal power

- life in Pentecostal power prompts me to proclaim that I am healed from the corruption and loathsomeness of sin, delivered and emancipated from the enslavement of sin, and all vileness of sin is expelled from my life through the power of life in Jesus

- I refuse and reject the insinuations and insults of the Devil, who uses craft and cunning to harass and hassle me over sin; instead, life in Pentecostal power enables me to boldly assert that my sins are underneath the blood of the Lamb of Calvary (Eph. 1: 7), as far removed as darkness is from dawn, and as the east is from the west (Psa. 103: 12), they're in the depths of the sea (Mic. 7: 19)

- the spirit of joy and thanksgiving rests mightily upon me; I celebrate Jesus for freeing me from the tyranny of sin, and, enjoying this liberty and life, I praise Him intensely for my release from the shackles of sin, and I will unashamedly tell others of what it is to live free

- I am not broken, but born again and blessed; not cursed, but changed and charged; not denied, but delivered with a Divine destiny; not entangled again, but ecstatic and elated to be free from sin to live in Pentecostal power

BE IT THEREFORE RESOLVED by me this day that

- I maintain the choice to be free from the allurements of sin to live in Pentecostal power

- I resist the idea or thought of relinquishing my freedom to live in Pentecostal power to become enslaved again to the yoke of sin (Gal. 5: 1).

BY THE AUTHORITY VESTED IN ME, LIVING IN PENTECOSTAL POWER, I DRIVE THESE DECREES, DECLARATIONS, AND RESOLUTIONS AS STAKES IN THE GROUND; I am fully persuaded that they are established and settled in the earth; they have the benediction and blessing of Heaven's holy court; the powers of evil set against them are plundered and pulverized by Pentecostal power, and I am confident that the light shall shine upon my ways (Job 22: 28).

In the ransoming, redeeming, and releasing name of the blessed Godhead Three-in-One – Father, Son, and Holy Ghost!

AND IT IS SO!

Day 133

FORASMCH as I have once again been a beneficiary of the compassion, grace and mercy of my Heavenly Father, who has allowed me to breathe with life at the dawning of a new day; and

WHEREAS, I marvel at God today for the astonishing things that He has done for me, and to praise, thank, and worship Him with my whole heart is not a problem, but an absolute pleasure and privilege; and

WHEREAS, my focus surrounds the theme "The Fire is Here" (Leviticus 6 & Acts 2) - the fire of the Holy Spirit promised of the Father for all His children, and to as many as He calls (Acts 2: 39); and

WHEREAS, my heart is gladdened to know that the power of God's Holy Spirit continues to manifest and work in my life, and I have rapturous joy in knowing that physical healing, spiritual breakthrough, and bondage-breaking victory has come to my life - these are all cause for intentional praise to Almighty God; and

WHEREAS, the fire of Pentecost burns and rages within me, and the Holy Ghost continues to manifest Himself so powerfully for me, through me, and to me.

I DECREE AND DECLARE this Day 133 that

- I call forth and speak a fresh and new cleansing and purging within by the power of the Holy Ghost, and I will not be satisfied or settle for less than a sustained manifestation of His presence, which is the difference in my life

- I prophesy that the righteous right hand of God harnesses, helps, and holds me in all aspects of my life, and that my submission to the voice of the Holy Ghost who motivates and moves us to Kingdom activation, yields a bountiful harvest of lost souls (Prov. 11: 30)

- I prophesy enlargement of my borders and territory for the Kingdom (Isa. 54: 2); that the secret things of God are downloaded to me by the Holy Ghost (Psa. 25: 14), and that doors of Gospel opportunities will for me open for the glory of God (1 Cor. 6: 9)

- the accuser of the brethren, adversary #1 of my soul, has no authority over me, and by the Holy Ghost, I rebuke (Zech. 3: 2) every wile and work of darkness, and I consign his evil schemes to the pit of hell

- the living sacrifice and service of my life yields supernatural dividends; the Kingdom of God is extended in the earth, and miracles, signs and wonders follow the flame and fire of Pentecost within me as I live credibly and righteously for God (Psa. 84: 11).

BE IT THEREFORE RESOLVED by me this day that

- I remain connected to the Holy Ghost, my source of Pentecostal fire and power

- I remain consecrated to the things of God, and will not be deterred or disturbed by enemy hostility

AS A KING AND PRIEST WITH GOD, (Rev. 1: 6), AND BY THE POWER OF THE FIRE OF PENTECOST, I DRIVE THESE DECREES, DECLARATIONS, AND RESOLUTIONS AS POSTS OF FIRE IN THE GROUND; they are established and settled by the fruit of my mouth (Prov. 18: 21); they have the affirmation and agreement of Heaven; the Devil will have to flee and drop his weapons set against them, and I am confident that the light shines upon my ways (Job 22: 28).

In the glorious, gracious, and illustrious name of the Triune God - the Father, Son, and Holy Ghost! Blessed Godhead, Three-in-One!

AND IT IS SO!

Day 134

FORASMUCH as I am alive today because of the goodness and gracious loving care of my loving Heavenly Father, whose holy angel encamped about me during the night, because I fear Him (Psa. 34: 7-9); and

WHEREAS, it is of the Lord's mercies that I am not consumed; great is His faithfulness toward me (Lam. 3: 23); and

WHEREAS, I am honored and humbled that God has chosen me from the foundation of the world by His own counsel and will to walk the earth as His child (Eph. 1: 3-11); and

WHEREAS, my excitement and expectancy in the Lord is palpable; God Almighty is in my midst, and like a surging, unstoppable Niagara, the unprecedented move of God's Omnipotence has begun; sudden Pentecostal sounds, scenes, and speech have descended from Heaven and set upon me (Acts 2: 3); "The Fire Is Here", and I am blue-hot with desire and passion to experience what the prophet Joel prophesied (Joel 2: 28-30; Acts 2: 16); and

WHEREAS, I acknowledge and affirm that the five-fold ministry gifts given to the Church by Christ for Kingdom activation and advancement in the global village are relevant for today (Eph. 4: 11), all for the perfecting of the saints, the work of the ministry, and for the edifying of the body of Christ (Eph. 4: 12).

I DECREE AND DECLARE this Day 134 that

- I will not be ignorant, out of touch, or uninformed about the five-fold ministry gifts that Christ gave to the Church to advance the causes of the Kingdom in the earth, and God audaciously graces those who engage in the empowerment, enlightenment, and enrichment of the saints

- the divine order and protocol of Heaven is firmly established in Christ's Church, and I silence the noises of chaos and confusion brought against His Church by Satan whose chief aim is to cause its demise and destruction (Isa. 54: 17)

- the gates of hell cannot and will not prevail against the Church that Jesus built, and is the Head of, and I celebrate and honor the gifts of the apostle, the prophet, the evangelist, and pastors and teachers, whom Jesus sets in ministry office by the power of the Spirit

- the apostle will blaze new horizons and trails of Gospel penetration in the earth; the prophet will proclaim and pronounce the heart, mind and will of God to the masses with pin-pointed accuracy through the enablement and equipment of the Holy Ghost; the evangelist will herald the good news of Jesus Christ to the spiritually languishing and lost, and the pastor/teacher will provide sound biblical instruction and teaching, and, by the help of the Holy Ghost, create an atmosphere of hunger and thirst for growth, learning and maturity in the hearts of the people (2 Pet. 3: 18)

- effectiveness and excellence in the Kingdom abounds through the five-fold ministry gifts/servants; each compliments each without competing against each, and, as Jesus said, the reach and scope of ministry impact and influence by them in the global village is without question (Jn. 14: 12).

BE IT THEREFORE RESOLVED by me this day that

- I will remain loyal and submitted to the order of Jesus' construction of His Church in the earth, knowing that the gates of hell shall not prevail against it

- I remain in holy, hot pursuit of all that God has planned for me (Jer. 29: 11), and every evil saboteur will have no ground or space in my life because of the fire of Pentecost.

BY THE AUTHORITY OF MY POSITION AS A KING AND PRIEST WITH GOD MY FATHER (Rev. 1: 6), I DRIVE THESE DECREES, DECLARATIONS, AND RESOLUTIONS AS STAKES IN THE GROUND; they are established and settled in the earth by the fruit of my lips (Prov. 18: 21); the will of the Father, work of the Son, and witness of the Spirit guarantee their fulfillment, the fire and wind of the Spirit causes the wiles and works of Satan against them to waste and wilt away, and I am confident and persuaded that the light shines upon my ways (Job 22: 28).

In the majestic, marvelous, and mighty name of the Triune Godhead. Blessed Trinity!

AND IT IS SO!

Day 135

FORASMUCH as my Sovereign Heavenly Father has extended grace and mercy to me to be alive and well to see the dawning of another day; and

WHEREAS, I give high praise and thanksgiving to God for faithfully caring for and watching over me during my journey of faith in the earth, tabernacling with me daily, and my close and intimate relationship with Him is beyond description; and

WHEREAS, despite the ravages of trouble and turmoil in the world today, God has held me fastened and secure in the palm of His strong hand; and

WHEREAS, I am riveted to the scriptural truth that God continues to demonstrate and manifest His glorious power in the earth through the operation of the five-fold ministry gifts in the Church; and the unalterable and undeniable connection between these ministry-gift servants and the fire and gift of the Holy Ghost that fell upon the 120 who assembled in the Upper

Room on the Day of Pentecost as their warrant for effective service for the Kingdom; and

WHEREAS, a strong anointing and grace is upon those whom God has chosen to minister His Word in the global village (the apostle, the prophet, the evangelist, the pastor/teacher), a powerful presence of the fire of the Holy Ghost has permeated the earth, and today, I acknowledge the "Pastor", the gift whom God has given to the body of Christ after His own heart (Jer. 3: 15).

I DECREE AND DECLARE this Day 135 that

- the pastors/shepherds called and chosen by God lack or come short in no thing, but by the ability of the Spirit, they will lead the sheep (God's people) with anointing, credibility, and care; reflecting the relational bond between a shepherd and the sheep

- I speak a wall of fire about them for their protection; the brooding of the Holy Spirit over them for attention to His voice; the blood of Jesus upon them as their covering from evil and vice, and the glory of the Lord manifests through them as they provide care to those whom they shepherd

- their labor in God's vineyard is graced and laced by the love of God; they have a mind-set that gives up and throws in the towel on no one, and their impact and influence in the global village produces lasting, godly fruit

- I reject, renounce, and resist the strategies of evil against the Pastor, and they will experience the supernatural move of God in their midst with frequency and regularity

- I speak a broadening of the Pastor's borders and horizons; the strengthening of their stakes in the Gospel; the extension of the Kingdom through them; their hands wax strong and valiant; the

Word of God is a sharp, two-edged sword in their mouths; they are held and helped by the power of the Holy Ghost, and the anointing and grace to minister in the earth drapes and drenches them to lead sheep for the glory and honor of the King.

BE IT THEREFORE RESOLVED by me this day that

- I remain loyal to the gift to the Church called Pastor

- I choose to highly esteem, honor, pray for, and visibly support the Pastor

BY VIRTUE OF MY COVENANT-POSITION AS A KING AND PRIEST UNTO GOD (Rev. 1: 6), I DRIVE THESE DECREES, DECLARATIONS, AND RESOLUTIONS AS SURE STAKES IN THE GROUND; they are established and settled in the earth by the fruit of my mouth; Heaven embraces and graces their fulfillment; the Devil is impotent and powerless to stop them, and I am confident that the Light shines upon my ways (Job 22: 28).

In the caring, comforting, and consoling name of the Father, Son, and Holy Ghost! Blessed Godhead, Three-in-One!

AND IT IS SO!

Day 136

FORASMUCH as the Lord, by His faithfulness and grace, allowed me to rise from rest to see the light of another day; and

WHEREAS, God is too faithful to fail or forsake me, too loving to leave or let me go (Heb. 13: 5), and too wise to make a mistake about me; and

WHEREAS, I lift my hands today in thankful adoration of my Heavenly Father, who has blessed me to have sweet fellowship in the Spirit with Him; and

WHEREAS, it is in sometimes difficult to comprehend, let alone explain, how much the Lord's grace and mercy has impacted my life; I simply take time to give Him all the glory and honor for His marvelous works in my life; and

WHEREAS, the beauty of my life is not the work of man; "this is the Lord's doing; it is marvelous in my eyes" (Psa. 118: 23); "this is that which was spoken by the prophet Joel, that God will pour out of His Spirit upon all flesh: sons, daughters, young men and old men, servants, and handmaidens (Joel 2: 28, 29;

Acts 2: 16-18), and He did not leave me out as the herald, the evangelist, proclaimed the love of Jesus to me.

I DECREE AND DECLARE this Day 136 that

- the voice of the evangelist, a herald of the Gospel of Jesus Christ in the earth, will not be silenced, stilled, or stopped; instead, His servants will lift their voices like trumpets to make the clarion call that He can save anybody, from anything, at any time, and anywhere

- the power of the Holy Ghost will manifest through them with miracles, signs following, and wonders; the presence of God will drench them with stamina and strength to engage the harvest, and the pull of the Gospel message will be so convicting and strong that it will reach the "whosoever"

- despite adversaries, devices from the dark domain, evil spirits, and harassment and hostility from enemy #1, effectual doors shall open to the evangelist, and Pentecostal anointing and holy fire encases and envelopes them; and by the dynamism of the Holy Ghost, they shall reap the white fields of harvest in the earth for the glory of the Kingdom of God

- I banish, bind, and break mindsets of apathy, disrespect and dishonor aimed at the evangelistic gift to the Body of Christ; instead, I call forth and loose a sweeping, world-wide resurrection, return and receptivity of the evangelist's voice to the global platform, and the opening of doors and fields of opportunity for the maximum use of this important and necessary ministry gift to the world

- the Lord graces His servants the evangelists to be fully armed, anointed arrows in His quiver, to be straight sharpshooters of the message of hope and salvation to the lost, and to be a nightmare to the devilish and diabolical designs of the Devil.

BE IT THEREFORE RESOLVED by me this day that

- I readily respond to the anti-God messaging in the world that I will take the gospel message to the world no matter what

- I remain committed and submitted to world evangelization, and to the support and sustenance of Christ's gift to the Church and the world, His servants, the evangelists

WITH DILIGENCE AND DUTY AS A KING AND PRIEST UNTO GOD (Rev. 1: 6), I PILE-DRIVE THESE DECREES, DECLARATIONS, AND RESOLUTIONS AS ESTABLISHED AND SETTLED STAKES IN THE GROUND; by the fruit of my lips, I speak their fulfillment (Prov. 18: 21); the Triune Godhead grants them their stamp of approval; the force of the power of God demolishes and totally destroys the works of Satan against them, and I am fully persuaded that the Light shines upon my ways (Job 22: 28).

In the name of my safe and secure Sovereign God, the Father, Jesus, the Son, and the Holy Ghost! God in three Persons, blessed Trinity!

AND IT IS SO!

Day 137

A CELEBRATION OF YOUTH

"Let no man despise thy youth..."
- 1 Tim. 4: 12

FORASMUCH as our kind and loving Father watched over me through the night, and then allowed me the privilege to live, and move, and have my being another day (Acts 17: 28); and to arise with a heart determined to live for, and serve Him acceptably with reverence and godly fear (Heb. 12: 28); and

WHEREAS, I proclaim like king David, "Thine O Lord, is the greatness, and the power, and the glory, and the victory, and the majesty....thou art exalted as head above all" (1 Chron. 29: 11); and

WHEREAS, like Abraham did with his son Isaac (Gen. 22: 5), the older generations and the Present Next Generation joins hearts today to praise and worship Almighty God in spirit and in truth (Jn. 4: 23, 24); and

WHEREAS, I acknowledge, honor and salute the present Next Generation of God's called out ones, young people, who valiantly walk the path of consecration and separation unto God amongst their peers in the midst a crooked, perverse, and ungodly world; and

WHEREAS, I embrace and endorse the Christian youth who have made a conscious and personal choice to live for the Lord despite relentless pressure from the Devil to sin, and the testimonies of God's sustaining grace and keeping power in their lives prompt praise and thanksgiving to Almighty God for the great things He has done in them, for them, through them, and to them.

I DECREE AND DECLARE this Day 137 that

- like Daniel, the youth have an audacious, bold, courageous, and excellent spirit that graces them to stand tall, and to shine as lights for Jesus in the midst of the darkness of sin in this world (Dan. 5: 12)

- despite their youth, God's Holy Spirit dwells in them, and empowers them to live credibly, differently, and godly, and should others look down upon them because of their age, they will recall the words of Paul to young Timothy - "let no man despise thy youth" (1 Tim. 4: 12)

- their age is not a barrier or blockage to their usefulness for the Kingdom in the global village; and through their example and influence, others of their age and associations will be won to the Lord and radically saved from sin

- I break up, cast out, thrust out, pull down and pulverize every evil work against the youth, and by the power of the Spirit of God, and the intercepting and interrupting work of angelic assistance on their behalf, the youth flourish and grow as strong trees of righteousness in the earth

- a strong mantle of prayer covers them; discipline to bear the yoke while still a youth blankets them like thick clouds (Lam. 3: 27); the rain of God's presence, like a strong and relentless waterfall, drenches their entire being; like arrows from the master sharpshooter, their praise of the Lord pierces the darkness around them, and I declare that they are the devil's worst nightmare; he underestimates them because they are young; however, the Word of God abides in them, and they have overcome the wicked one (1 Jn. 2: 14).

BE IT THEREFORE RESOLVED by me this day that

- I remain excitedly expectant that the youth will make significant and monumental strides for the Kingdom of God among their peers in the earth

- I remain actively prayerful for the youth as they are gifted, graced and groomed by God to receive the baton of Kingdom leadership in the global village, I will not despise their youth!

BY THE AUTHORITY VESTED IN ME AS A KING AND PRIEST UNTO GOD (Rev. 1: 6), I DRIVE THESE PROPHETIC DECREES, DECLARATIONS, AND RESOLUTIONS AS STAKES IN THE GROUND; they are established and settled by the fruit of my lips (Prov. 18: 21); Heaven's holy court of order and protocol endorses them as legitimate and lively in the earth; the wiles and works against them that Satan conspires are debilitated, diffused, and utterly destroyed, and I am persuaded that the light still shines upon my ways (Job 22: 28).

In the name of the most majestic, magnificent, and marvelous God the Father, the Son, and the Holy Ghost! Blessed Trinity!

AND IT IS SO!

Day 138

FORASMUCH as the Lord woke me up this morning to see the light of another day; He caused the Son to shine in my heart, and He clothed me in my right mind; and

WHEREAS, I have so many reasons to praise and worship my Heavenly Father, that, even if I had a thousand tongues, they would not be enough to sing my Redeemer's and Savior's praise; and

WHEREAS, I have unspeakable joy to affirm that by the grace and the will of God, I have been called and chosen by Almighty God to live in the earth as His child, and this is an honor and privilege I do not take as a light or trite thing; and

WHEREAS, today I exalt and extol the excellence and greatness of my God; I declare His majesty; He reigns magnificently, rules victoriously, and in humble adoration, I bow my heart before His holy presence.

I DECREE AND DECLARE this Day 138 that

- I will use praise and worship of God as my weapons of choice when the battles of life get hellish and hot, according to the Scriptures, the battles belong to God (2 Chron. 20: 15); so, I take my hands off, and leave the battle with my hands up

- as only sharp instruments do well on the war front, I am shaped and sharpened by the Holy Ghost through the spiritual disciplines of fervent prayer, unwavering faith in God, an insatiable appetite for the Word of God, an ear to hear what the Spirit says to me, and a heart to diligently and obediently do as I am told by Him

- as a sharp, new threshing instrument having teeth (Isa. 41: 15), and by the power of the Holy Ghost, I root out, pull down, destroy, and throw down every idolatrous thing, and I will do what is right in the sight of God - walk in His ways, and turn not aside to the right or left (2 Kin. 22: 2)

- I will consistently, unashamedly, and unflinchingly speak the truth, the whole truth, and nothing but the truth in the global village: Heaven is still real, hell is really hot, the Bible is still right, sin is still wrong, repentance is still necessary for the forgiveness of sin, Jesus is still the only Way (Acts 4: 12; Jn. 14: 6), His sinless blood still cleanses (1 Jn. 1: 9); Eph. 1: 7), the devil is still a liar (Jn. 8: 44), and "in all things I am more than a conqueror through Him who loved me" (Rom. 8: 37)

- I am not a coward, but courageous (Josh. 1: 7); the head, and not the tail (Deut. 28: 13); anointed, not desecrated (Isa. 10: 27); on fire for God, and not lukewarm (Acts 2: 3); souled out, and not for sale (Mk. 12: 30); a victor, not a victim (1 Jn. 5: 4) - I WIN!

BE IT THEREFORE RESOLVED by me this day that

- I willingly yield to being yoked with Jesus in the global village; He's the only hope and option I have in this crooked and perverse world

- I choose to let His light shine in and through me, rather than seek to having the limelight shine on me.

BY THE AUTHORITY OF MY POSITION AS A KING AND PRIEST UNTO GOD (Rev. 1: 6), I DRIVE THESE PROPHETIC DECREES, DECLARATIONS, AND RESOLUTIONS AS STAKES IN THE GROUND; by the fruit of my lips (Prov. 18: 21), they are established and settled; the God of Heaven and earth breathes upon, and blesses them; the Devil and his hordes are wasted, withered and wounded, and I rejoice that the light shall shine upon my ways (Job 22: 28).

In the comforting, compelling, and complete name of Heaven's best: Father, Son, and Holy Ghost! Blessed Godhead, Three-in-One!

AND IT IS SO!

Day 139

FORASMUCH as my kind and loving Father watched over me throughout the night, caused death to behave itself once again (Jesus holds the keys - Rev. 1: 18), and breathed life into my being once again to see the light of another day; and

WHEREAS, it is no small thing that my Heavenly Father continues to manifest His excellent greatness in my life; I have fared sumptuously in His banqueting house, and His banner over me is love (SS. 2: 4); and

WHEREAS, God has graced me with the momentum of the Holy Ghost, and the many ways that He has manifested His power in my life far exceeds my finite comprehension and understanding - "His ways are past finding out" (Rom. 11: 33); and

WHEREAS, God is the God of order; He is not limited by space or time; man's intellect or thinking; instead, He does all things after the counsel and purpose of His own will (Eph. 1: 11); and

WHEREAS, it is God's order and will that I "Keep the Fire Burning", a command He gave the Levitical priesthood in Leviticus 6 pertaining to the Old Testament sacrificial system; and

WHEREAS, Jesus our High Priest, the ultimate Sacrifice, provided the example of Himself by sacrificing His own body at Calvary, and now, I am commanded to offer my body as a living sacrifices, holy, and acceptable unto Him (Rom. 12: 1).

I DECREE AND DECLARE this Day 139 that

- as I fear (reverence) and respect God, who is a consuming fire (Heb. 12: 29), and who is not mocked (Gal. 6: 7), I make every effort to avoid offering strange fire unto Him

- I reject the idea and notion that it is acceptable to God to offer strange fire on the altar, like Nadab and Abihu did (Lev. 10: 1), a sacrifice that He has not ordered, and will not accept, that is outside the boundaries of His holiness

- I will KEEP the fire on the altar of my heart burning, and will fight against carnal means to satisfy God, and will refrain from engaging in all manner of behavior and conduct that will contaminate and corrupt the sacred altar in my life

- I will maintain the correct heart temperature and posture before God, so that His fire will fall and burn within me at all times

- like natural fire has an effect on things based on its heat, in the Spirit, I call forth the blue flame fire (a combination of all flame colors at 2600-3000 degrees) of the Holy Ghost burning in my life, so that everything about me, everyone connected to me, and everywhere around me, comes under His complete control, impact and influence

BE IT THEREFORE RESOLVED by me this day that

- keeping the fire burning upon the altar of my heart is priority #1 in a world that offers choices and options to pleasing God

- I remain committed to keeping my heart pure, and my hands clean, so that my sacrifices to God are acceptable to Him, and in conformity to His holiness.

I AM DETERMINED TO KEEP THE FIRE BURNING; THEREFORE, I DRIVE THESE DECREES, DECLARATIONS, AND RESOLUTIONS AS FIRE STAKES IN THE GROUND; they are established and settled by the fruit of my mouth (Prov. 18: 21); the order and protocol of Heaven grants them assent and authority in my life; the fire of Pentecost from Heaven completely devours, dominates and destroys every satanic scheme and system from hell set against them, and I am confident that the light continues to shine upon my ways (Job. 22: 28).

In the Almighty, All-Sufficient, All-Supreme name of the Father, the Son, and the Holy

Ghost! Blessed Godhead, Three-In-One!

AND IT IS SO!

Day 140

FORASMUCH as a new day has dawned, I am still alive with the use of my faculties and a sound mind, and my name is still written in the Lamb's Book of Life; all the handiwork of our gracious, kind and loving Heavenly Father - to Him be glory, praise, and honor; and

WHEREAS, this is a day that is full-term pregnant with possibilities and potential as God's child in the earth, and the unlimited power of our Sovereign God, and His ability to do the exceeding, abundantly, above all that we can ask or think fills me with anticipation, expectation, and hope that is beyond my imagination or thinking; and

WHEREAS, this is another day of joy, and I am happy to render praise, thanksgiving, and worship to God, and to give my body as a living sacrifice, holy and acceptable unto Him, which is my reasonable service (Rom. 12: 1); and

WHEREAS, I do not devalue or diminish the importance and primacy of Holy Ghost baptism and fire as saints of God in the global village (Matt. 3: 11), nor do I take lightly how effective the power of God's Holy Spirit in me makes me as an ambassador of His Kingdom in the earth (2 Cor. 5: 20); and

WHEREAS, I desire today to "KEEP FIRE BURNING" (Lev. 6: 13-23; Acts 2: 1-4).

I DECREE AND DECLARE this Day 140 that

- I will not allow the coolants of compliance, compromise, and concession promoted by this anti-God world to drain, drench, and drown Holy Ghost fire in me

- the unquenchable Holy Ghost fire and power resident in me makes me uncontrollable, unrestrainable, and unstoppable by the systems of this godless world, and by His mighty burning fire, I run through troops, and leap over walls (Psa. 18: 29)

- all thrones, dominions, principalities, and powers are subject to God's holy order, and I proclaim that the burning, holy fire of God's Spirit brings them all to nothing, and they submit to His righteous rule and Sovereign supremacy

- I curse the spirits of Absalom (2 Sam. 13-19), Adonijah (1 Kin. 1: 5-10), and Ahithophel (2 Sam. 15: 12) to the root; the wicked enterprises of Satan that seek to promote cheap options and substitutes, and that aim to extinguish true, biblical Holy Ghost fire and power in God's Kingdom

- I submit to the deep, inner burning of Holy Ghost fire within me; He provides the fire, I the sacrifice, and I keep burning for Him.

BE IT THEREFORE RESOLVED by me this day that

- I wholeheartedly embrace the Joel 2: 28, 29 and Acts 2: 14-21 encounter with Holy Ghost fire and power, and His fire within braces and graces me for Kingdom effectiveness in the earth

- I willingly embrace the enablement and equipment of this holy flame as a Kingdom citizen in the earth, and I keep the fire burning on the altar of my heart.

BY THE AUTHORITY AND BOLDNESS THAT THE HOLY GHOST BAPTISM AFFORDS, I PILE-DRIVE THESE DECREES, DECLARATIONS, AND RESOLUTIONS AS STAKES IN THE GROUND; they are established and settled by the words I speak (Prov. 18: 21); Heaven's holy court seals and stamps their legitimacy and life; Satan's attempts to stop them are blown off course by Ruach Elohim (Spirit of God - Gen. 1: 2), and I rest in confidence that the light shines upon my ways (Job 22: 28).

In the name of El Elyon, El Shaddai, YHWH: Father, Son, and Holy Ghost! Blessed Godhead, Three-in-One!

AND IT IS SO!

Day 141

FORASMUCH as God has raised me up today, redeemed me from sin's destruction, rescued me from myself, and armed me with a ready mind to live for Him another day in the midst of a crooked and perverse world; and

WHEREAS, today I am bubbling and bursting with excitement and joy when I think of the good and marvelous things God has done, is doing, and will continue to do, in my life during my amazing, awesome journey as a Christian in the global village; and

WHEREAS, Pentecostal fire blazes and burns on in me, and this uncontainable and uncontrollable fire cannot and will not go out, even in the face of devilish extinguishers from the wicked one; and

WHEREAS, as a firebrand child of God, I take personal responsibility to remain radically positioned for retooling by the influence of the Holy Spirit's fire and power; and

WHEREAS, I choose to remain on the fire wall, to "KEEP THE FIRE BURNING".

I DECREE AND DECLARE this Day 141 that

- I immerse myself in the end-time revival of Holy Ghost fire, manifestation, and power, and my supplications, prayers, intercessions, giving of thanks, and sacrifice of myself (1 Tim. 2: 1; Rom. 12: 1) keeps the fire on the altar of my life from ever from becoming a flickering flame

- as a New Testament Christian, and endowed with Pentecostal fire, I blaze a holy trail of Gospel seeds in the earth, and await the hand of God's enlargement and expansion in His Kingdom

- I rebuke and reject every strange fire that tinkers, trifles, or troubles the fire of God's holiness, and the holy fire of God's power brings a swift end to the ways and works of evil

- Holy Ghost fire consumes every agent and alliance of hell, and every diabolical device of the dark domain, and the fire annihilates and obliterates all satanic interferences and interruptions against God's established order in the earth

- the wind of Holy Ghost revival causes the fire to spread in the global village uncontrollably and irresistibly, and I call the unsaved of earth to be drawn to this undeniable, unquenchable fire for salvation and deliverance from the soul-destructiveness of sin.

BE IT THEREFORE RESOLVED by me this day that

- I resign myself to functioning only by Holy Ghost fire in the global village for maximum effectiveness and impact for the Kingdom of God

- I stand ready to engage in spiritual warfare for the King under the auspices and authority that being endowed with Holy Ghost fire and power affords.

BY THE POWER VESTED IN ME AS A HOLY GHOST FILLED, FIRE-BAPTIZED CHRISTIAN; AND AS A KING AND PRIEST UNTO MY GOD AND FATHER (Rev. 1: 6), I DRIVE THESE PROPHETIC DECREES, DECLARATIONS, AND RESOLUTIONS AS STAKES OF FIRE IN THE GROUND; by the fruit of my mouth (Prov. 21: 18), they are established and settled; Heaven fully embraces and endorses them; the fire pushes back and pulverizes the plots and ploys of the evil one against them, and I am confident that the light shall continue to shine upon my ways (Job 22: 28) as we KEEP THE FIRE BURNING!

In the All-Championing, All-Conquering, and All-Consuming name of the Father, the Son, and the Holy Ghost! Blessed Godhead, Three-In-One!

AND IT IS SO!

Day 142

FORASMUCH as my gracious, kind, and loving Heavenly Father has breathed on me to be alive for another day; He has beckoned me from sin to salvation, blessed me with all spiritual blessings in Heavenly places in Christ Jesus (Eph. 1: 3), and blocked the works of the Devil against me; and

WHEREAS, I am happy to be called a child of God, glad that God chose me from the foundation of the world (Eph. 1: 4), and He continues to garrison and guard me during my journey of faith in the earth; and

WHEREAS, I have every reason and right to highly exalt and extol the name of my loving Lord for His wonder-working power in my life; and

WHEREAS, I am stirred to "KEEP THE FIRE BURNING" (Lev. 6 & Acts 2), and my spirit is kept buoyant by the penetrating, plain and pure Word of God, and Holy Ghost fire continues to burn blue-hot within; and

WHEREAS, Holy Ghost fire attracts, compels and draws the unsaved, and those who passionately seek to burn for the Lord in these perilous times, so that glory and honor goes to Him.

I DECREE AND DECLARE this Day 142 that

- Holy Ghost fire that burns within me ignites a flaming trail of Kingdom impact and influence in the global village

- I will not allow age, economics, position, or social status (Joel 2: 28, 29) to cool or quench the fire; instead, the fire burning within me motivates and moves me to engage in the ministry mandate and mission in the earth by the might and militance of the Holy Spirit

- with holy anticipation and expectancy, I report for Kingdom duty, and Holy Ghost fire enables and graces me to actively engage in my God-given assignment and deployment as a carrier and custodian of the flame (Acts 2: 6)

- I will not abandon my post, become distastefully lukewarm (Rev. 3: 16), lay down my Gospel tools in battle (Psa. 78: 9), or allow strange fire (Lev. 10: 1) to infiltrate, intrude into, or invade my worship for anyone, for anything, for any reason, or at any time

- Holy Ghost fire within me is not an illusion, a figment of my imagination, or a cheap imitation; instead, the real fire on the altar of my lives comes from God, a consuming fire, and I will KEEP THE FIRE BURNING during this end-time revival until scores of souls are delivered from the power of darkness, and translated into the Kingdom of the Son (Col. 1: 13).

BE IT THEREFORE RESOLVED by me this day that

- I remain vigilant and watchful against fake fire and imposters assigned from hell that attempt to quell and quench Holy Ghost fire that burns within me

- I remain a militant custodian and guardian of holy, Pentecostal fire, and I will, by all means, KEEP THE FIRE BURNING

BY THE AUTHORITY VESTED IN ME AS A HOLY GHOST FILLED, FIRE-BAPTIZED, SANCTIFIED KING AND PRIEST UNTO GOD (Rev. 1: 6), I DRIVE THESE PROPHETIC DECREES, DECLARATIONS, AND RESOLUTIONS AS PILLARS OF FIRE IN THE GROUND; they are established and settled by the fruit of my lips (Prov. 18: 21); Heavenly benediction and blessing affirms them; the hateful hostility of hell is scathed and scorched by Holy Ghost fire, and I am confident that the light shines upon my ways (Job 22: 28).

In the amazing, astonishing, and astounding name of the Father, the Son, and the Holy Ghost! Blessed Trinity! Three-in-One!

AND IT IS SO!

Day 143

CELEBRATING YOUNG PEOPLE

FORASMUCH as the Lord kept death away from me during the night, and breathed His breath in me again to have life, and to see the dawn of a new day; His compassions never fail; great is His faithfulness; therefore, I hope in Him (Lam. 3: 22-24); and

WHEREAS, today I boldly and bravely proclaim my adoration and love for my Sovereign Heavenly Father, and the marvelous works of His strong hand upon my life during my walk of faith are worth declaring; and

WHEREAS, I lovingly embrace the value and worth of young people, the Present Next Generation; God's hand rests mightily upon them, and they deserve to be regarded and respected for their choice to remember and serve the Lord in their youth (Eccl. 12: 1); and

WHEREAS, young people have value and a place in the Body of Christ to activate the calling and gifts of God upon them in the global village for the extension of His Kingdom; and

WHEREAS, nothing can stymie or stop God from manifesting His power in the earth through young people, and testimonies abound how He has moved, and continues to move, through the dedicated and loyal young people in the global village, whose courage validate and verify the hand of God upon them.

I DECREE AND DECLARE this Day 143 that

- the Present Next Generation shall live, thrive, and not die, to declare the works of the Lord through their lives (Psa. 118: 17)

- I peel away and push back the pain and shame of their youth, and call forth the arrows of the Lord to walk in Holy Ghost boldness as called, choice and chosen vessels unto the Lord (Jn. 15: 16)

- I call forth the young arrows in God's quiver to walk in purity like Joseph (Gen. 39: 9), be mighty and militant for the Kingdom of God like Joshua (Josh. 8: 1-23), be anointed with a double anointing to do the miraculous like Elisha (2 King. 2: 12-15), and to walk in subjection and submission to their parents like Jesus (Luke 2: 51, 52)

- a great move and revival of God's power will be manifested among the Present Next Generation around the world, and in this region, the glory and power of God will sweep over the youth in unavoidable and unprecedented proportions

- my intercessions, prayers and supplications for the Present Next Generation will be effectual, and they shall prevail, and they shall be a terror and torment to the gates of hell because of the anointing of the Holy Ghost upon them, and He causes an uproar and an uprising against the minions of the Devil because of anointed young people.

BE IT THEREFORE RESOLVED by me this day that

- I stand together and united with the youthful champions of the causes of Christ in the global village, and I will march to the drumbeat and rhythm of Heaven to effect change for Him in the earth

- I remain valiant, vibrant, and victorious in the earth because of Jesus, and Holy Ghost firepower is a canopy over me as I take territory for the King.

BY THE AUTHORITY AND AUDACITY OF HOLY GHOST ANOINTING AND POWER, I DRIVE THESE PROPHETIC DECREES, DECLARATIONS, AND RESOLUTIONS AS IRREVOCABLE STAKES IN THE GROUND; by the fruit of my lips (Prov. 21: 18), they are established and settled in the earth; they have the full backing and benediction of Heaven's high and holy order; the death knell pierces and plunders the designs and devices of evil, and I am confident that the light shall shine upon my ways (Job 22 28).

In the accelerating, activating, and authorizing name of the Father, Son, and Holy Ghost! Blessed Godhead, Three-In-One!

AND IT IS SO!

Day 144

FORASMUCH as it has pleased Almighty God to watch over me throughout the night; then, He graciously and mercifully enabled me to arise to the light of another day to live joyfully for Him; and

WHEREAS, my life's experiences have been engineered by the gracious hand of God, and my epic spiritual journey is a joyful and jubilant one; and

WHEREAS, I have experienced momentous and unforgettable days of powerful Holy Ghost revival, and God continues to deliver, heal, restore me into a vessel to His honor; and

WHEREAS, although the world spirals downward in debauchery and decadence in sin, God has an army in the earth that marches unified and in spiritual syncopation; and, as I engage as a member of this army, I behold the mighty works of His Omnipotence and Sovereignty.

I DECREE AND DECLARE this Day 144 that

- I will endeavor (make every effort) and strive to keep Christian unity in the bond of peace (Eph. 4: 3), and to follow the example and model of God the Father, the Son, and Holy Ghost, who, from the beginning of Creation, said, "Let US make man in our image, after our likeness:..." (Gen. 1: 26)

- as one who has experienced Pentecostal power, as read in Acts 2: 1-4, this "one accord" that encourages and ensures my ardent commitment to true biblical unity, obligates God to pour out of His Spirit, and to rain down fire from His holy throne upon me

- I acknowledge, honor, and respect those whom God has graced to lead me, and who operate in the five-fold ministry gifts Jesus gave to the Church (Eph. 4: 11-13), and by the power of Pentecost, they are activated and authorized by Heaven to function effectively and with supernatural anointing and power in the earth for the glory of God, and the extension of His Kingdom

- I will not compete and contend against my brother/sister; instead, I will commend and complement them as read in Rom. 12: 10, "in honor preferring one another", and "let each esteem other better than themselves" (Phil. 2: 3)

- knowing that Satan is the chief adversary and antagonist to true Christian unity, I close rank, and march arm-in-arm, hand-in-hand, and heart-to-heart with others in genuine Christian unity, going forth, "conquering and to conquer" (Rev. 6: 2).

BE IT THEREFORE RESOLVED by me this day that

- U-N-I-TY (tie) is my password and watchword as I seek to champion the causes of the King and His Kingdom in the global village

- I remain steadfast and sure in my endeavors to preserve unity in the spirit and power of Pentecost.

BY THE HOLY GHOST AND POWER OF PENTECOST, I DRIVE THESE DECREES, DECLARATIONS, AND RESOLUTIONS AS IRREVOCABLE STAKES IN THE GROUND; by the fruit of my mouth (Prov. 18: 21), they are established and settled in my life; the unified Godhead of Heaven grants their approval and assent; the designs and devices of the dark domain against them are reduced to dust, and I am confident and persuaded that the light shines upon my ways (Job 22: 28).

In the unequalled, unified, and unrivaled name of the Father, Son, and Holy Ghost! Blessed Godhead, Three-in-One!

AND IT IS SO!

Day 145

FORASMUCH as I am alive today - God did it; I am saved and sanctified - God did it; I am Holy Ghost filled and fire baptized - God did it; I am ransomed and redeemed - God did it; the Lord has done this, and it is marvelous in our eyes (Psa. 118: 23); and

WHEREAS, my heart is filled and overflowing with rapturous joy as I muse and ponder the mighty works of the Lord in my life; and

WHEREAS, God continues to manifest His power, showing Himself strong on the behalf of those whose hearts are perfect toward Him (2 Chron. 16: 9), and the marvelous and miraculous manifestations of His excellent greatness in my life are beyond doubt; and

WHEREAS, the Oneness of the Father, Son, and Holy Ghost serves as the ultimate marker and template of perfect unity, and it is by this unity that, as a member of the Church of the Living God, I am obligated to live in oneness with others, and to preserve the spirit and power of Pentecost in the earth; and

WHEREAS, it is this oneness and unity of the Spirit that I choose to join in fellowship and unity without regard to denominational affiliation, but in celebration of the spiritual heritage as the ecclesia of God and his Kingdom causes in the earth.

I DECREE AND DECLARE this Day 145 that

- I debunk and disallow every contaminating and corrupting thing (Gal. 5: 9) that opposes Christian unity in the Spirit; instead, I receive fresh holy fire from God that extinguishes the enemy's assaults against me

- the sanctifying work of God's fire in the inner man moves me to preserve the purity of the Spirit, the power of the Spirit, and the productivity of the Spirit in the power of Pentecost (Mal. 3: 3)

- I refuse and reject demonic and diabolical anarchy, disharmony, and mutiny that attempts to arise in the Body of Christ against true Christian unity, and I send forth the blazing and burning Holy Ghost fire to rage and rip through every high thing and stronghold of the Devil (2 Cor. 10: 5)

- my efforts toward the preservation of unity in the spirit and power of Pentecost blazes a fire in and through me that makes God's power inescapable, irresistible, and unavoidable

- I unashamedly preserve the unity of the Spirit in the power of Pentecost, and I do not accept or allow extras, options or substitutes to true Pentecostal unity to infiltrate or invade Christian ranks that will cause stumbling-blocks to the proclamation of the Gospel of Jesus Christ to the world.

BE IT THEREFORE RESOLVED by me this day that

- I remain committed to fueling, fanning and preserving Holy Ghost fire that causes me to blaze and burn for the Lord in the global village

- I live in the fire, march and move by the fire, rejoice and sing because of the fire, and preach with the fire, and I will NOT let it go out (Lev. 6: 13)!

BY THE AUTHORITY OF HOLY GHOST FIRE ENABLEMENT, I DRIVE THESE DECREES, DECLARATIONS, AND RESOLUTIONS AS INEXTINGUISHABLE POSTS IN THE GROUND; they are actualized, established, and realized by the words I speak (Prov. 18: 21); the Triune Godhead of Heaven sanctions their fulfillment; Holy Ghost fire causes a deadly and destructive insurrection against the Devil's weapons aimed at them, and with confidence, I walk in the light that shines upon my ways (Job 22: 28).

In the fearsome, fiery and flaming name of the Father, Son, and Holy Ghost! Blessed Triune Godhead, Three-in-One!

AND IT IS SO!

Day 146

FORASMUCH as God has blessed and graced me to arise another day with life and use of my limbs, a mind to glorify, honor and praise Him for the marvelous things He has done for me, and to keep myself in is love today; and

WHEREAS, "Where would I be if Jesus did not love me? Where would I be if He did not care? Where would I be if He had not sacrificed His life? Oh, but I'm glad, so glad He did," (Andrae Crouch); and

WHEREAS, on this brand new day, with a grateful and thankful heart, I lift up holy hands in the presence of the Lord, and I celebrate the excellency, majesty and might of His name; and

WHEREAS, God's faithfulness and power has brought me thus far, and I am honored and humbled that He would choose me to occupy a place in His Kingdom on the earth as a fellow citizen (Eph. 2: 19; 1 Pet. 1: 2: 9); and

WHEREAS, kind affection with brotherly love, honor and respect of one another (Rom. 12: 10), righteousness, peace, and joy in the Holy Ghost (Rom. 14: 17), enablement by the Spirit of God to impact and influence the global village for Christ, and fellowship in the Spirit (Phil. 2: 1,2), give rise to a momentous wave of Shekinah glory in the earth; and a wave of glory that rolls over and cascades onto the atmospheres and circumstances of my life, which takes me from glory to glory (2 Cor. 3: 18); and

WHEREAS, this holy fire, glory, and power of God from Heaven above is the basis and bedrock of oneness and unity in the Spirit, and it is the ardor and passion of my heart to preserve this unity in the spirit and power of Pentecost.

I DECREE AND DECLARE this Day 146 that

- true unity in the spirit and power of Pentecost means that I employ no carnal methods whatsoever to preserve Christian unity; therefore, I dismiss humanism, legalism, and relativism, which originate from the Devil, and are antagonistic to God and holy things

- I follow the leadership of the Holy Spirit, who guides me into all truth (Jn. 16: 13), and I leave a meaningful Christ-like legacy in the earth by the power of the Holy Spirit, and I live under the Acts 1: 8 prophetic declaration of Jesus... "ye shall be witnesses unto me..."

- I call for the "the 21st Century Church live to in 1st Century power" (Bishop Ishmael P. Charles), and this 1st Century power is centered and focused on the true biblical, Pentecostal spirituality that promotes the name of Jesus (Jn. 15: 26)

- I drape and drench my spirit in Jesus' prayer for believers, "that they all may be one", as He is with the Father (Jn. 17: 21, 22), and preserving unity in the spirit and power of Pentecost is my constant theme and song during my earthly sojourn

- I am undeterred, unperturbed, and unruffled by the contrary winds of Satan that assail and attack my endeavors to preserve Christian unity; instead, these cement and concretize a steadfast and steely commitment within me that preserves unity in the spirit and power of Pentecost (Acts 20: 24).

BE IT THEREFORE RESOLVED by me today that

- I keep Jesus as the central, core, and pivotal theme in my engagement in His causes in the global village

- I am ablaze and burning by the fire of Pentecost (Acts 2: 3), and I remain unmoved from my position to preserve unity in the spirit and power of Pentecost

BY THE AUTHORITY OF THE POWER OF PENTECOST, I DRIVE THESE DECREES, DECLARATIONS, AND RESOLUTIONS AS IRREFUTABLE, IRRESISTIBLE STAKES IN THE GROUND; I believe in them, and they are established and settled in the earth by the fruit of my mouth (Prov. 13: 2); I rest in Heaven's affirmation of them; Holy Ghost fire reduces every demonic work set against them to rubble and ruin, and blows them away as stubble (Isa. 54: 17; Isa. 40: 24), and the light shall shine upon my ways (Job 22: 28).

In the regal and resplendent name of God – my Father, Jesus the Son – my Friend, and Holy Ghost – my Helper. Blessed Godhead! Three-In-One!

AND IT IS SO!

Day 147

("anexomai" - Strong's): "to live out the faith that God works in"

FORASMUCH as the Father woke me up this morning breathing life, and started my on my way; He put a song of praise in my heart, and this sentiment is expressed from my mouth as a sacrifice of praise to Him continually (Heb. 13: 15); and

WHEREAS, I continue to bathe in the bountiful blessings and benedictions of Heaven, and am joyful and jubilant because of the love and life of Jesus in me, the hope of glory (Col. 1: 27); and

WHEREAS, a very powerful, life-changing spiritual revival from Heaven like a contagion is in the earth; God's mighty power is sweeping across the four corners of the globe; people are being delivered, healed, and redeemed/saved from sin; and

WHEREAS, demonstrations and manifestations of God's Omnipotence in the earth are undeniable and unparalleled –

God's "ways are past finding out" (Rom. 11: 33), and His doings are "marvelous in our eyes" (Psa. 118: 23); and

WHEREAS, with all of the challenges, changes and choices available today to the Christian Church in a world spiraling out of control, nothing is more pressing upon the Body of Christ than unity (Eph. 4: 3); and

WHEREAS, the heart of Jesus's Church in the earth is unity in the spirit and power of Pentecost, the prerequisite of, and precursor to, miraculous manifestations of God's power in the earth.

I DECREE AND DECLARE this Day 147 that

- by earnestly endeavoring to preserve Christian unity in the spirit and power of Pentecost, families, homes, neighborhoods, towns, parishes, cities, and countries will all be affected and impacted by the convicting power of the Spirit of God (Jn. 16: 8)

- as the fire "sat upon each of them" (Acts 2: 3), Holy Ghost fire and power "sets upon" me, and through Christian unity, God engineers a trail of spiritual power in the earth, and I will see, and participating in, a revival of epic proportions that will blanket the globe for the glory of God

- I call forth the authentic, undiluted power of Pentecost to drape and encamp church congregations and pulpits in the global village, and the Holy Spirit will manifest Himself amongst His people in ways unheard or unthought of, and the unavoidable fire of Pentecost will engulf all who seek Him (Jer. 29: 13)

- as I submit and surrender to His direction and leading (Prov. 3: 5, 6; Rom. 8: 14), a deluge and a drenching of Holy Spirit anointing will come upon me, and this anointing will cause an insurrection and terror to the gates of hell

- I curse every spirit of collusion, condemnation, and corruption from Satan that seeks to thwart and trifle with the power of Pentecost, and without fear (2 Tim. 1: 7), I advance the Gospel mandate and mission in the might and militance of Pentecost.

BE IT THEREFORE RESOLVED by me this day that

- I maintain the forward thrust and momentum of Holy Ghost movement in the earth, and will not be seduced or swayed by anything other than true Pentecostal power to proclaim the message of Jesus Christ, and the redemption and salvation He gives to the lost

- I take refuge in no other power but God's, and knowing that I am safe and secure in Him prompts every effort within me to preserve unity in the spirit and power of Pentecost.

BY THE AUTHORITY OF PENTECOSTAL POWER VESTED IN ME BY GOD, WHOSE FIRE "SETS UPON" ME (Acts 2: 3), I BOLDLY DRIVE THESE DECREES, DECLARATIONS, AND RESOLUTIONS AS PENTECOSTAL STAKES OF FIRE IN THE GROUND; they are established and settled by the fruit of my mouth (Prov. 18: 21); they are graced and guaranteed by the blessing of Heaven; Holy Ghost fire that secures and surrounds them ambushes and annihilates Satan's weaponry against them, and I am fully persuaded that the light shines upon my ways (Job 22: 28).

In the winning, wonderful, and wonder-working name of the Father, Son, and Holy Ghost! Blessed Godhead, Three-In-One!

AND IT IS SO!

Day 148

FORASMUCH as the Father's compassion, faithfulness, grace and mercy is extended to me today to be alive, moving, and having my being because of Him (Acts 17: 28); and

WHEREAS, this is a great day to praise the Lord, to exalt His greatness and majesty, to celebrate, cry out and shout, "Glory to God in the highest"; and

WHEREAS, I have joy unspeakable in my soul for what the Lord has done in my life, and I dedicate and devote myself to His commands and marching orders for my journey of faith in the global village; and

WHEREAS, I acknowledge the holy presence of the Triune God who tabernacles with me; He has fed me manna from His bountiful supply, led me beside the still waters, and placed His love in me by the Holy Ghost (Rom. 5: 5); and

WHEREAS, the priority of unity in the Spirit in the Body of Christ cannot be overestimated and overstated; it is an absolute necessity for Christ's Body to endeavor to keep the unity of the Spirit in the bond of peace (Eph. 4: 3).

I DECREE AND DECLARE this Day 148 that

- I walk, war and win in the global village in the fire and power of Pentecost, which is not an event, but an encounter with God that makes me progressive, radical and militant for the causes of the Kingdom of God

- I am called and chosen by God to have effect and make impact for Him (Jn. 15: 16), harnessed and held by Jesus, who calls me His friend (Jn. 15: 15), and equipped, empowered and enabled by Holy Ghost anointing that draws attention and attraction to Jesus, and not myself

- they that are with me are more than they who are with them (2 Kin. 6: 16); I do not fight with or am fretful toward others; instead, I raise the banner of unity in the Spirit, and I unapologetically hold fast to the liberating power of God, who is for me (Rom. 8: 31)

- I know my calling from God (1 Cor. 1: 26), I have the intelligence of the Spirit (Rom. 8: 16), angels are on assignment for me (Psa. 103: 20), and Holy Ghost anointing braces and graces me to dominate and take territory for the Kingdom in the earth

- I will not lag behind or experience lack in matters of the Spirit; my speech for Jesus is as a sharp sword by God's anointing and power, and spirits of evil are subject to Christ because I ardently and defiantly preserve unity in the spirit and power of Pentecost.

BE IT THEREFORE RESOLVED by me this day that

- in nothing will I be moved from my position and posture of faith and unity in the Spirit

- I remain steadfast in my endeavors to preserve unity in the spirit and power of Pentecost

BY THE AUTHORITY AND POWER THAT HOLY GHOST FIRE AFFORDS, I DRIVE THESE PROPHETIC DECREES, DECLARATIONS, AND RESOLUTIONS AS IRREFUTABLE POSTS OF FIRE IN THE GROUND; they are established and fulfilled in the earth by the words that I speak (Prov. 18: 21); Heaven's throne grants them holy assent; Holy Ghost fire banishes and bars satanic aggression against them, and I am confident that the Light shines upon my ways (Job 22: 28).

In the name of the Sovereign, splendid, and superior Father, the Son, and the Holy Ghost! Blessed Godhead, Three-In-One!

AND IT IS SO!

Day 149

FORASMUCH as it pleased my Heavenly Father to awaken me from a peaceful night of rest, it pleased Him to touch me again with His finger of love, and to bestow upon me the blessing of life and liberty; and

WHEREAS, God continues to hold me in the palm of His mighty hands of grace; He stays with me and continues to transport me along the journey of fellowship with Him from glory to glory (2 Cor. 3: 18); and

WHEREAS, the significance of my life is not who I am, but how big God is in me, and the grace He provides to me daily is the reason why I make impact for Him in the global village; and

WHEREAS, a sweeping, supernatural revival is upon me; this is not a duplication or replication of yesterday, but a new thing (Isa. 43: 19), a fresh thing, a mighty thing, a God thing, an unforgettable and unregrettable thing, and it is marvelous in my eyes (Psa. 118: 23); and

WHEREAS, this move of God in my life requires that I live credibly, consistently, and in harmony with others in the global village, and to endeavor earnestly to keep this unity in the spirit and power of Pentecost; therefore, the natural is out, and the supernatural is in - the agenda and secret to expansion and extension of the Church of the Living God in these last and evil days.

I DECREE AND DECLARE this Day 149 that

- I will not move from my endeavors to maintain Christ-like unity in the spirit and power of Pentecost, and the manifestation of God's omnipotence in the earth is my anthem and song

- I will not faint, fear, or fret; instead, my faith in God's power makes me audacious, brave, courageous, and diligent enough to proclaim Jesus despite the contrary winds that assail me

- Holy Ghost power manifests and moves in my circumstances and situations, and He overrules and overrides every diabolical device or design meant to derail and deter my progress in the Spirit

- I will reflect true Christian unity come what may in my life; I will not be contentious, pretentious, or vexatious; instead, I will exude the aroma and fragrance of the Fruit of the Spirit inwardly (to ourselves), outwardly (toward others), and upwardly (toward God)

- I will live in the spirit, fire and power of Pentecost, the Church's birthing place (Acts 2), the altar of my heart is ablaze with the fire that shall never go out (Lev. 6: 13), and God, a consuming fire (Heb. 12: 29), sends and sets His fire upon me as I offer myself as a living sacrifice unto Him (Rom. 12: 1).

BE IT THEREFORE RESOLVED by me this day that

- unity is the bedrock and foundation of my "raison d'etre" (reason for being), and I keep it in the spirit and power of Pentecost

- I remain on fire for God, and will not allow it to reduce to ashes, become a flickering flame, or go out completely

WITH HOLY GHOST ARDOR AND AUTHORITY, I DRIVE THESE PROPHETIC DECREES, DECLARATIONS, AND RESOLUTIONS AS HOLY STAKES OF FIRE IN THE GROUND; they are established and settled in the earth by the fruit of my mouth (Prov. 18: 21); Heaven's throne affirms and authorizes their fulfillment in the earth; Holy Ghost fire tangles, ties up, and torches every demonic scheme set against them, and I am confident that the light shall shine upon my ways (Job 22: 28).

In the magnificent, mighty, and mountain-moving name of the Father, Son, and Holy Ghost! Blessed Godhead, Three-In-One!

AND IT IS SO!

Day 150

CELEBRATING YOUNG PEOPLE

FORASMUCH as Almighty God has breathed upon me to arise to see the light of another day, strengthened me to live, move, and have my being, and graced me to function in the global village as His ambassador (2 Cor. 5: 20); and

WHEREAS, I am more than excited to exalt, extol and exuberantly praise and worship His holy name for divinely calling, choosing, and ordaining me as His child; and

WHEREAS, life in the Spirit for me gets better; God keeps pouring His power upon me; as the song exclaims, "Sometimes, I just don't know what to do"; and

WHEREAS, young people are a gift and a treasure; their presence in our lives allows us the delight and joy of guiding, leading, and mentoring them, and their ministry is enthralling and exciting as they flourish for the Lord in the global village; and

WHEREAS, the Present Next Generation is full term with possibilities, potential and promise from God (Jer. 29: 11), and their excellence in ministry and service for the King in the global village is worthy of celebration and commendation - to God be the glory!

I DECREE AND DECLARE this Day 150 that

- I speak the continued manifested hand and help of God upon the young people, and a powerful anointing from God will grace them with the necessary spiritual tools and equipment to take their generation from the devil for Jesus

- their mouths are as a sharp swords; they are hidden in God's hand and quiver, and they are as polished shafts (Isa. 4: 2) harnessed and held by Omnipotence

- as arrows in the hand of a mighty man (Psa. 127: 4, 5), I speak Holy Ghost acceleration and authority upon the young people, and the arrow hits the bullseye of their futures with accuracy and precision, guaranteeing the sure promises of prosperity and success from God to envelope their lives for His glory (Josh. 1: 8)

- they are saturated and soaked with Holy Ghost audacity, boldness, character, and determination, and their presence in the global village as the present next generation representatives of the Kingdom makes an incredibly influential and irresistible mark for Jesus

- the favor of God is upon them, the fire of God is in them, the fertility of God blesses them, and the fruitfulness of God embodies them.

BE IT THEREFORE RESOLVED by me this day that

- I remain determined to ensure that the youthful arrows maintain their place of potential and promise in God's Kingdom agenda in the earth

- I purpose to prayerfully consider them, cover them, regard them, respect them, take them by their hand, and treasure them in my heart

BY THE AUTHORITY VESTED IN ME AS A KING AND PRIEST UNTO MY GOD AND FATHER (Rev. 1: 6), I DRIVE THESE DECREES, DECLARATIONS, AND RESOLUTIONS CONCERNING YOUNG PEOPLE AS IMMOVABLE STAKES IN THE GROUND; they are established and settled in the earth by the fruit of my mouth (Prov. 18; 21); Heaven affirms and approves their establishment; the fury of hell against them turns in on itself to utter destruction and doom, and I confidently assert that the light shines upon their ways (Job 22: 28).

In the Sufficient, Superior, and Supreme name of the Father, Son, and Holy Ghost! Blessed Trinity!

AND IT IS SO!

Day 151

FORASMUCH as my Sovereign God has demonstrated His compassion, grace and lovingkindness to me, and breathed life into my body to see the light of another day in the land of the living (Psa. 27: 13, 14); and

WHEREAS, God is good; I am a beneficiary of His goodness, and, with His tender mercy, they follow me every day (Psa. 23: 6); and

WHEREAS, I honor and highly exalt the name of the Lord, whose awesome presence continues to dwell and tabernacle with me, and in His presence I enjoy fulness of joy (Psa. 16: 11); and

WHEREAS, as the Psalmist declared, "...we (I) shout for joy over your salvation, and in the name of our God set up our banners!..." (Psa. 20: 4, 5); and

WHEREAS, as a firebrand of Pentecostal power, I "clap our (my) hands, and shout unto God with the voice of triumph!" (Psa. 47: 1); "...for He hath triumphed gloriously! The horse and his rider hath He thrown into the sea" (Ex. 15: 21); and

WHEREAS, His conquest and overwhelming victory over the enemy for me fills me with unbreakable confidence in Him, "So that we (I) can boldly/confidently say, "The Lord is my helper..." (Heb. 13: 6), "...who is able to do exceeding abundantly above all that we ask or think..." (Eph. 3: 20).

I DECREE AND DECLARE this Day 151 that

- as a soldier in God's army, I choose to be strong in the Lord, and in the power of His might (Eph. 6: 10), and I fearlessly and valiantly follow the orders of my Commander-in-Chief

- God's Church is on the move in the earth; its mission is deathless and indestructible, and I take dominion over principalities and powers, and they are subject to God's glorious name and power

- the Kingdom agenda will be fulfilled in the global village; Satan's wiles will not prevent the power of the Almighty to manifest, and God's glory fills the earth as the waters cover the sea (Hab. 2: 4)

- I am called for Kingdom purpose, clothed in Kingdom anointing, covered by regal, untainted blood, and, like the rider on the white horse, I go forth conquering and to conquer (Rev. 6: 2)

- I am safe and secure, saved and satisfied, strong and stable, and I march onward, keeping the upward look - God's Church on the move is unconquerable and unstoppable!

BE IT THEREFORE RESOLVED by me this day that

- I remain unrelenting and unyielding with my engagement in the Kingdom agenda on the earth

- I keep my eyes on Jesus, my ears open to hear God's voice, and my heart and hands pure as revival sweeps across the earth

BY THE AUTHORITY GIVEN TO ME BY MY KING, I DRIVE THESE PROPHETIC DECREES, DECLARATIONS, AND RESOLUTIONS AS IMPREGNABLE STAKES IN THE GROUND; they are established and settled in the earth by the fruit of my mouth (Prov. 21: 18); Heaven graces and guarantees their fulfillment; the wind of the Spirit blows satanic ways and wiles off course and into oblivion, and I am confident that the light shall shine upon my ways (Job 22: 28).

In the vanquishing, valorous, and victorious name of the Father, Son, and Holy Ghost! Blessed Trinity!

AND IT IS SO!

Day 152

FORASMUCH as my kind and loving Father has breathed His breath into my body one more time to arise from overnight rest to see the light of another day; and

WHEREAS, God is due all the glory, high honor and praise for His wonderful works toward me (Psa. 107: 8); and

WHEREAS, I sing unto Him, I (lift my voice and) sing psalms unto Him, and talk of all His wondrous works (Psa. 105: 2); and

WHEREAS, I remember the Lord's wonders in my life, and every morning I spend devotional quiet time with Him, and He feeds me my daily bread; and undoubtedly, the move of His Spirit and power in my life is indisputable and undeniable; and

WHEREAS, I proclaim and pronounce that God's Church is on the move, marching, mobilized and motivated by His holy presence and power; and

WHEREAS, from the beginning of time as we know it, to create His earth, "the Spirit of God moved upon the face of the waters" (Gen. 1: 2).

I DECREE AND DECLARE this Day 152 that

- my God is irresistible and unstoppable, and I rest my circumstances and situations upon Him to move as He wills

- like the "Shekinah" cloud of God's presence over the children of Israel in the wilderness (Ex. 13: 21, 22), I position myself under the cloud, and will not take a detour for anyone or anything for any reason whatsoever

- Jesus' Church is full of faith and power; it is fortified and secured by His precious blood, and the gates of hell cannot and shall not prevail against her (Matt. 16: 18)

- I call forth a move of His might and power upon everything and everyone associated with me, and through Holy Ghost impetus, I blaze an unforgettable trail of Gospel influence in the global village that will yield an enormous harvest of souls for the Kingdom

- the Church will be known in the earth for its unity in the Spirit; the aroma and fragrance of the Fruit of the Spirit emanating from its Body (Gal. 5: 22, 23); her embodiment, embracing, and engagement in the five-fold ministry gifts by Holy Ghost power, and a movement in the hands of the moving, manifesting Sovereign God that confounds and crushes the wiles and works of Satan

BE IT THEREFORE RESOLVED by me this day that

- I remain secure and stable in God's hands, and am in nothing terrified by my adversaries (Phil. 1: 28) who oppose the Church on the move

- I remain unabashed and unashamed to be called a member of Christ's Body, the Church; I remain on the move, and am unwavering in my choice to "be strong in the Lord, and in the power of His might" (Eph. 6: 10)

BY THE AUTHORITY VESTED IN ME AS A MEMBER OF CHRIST'S CHURCH ON THE MOVE IN THE EARTH, I DRIVE THESE PROPHETIC DECREES, DECLARATIONS, AND RESOLUTIONS AS IMPREGNABLE STAKES IN THE GROUND; they are established and set in the earth by the words of my mouth (Prov. 18: 21); the agreement and authorization of Heaven enlivens them; every demonic and diabolical device against them is disemboweled and dismembered, and I am persuaded that the light shall shine upon my ways (Job 22: 28).

In the manifesting, mighty, and moving name of the Father, Son, and Holy Ghost! Blessed Godhead, Three in One!

AND IT IS SO!

Day 153

God's got an Army, marching through the land
Deliverance is their song, there's healing in their hand;
There's everlasting joy, and gladness in their heart;
And in this Army I've got a part.
(E. Leroy Baker)

FORASMUCH as my kind Father, by His finger of love, has blessed and touched me to arise to the light of another day with a sound mind; and

WHEREAS, I joyfully acknowledge the excellence and greatness of God in my midst, and the awesome manifestations of His power in my life fills me with unspeakable joy that is worth talking about; and

WHEREAS, the Church of the Lord Jesus Christ in the earth, the called out ones foreordained before the foundation of the world to become heirs of salvation (Eph. 1: 4, 5; Heb. 1: 14), is an Army on the move with a mandate and a mission (Matt. 28: 19, 20) to win the lost; and

WHEREAS, the Church's mission in the world is one of precedence and priority; evil spirits unfriendly to grace have launched an all-out assault on the Gospel; therefore, God calls His Church to be on the move with His cause with haste, for the night comes when no man can work (Jn. 9: 4); and

WHEREAS, I hear and give heed to God's clarion and call to rally around the banner in the global village.

I DECREE AND DECLARE this Day 153 that

- as God is an advancing, moving and progressing God, I buckle up my boot straps with the preparation of the gospel of peace (Eph. 6: 15), and, as a soldier in His Army, I march forward and onward toward the conflict under His command

- my borders for Christ and the Gospel message are expanding and extending daily, Gospel territory in the earth is enlarging, and forthwith, I take prisoners out of the pit wherein is no water, (Zech. 9: 12) and speak hope into their lives for the glory of God

- the strong, moving wind of the Spirit blows a reawakening and revival of epic proportions into my circles of association and beyond (Jn. 3: 8); I speak to the very dry bones in the valley, and prophecy to the four winds to breathe upon the slain, and they shall stand on their feet, an exceeding great army (Exek. 37: 1-10)

- as a member of Christ's Church on the move in the earth, I reject and renounce the fake, the false, and the feign, and Holy Ghost fire burns predatory counterfeit and imitation spirits away that have no part or place amongst its sanctified ranks

- God will be glorified, Jesus will be magnified, Holy Ghost power will be intensified, the devil will be horrified, and the

Church on the move in the earth will be edified (Eph. 4: 16) - and it is so!

BE IT THEREFORE RESOLVED by me this day that

- I keenly keep in step and follow the moving cloud of God's glory that tabernacles with the Church on the move in the earth

- I keep my spirit pure, and my hands and heart clean, God's marching orders to His Church on the move are not for the impure and unclean

WITH AUDACITY AND AUTHORITY, I DRIVE THESE PROPHETIC DECREES, DECLARATIONS, AND RESOLUTIONS AS STAKES IN THE GROUND; they are established and settled in the earth by the fruit of my mouth (Prov. 18: 21); they have the grant and guarantee of Heaven; Satan's attempts to stop them are doomed, done and dusted, and I am confident and persuaded that the light shall shine upon my ways (Job 22: 28).

In the regal, reigning, and relentless name of God, my Father, Jesus, my Friend, and the Holy Ghost, my Guide! Blessed Godhead, Three-in-One!

AND IT IS SO!

Day 154

The move is on my Lord, the move is on;
I can hear the rustling of the mulberry tree,
And I know, I know the move is on.
(Unknown)

FORASMUCH as my benevolent Father of grace and mercy has blessed me to be alive today with a sound mind, and the activity of my limbs; and

WHEREAS, today my soul is engulfed with joy as I exalt, honor, praise and worship my Sovereign Heavenly Father for the marvelous things that He has done for me, in me, through me, and to me; and

WHEREAS, my life is abundant and victory-laden because I have the honor and privilege, by grace, to spend intimate and personal moments with God every day without condemnation (Rom. 8: 1); and

WHEREAS, I am thankful that I encounter and experience God in dynamic and fresh ways (Isa. 43: 19), and to give testimony and witness of powerful manifestations by the Holy Ghost in my life fills me with excitement; and

WHEREAS, without doubt, I am led daily by Elohim Sabaoth, YHWH, the Lord of Hosts.

I DECREE AND DECLARE this Day 154 that

- the power of God the Holy Ghost has begun a worldwide ingathering of the lost through a revival of righteousness in the global village, and by Him, the dejected, disconsolate, and downcast are gathered into His fold for acceptance, joy, and lifting to deliverance and salvation

- by the Spirit, as a member of Christ's Church on the move in the global village, I am intentional with the message of Jesus (Acts 4: 12), intense about its mission to win souls (Prov. 11: 30; Luke 4: 18, 19), and I have the intelligence of Heaven to engage the Kingdom mandate in the world (Isa. 61: 1-3)

- I will not encroach upon the Holy Ghost foolishly or presumptuously with strange fire (Lev. 10: 1), embellish the Holy Ghost with form and no fire (2 Tim. 3: 5), or embarrass Him with Spirit-less emotion and excitement (Judg. 16: 20); rather, as a Christian on the move, I am empowered, enabled, and endowed by the authentic, genuine, and pure firepower from Heaven for Kingdom impact and influence in the earth

- the word is out - it is not a rumor or a whisper, an idea or lofty thought – I am mobilized and motivated, manifesting, marching, and on the move by Pentecostal firepower, and I consign every demon from hell to the depths of darkness where they belong

- I walk by the Spirit, war in the Spirit, witness through the Spirit, work because of the Spirit, and win by the Spirit - the move is on!

BE IT THEREFORE RESOLVED by me this day that

- I will remain on the move as a member of the Lord's Church, and buoyed by the call of God, the character of Christ, and the competence of the Holy Ghost

- I will remember the name of the Lord at all times, represent Him radically, yet righteously, and BE the Church on the move in the earth

BY THE AUTHORITY OF THE MANDATE AND MISSION OF GOD TO ME, I DRIVE THESE PROPHETIC DECREES, DECLARATIONS, AND RESOLUTIONS AS MEMORABLE STAKES IN THE GROUND; I establish and settle them as fulfilled by the words I speak (Prov. 18: 21); Heaven backs and blesses them as affirmed and approved; the tactics and torments of Satan against them are immobilized and rendered impotent, and as a Christian on the move by the fire and power of the Holy Ghost in the earth, I am fully persuaded that the light shines upon my ways (Job 22: 28).

In the never-failing, always-faithful, ever-fruitful name of the Father, Son, and Holy Ghost! Blessed Godhead, Three-in-One!

AMEN!

Day 155

FORASMUCH as the Lord God of glory has breathed upon me, smiled on me, kept the death angel away from me, and touched me with His finger of love to arise from overnight rest to see the light of another day; and

WHEREAS, it is no trivial thing that God has called me into His marvelous light from the darkness of sin, and graced me with the anointing authority to impact the world; and

WHEREAS, I am thankful that the "greater works than these shall ye do" prophetic words of Jesus to Philip (Jn. 14: 12) applies to me, and my reawakening, repositioning, and revival is not by chance; rather, it is the Spirit of God who drew me to desire and yearn more of Him; and

WHEREAS, I jubilantly and triumphantly lift my Savior up for all the world to see; I am unashamed of the Gospel (Rom. 1: 16), unwavering in my total confidence in His might and power (Heb. 10: 35), and I unflinchingly uphold His royal banner in the global village (Psa. 60: 4), for it shall not suffer loss.

I DECREE AND DECLARE this Day 155 that

- a strong anointing of authority, boldness, and Holy Ghost dynamism graces me to function in the earth and, with rejoicing, I shall reap the harvest that God has promised me (Psa. 126: 6)

- I am not subject to decay, destruction or death by demonic strongholds; instead, my life is garrisoned, governed and guarded by the blood of Jesus, and by His blood I shall prevail (Rev. 12: 11)

- I cast down, pull down, and plunder every high and idolatrous thing that exalts itself against the knowledge of God in my life (2 Cor. 10: 5), and I strangle and suffocate every stronghold that seeks to erect its religious, repugnant head in me

- I affirm my unassailable and unstoppable status as a shielded (Psa. 84: 11) ambassador and representative of the Kingdom of God and His righteous causes in the earth (2 Cor. 5: 20)

- I live today in the power of the Spirit (Gal. 5: 25) and through the Son (1 Jn. 4: 9), I lean on the everlasting arms (Deut. 33: 27), I lack no good thing (Psa. 84: 11), and I love others lavishly and unconditionally (1 Jn. 4: 11, 21) – I am on the move!

BE IT THEREFORE RESOLVED by me this day that

- I remain a member of a movement (the Church), and not a monument, and I will "go" with haste, and not cower or back down in fear

- I remain resilient as a Christian on the move in the earth, and I steadfastly adhere to the precepts, tenets and truths of God's holy Word

BY THE AFFIRMATION AND APPROVAL OF MY SOVEREIGN FATHER, I BOLDLY DRIVE THESE PROPHETIC DECREES, DECLARATIONS, AND RESOLUTIONS AS IMMOVABLE STAKES IN THE GROUND; they are established and settled in the earth by the words I speak; Heaven seals and secures them; satanic schemes and systems set against them are shut down and silenced, and the Light shall shine upon my ways - I am on the move (Job 22: 28).

In the overcoming, overruling, and overwhelming name of the Father, Son, and Holy Ghost! Blessed Godhead, three-In-One!

AND IT IS SO!

Day 156

FORASMUCH as my loving Heavenly Father has lavished compassion, grace, love, and mercy upon me His child, and allowed me to breathe the air He owns, and to enjoy soundness of mind and the activity of limbs one more day; and

WHEREAS, I have so much to thank God for, my heart is bubbling and bursting with joy for the mighty and wonderful things He has done and is doing in my life as a Christian in the earth; and

WHEREAS, this rejoicing and thanksgiving in my heart can simply be described as "unspeakable, and full of glory" (1 Pet. 1: 8); and

WHEREAS, to think that I was adrift on life's stormy seas without a compass, a rudder, or an anchor, I was subjected to every wind of error and sin that blew into my life; BUT, Jesus came into my life, cleansed and washed me in His stainless blood (Rev. 1: 5), the tempter's power over me was and is broken, I am now an heir of God, a joint heir with the Son (Rom. 8: 17), and a citizen of the Kingdom (Eph. 2: 19); and

WHEREAS, I am a member of Christ's Church on the move in the earth - a healthy, unified, and unstoppable movement in the hands of Omnipotence, and I am ready to engage in reaping the white harvest (Jn. 4: 35) and to bring in the sheaves with rejoicing (Psa. 126: 6).

I DECREE AND DECLARE this Day 156 that

- my inheritance in Christ's Body, the Church on the move, is valuable and worth too much; therefore, I will not engage in that which tampers and tinkers with my value as a believer

- I am not a misfit or mistake; I do not wander in the earth without meaning; instead, I am on the move, my spiritual weapons of warfare are mighty through God (2 Cor. 10: 5-7), and the power of the Holy Ghost manifests miraculously through me for last day godly impact and influence (Mk. 16: 20)

- I resist satanic backlash and residue against me, and I reject evil conspiracies, and sinister subterfuge and schemes of Satan designed to topple me from grace; they shall not prevail or prosper (Isa. 54: 17)

- I am real, relevant, and righteously radical, and I will reach the unreachable and love the unlovable, one soul at a time for the Kingdom

- Holy Ghost firepower living in me does not engage in the Gospel mandate and mission for a draw, a loss, or a stalemate; instead, I and the members of the Lord's body (1 Cor. 12: 12) are many, mighty, militant, and on the move for the Lord in the earth - WE WIN!

BE IT THEREFORE RESOLVED by me this day that

- I remain connected to the power source, and I draw from the power that never lacks, runs dry, or runs out

- inhabited and indwelled by the Holy Ghost, my intellect remains enlightened by the Spirit, and Divine empowerment and enablement hold me steadfast and unmovable

BY THE BOLDNESS, BRAVERY, AND BRAZENNESS OF THE HOLY GHOST, I DRIVE THESE PROPHETIC DECREES, DECLARATIONS, AND RESOLUTIONS AS SOLID STAKES IN THE GROUND; I believe that they are established and settled by the fruit of my lips (Prov. 18: 21); Heaven rapturously applauds and approves them; the dark domain is subject to delirium and doom because of them, and I am confident, and militantly so, that the light shall shine upon my ways (Job 22: 28).

In the name of the Omnipotent, Omnipresent, Omniscient Father, Son, and Holy Ghost! Blessed Trinity!

AND IT IS SO!

Day 157

A DECLARATION FOR YOUNG PEOPLE

FORASMUCH as God tarried the coming of His Son during the night, He touched me to arise from rest, and breathed life into me one more day to move and have my being (Acts 17: 28); and

WHEREAS, I adore and worship the God of my salvation for the honor and privilege by His grace to effect change, have impact and influence the world for His glory; and

WHEREAS, God is moving by His Spirit through miracles, signs and wonders all over the earth; a mighty move of His power has caused a great spiritual reawakening and revival, and His great hand and holy arm has gotten Him the victory; and

WHEREAS, God continues to mobilize and move me in the global village despite the negative effects of sin upon the world; He is moving and using some in His Church to plant, and some to water, but He gives the increase (1 Cor. 3: 6-8); and

WHEREAS, God uses whom He will (Rom. 9: 15), even the Present Next Generation, who has been called and chosen by

Him as vessels unto honor, sanctified and meet for His use in the global village (2 Tim. 2: 21), and the youth are acknowledged for their God-given grace and gifting, activated for Kingdom service, and anointed to live for Jesus and to bring forth fruit that remains (Jn. 15: 16)

I DECREE AND DECLARE ON THIS Day 157 that

- the Present Next Generation will submit and surrender to the Moses, Elijah, Paul, Deborah, Eunice, and Lois anointing, and become positioned to receive the mantle of Kingdom leadership and usefulness in the global village

- a strong desire and yearning will envelope the Present Next Generation for prayer, praise, worship, and the Word of God, and Holy Ghost enablement and equipment will be their primary passion and pursuit

- I rebuke and resist the contrary winds of Satan aimed to blow and veer the Present Next Generation off their God-ordained course (Jer. 29: 11), and the predominant and prevailing power of the Holy Spirit upon them harnesses and holds them to firm, fixed and focused (Zech. 4: 6; Gal. 5: 1-26; 2 Tim. 1: 7)

- they will not walk in anxiety, but in authority; they will not live under the burden of sin, but under the banner of salvation; they will not be weak in faith, but war and wax strong as firebrands of faith from the third-Heaven anointing

- the grace of God governs them, the friendship of Jesus guarantees them, and the companionship of the Hoy Ghost guides them as arrows from the Lord's quiver in the earth (Isa. 49: 2)

BE IT THEREFORE RESOLVED by me this day that

- I remain a strong encourager of the Present Next Generation as they are activated for Kingdom impact, influence and leadership in the earth

- I rest confidently that the high, holy and strong arm of the Lord motivates and moves the Present Next Generation to be dynamic change-agents in the global village whose lives will attract and draw their associates and peers to Jesus

BY THE AUTHORITY VESTED IN ME AS A KING AND PRIEST UNTO GOD MY FATHER (Rev. 1: 6), I DRIVE THESE PROPHETIC DECREES, DECLARATIONS, AND RESOLUTIONS AS STAKES IN THE GROUND THAT WILL NOT BE BREACHED; they are established by the fruit of my mouth (Job 22: 28a; Prov. 18: 21); they are backed and blessed by Heaven's holy court; the powers of the Devil are shaken and shut down because of them, and God's army, including the present next generation, is confident that the light shines upon their ways (Job 22: 28b).

In the peerless, penetrating, and powerful name of the Father, Son, and Holy Ghost! Blessed Godhead, Three-in-One!

AND IT IS SO!

Day 158

FORASMUCH as it was God's pleasure and prerogative to awaken me from rest throughout the night, and to allow me to breathe today - He's worthy of high honor and praise; and

WHEREAS, it is truly wonderful what the Lord has done by calling and choosing me out of the horror of sin, and giving me the freedom to glorify, honor, praise and worship Him, and to receive daily bread from His holy Word; and

WHEREAS, I am on a glorious sojourn in the Spirit and by the power of Pentecost; I expectantly awaits to see what divine manifestations God will show me as I trust His everlasting grace to keep me fixed and focused on Him; and

WHEREAS, I gladly announce that God has an army marching through the global village with audacity and Holy Ghost authority (of which I am a part), and this army is so trusting of its Commander-in-Chief that we boldly proclaim that He can do anything but fail us - His Church is on the move in the earth with the guarantee of His presence and power (Acts 1: 8);

I DECREE AND DECLARE this Day 158 that

- nothing that contends with me is out of God's ability to handle or fix; He's the God of the impossible (Lu. 1: 37), and there is no doubt that He "is able to do exceeding abundantly above all" for me (Eph. 3: 20);

- I am called, anointed, delivered, sanctified, and on the move for Him in the global village, and He is demonstrating His astonishing and awesome power through me for the world to see and witness who He is (Psa. 86: 10)

- I rebuke the words and works of the Devil against God's Church, and we rebut his diabolical lies (Jn. 8" 44) with the "It is written" words of our Savior (Matt. 4: 4-6)

- I speak breakthrough, deliverance, healing, liberty, total triumph, and victory over debilitating diseases, body disorders, failing health, illnesses, infirmities, and physical maladies by the power of the Holy Ghost, and by Jesus' stripes I am healed (Isa. 53: 5)

- there is no failure in God (1 Chron. 28: 20), and I expect nothing but the advancement of spiritual impact and influence for Him in the global village, and, by His grace and help, I will reap the harvest He has promised, and will recover and restore ALL (Joel 2: 25).

BE IT THEREFORE RESOLVED by me this day that

- I remain radically righteous, ready and resilient, reliant and resting in my Father's full giving of grace and mercy toward me

- I remain dedicated and devoted to God, my source of power and provision, who has called and chosen me in Him before the foundation of the world (Eph. 1: 4)

BY THE FAVOR AND GRACE OF MY HEAVENLY FATHER AND GOD, I DRIVE THESE DECREES, DECLARATIONS, AND RESOLUTIONS AS STAKES IN THE GROUND; they are established and settled in the earth by the words that I speak (Prov. 18: 21); they have the guarantee of fulfillment by the Triune God of Heaven; the plots and ploys of the evil one against them fail and fall to the ground defeated and destroyed beyond recognition, and I am confident that the light shines upon my ways (Job 22: 28).

In the overcoming, overpowering, and overwhelming name of the Father, the Son, and Holy Ghost! Blessed Godhead, Three-in-One!

AND IT IS SO!

Day 159

FORASMUCH as the Lord my God graciously and lovingly touched me with His finger of love and caused me to arise to see the light of another day with the gift of life; He is so faithful to me (2 Tim. 2: 13); and

WHEREAS, I shout aloud unto God with adoration, praise and thanksgiving for the marvelous and wonderful things that He has done in my life; I am changed, and not the same; look at what the Lord has done (Psa. 118: 23); and

WHEREAS, God has saved and sanctified me as His child, and given me a mission to engage the harvest, and to move with Him during a latter-day reawakening and revival that has shaken the world, and He has stirred me into Kingdom-activation and Gospel seed-planting in the earth; and

WHEREAS, I hear the heart of God and voice of the Spirit to me: "Christ's Church is on the move in the global village, reaping time of the harvest has come; "pray ye therefore the

Lord of the harvest that He will send forth laborers into His harvest" (Matt. 9: 38); and

WHEREAS, I cooperatively, unreservedly, and willingly respond to the call, "Here am I, send me" (Isa. 6: 8).

I DECREE AND DECLARE this Day 159 that

- I cleanse myself from all filthiness of the flesh and spirit, perfecting holiness in the fear of God (2 Cor. 7: 1), so that nothing in me hampers or hinders the move of God's Church in the earth

- every contrary spirit and wind that rises against God's Church I shut down, silence, and stop forthwith in the name of Jesus

- I march and push forward according to the plans, promises, and purposes of God (Jer. 29: 11), and His agenda to reconcile the unsaved unto Himself through Jesus takes preeminence and precedence over every agenda, agency and agent that is out of alignment with Him

- God's Church is on the move; I boldly and bravely incite a Holy Ghost insurrection and invasion of the enemy's camp, and I plunder and pulverize every entity and encampment of evil that the enemy attempts to erect and unleash against God's Church on the move

- God's anointed and consecrated Church on the move in the global village has a Gospel mandate, is manifesting by Holy Ghost power, is many and militant, and is missional and mobilized to work the works of Him who has sent me (Jn. 9: 4), and I will turn the world upside down for Jesus (Acts 17: 6).

BE IT THEREFORE RESOLVED by me this day that

- I remain submitted to the Heavenly Dove, and I earnestly endeavor to conduct myself in such a manner that the aroma and fragrance of the Fruit of the Spirit emanates from my living more than words can

- I remain passionate about contributing significantly to the advancement of the Gospel of Jesus in the global village, and I willingly submit myself to usefulness for the Master's glory and honor

BY VIRTUE OF MY STANDING AS A KING AND PRIEST UNTO GOD MY FATHER (Rev. 1: 6), I DRIVE THESE PROPHETIC DECREES, DECLARATIONS, AND RESOLUTIONS AS SOLID STAKES IN THE GROUND; I speak their establishment in the earth by the fruit of my mouth (Prov. 18: 21); they have the legal assent of the Godhead of Heaven; Satan's designs against them are decapitated and destroyed, and I valiantly march forward as a champion for Christ in the earth, knowing that the light shines upon my ways (Job 22: 28).

In the preferable, profitable, and powerful name of the Father, Son, and Holy Ghost! Blessed Godhead, Three-in-One!

AND IT IS SO!

Day 160

FORASMCH as the angel of the Lord encamped round about me throughout the night (Psa. 34: 7), and my all-Wise Sovereign Father allowed me to arise to see another day with life and liberty in Him; and

WHEREAS, today is a great day to praise the Lord for His goodness (Psa. 107: 31), and to sing forth the excellency and honor of His name, and to make His praise glorious in the earth (Psa. 66: 2); and

WHEREAS, I cannot contain the holy excitement and deep joy I have when I muse upon the glorious journey I have experienced as God has tabernacled with me during my journey in the earth as His child, I honor, praise, and worship Him with my whole heart; and

WHEREAS, my walk and work in the global village for the Lord is not finished; there is more fruit to bear for the Master, and the joy of serving others in the vineyard for the King is an honor and a privilege; and

WHEREAS, I am not overtaxed, tired, or troubled in the journey; instead, I am emblazoned with the marks of Holy Ghost revival, emboldened and fearless with Holy Ghost ardor, and empowered by Holy Ghost dynamism to make impact and have influence for Jesus as I triumphantly press toward the mark for the high calling of God in Christ Jesus (Phil. 3: 14).

I DECREE AND DECLARE this Day 160 that

- I am draped and drenched today by a "NEW" and "NOW" anointing to fulfill the mandate and mission of the Lord to me in the earth; yesterday is gone, and tomorrow may not be mine; therefore, I will function now, and not sit idle as a bystander and a wayside watcher (1 Sam. 4: 13)

- I am strengthened with might by his Spirit in the inner man (Eph. 3: 16), supported by angelic assistance (Heb. 1: 14), sustained by His amazing grace (Isa. 41: 13; Heb. 4: 16), and succored (helped) when I suffer (Heb. 2: 18), and I boldly proclaim God as my helper (Psa. 54: 4; Heb. 13: 6)

- I am not afraid, fretful, intimidated, or feel threatened by enemy hostility; the Holy Ghost dwells in me, He speaks through me, and He manifests His unstoppable power through me in the earth with miracles, signs, and wonders following the ministry assignments that God gives me (Acts 2: 43; 5: 12; 6: 8; 14: 3; 15: 12)

- I am on the move for Christ in the global village; I have WHO the world needs (Acts 4: 12), I wave HIS banner high (Psa. 20: 5; 60: 4; Isa. 11: 12), and I declare HIS rightful claim to my praise (Heb. 13: 15), His plans and purposes for me (Jer. 29: 11), so that I can champion the causes of His Kingdom in the earth with credibility, integrity, intensity and tenacity

- I am in the majority (2 Kin. 6: 16); I am victorious - my God towers far above and over every evil spirit and work, and I am well in Him.

BE IT THEREFORE RESOLVED by me this day that

- I remain steadfast in my faith and trust in God to speak to and guide me amidst the noise and voices that seek to disturb and perturb me from fulfilling my mission

- I remain bold and brave in the power given to me by the indwelling Holy Ghost, who seals me, and who is the earnest of my inheritance (Eph. 1: 13, 14)

WITH HOLY GHOST PERSUASION, I DRIVE THESE DECREES, DECLARATIONS, AND RESOLUTIONS AS STAKES IN THE GROUND; they are established and settled by the words I speak (Prov. 18: 21); Heaven blesses and bestows Divine benediction upon them; Satan may buffet them, but his agenda is banned, barred, and blocked by the blood of Jesus; I am mobile, motivated and on the move for the Lord in the earth, and I confidently affirm that the light shines upon my ways (Job 22: 28).

In the manifesting, matchless, and marvelous name of the Father, Son, and Holy Ghost! Blessed Godhead, Three-in-One!

AND IT IS SO!

Day 161

FORASMUCH as the Father's compassions, grace and mercy has been demonstrated once again to me, and I am in the land of the living one more day to live for Him; to God be the glory - and

WHEREAS, from the depths of my soul, I give the Lord praises and worship for His bountiful blessings upon me; and

WHEREAS, God's love looked for me, located me, lifted me, was lavishly poured into me, and now I sit together in Heavenly places in Christ Jesus as a joint heir with Him (Eph. 2: 6; Rom. 8: 17); and

WHEREAS, I am elated and exuberant that God has chosen me to be a part of His royal family of the blood-washed, forgiven, and redeemed (Heb. 13: 20; Rev. 7: 14); and

WHEREAS, as a member of the Church of the Living God, I have the missional mandate to move and manifest in the earth by the power and unction of the Holy Ghost, and I am activated and anointed to engage in Jesus' commission to "GO" (Matt.

28: 19): God's Church is on the move for Him in the global village.

I DECREE AND DECLARE this Day 161 that

- I lay side carnal means, mindsets, and motivations that do not laud and lift up the name of Jesus, or His causes and claims upon me as His representative in the earth

- I am on the move for the Master, and I will live with authenticity, credibility, dependability, and integrity, so that the Gospel of Jesus Christ and His Word is not blasphemed (Tit. 2: 5)

- I am more than a conqueror (Rom. 8: 37); I take authority over the wiles and works of the evil one (Luke 10: 19), and I cast and pull down vain imaginations that seek to be exalted over the Sovereignty and Supremacy of Jehovah in the earth (2 Cor. 10: 5-7)

- I am peaceable (1 Tim. 2: 2), prayerful (Lu. 18: 1), purposeful (Prov. 16: 4), and have potential (Jer. 29: 11); and through my living, the world will know that I have been with Jesus (Acts 4: 13), and that through Him I prevail (2 Chron. 14: 11)

- the strong hand of the Lord is upon me; there is a tsunami of Pentecostal power and glory at work in the global village, and I call forth supernatural breakthrough, miraculous deliverance, divine healing, total triumph, and overwhelming victory in the lives of those whom I make contact with.

BE IT THEREFORE RESOLVED by me this day that

- I will not back away, back down, back off, or back up from taking territory for the King in the earth – I will finish my assignment to plunder hell and populate Heaven!

- I remain devoted to draining the evil swamp of the Devil in the earth through the power of the Gospel of Jesus Christ, and I totally rely upon God's ability to save anyone, at any time, from anything, anywhere.

BY THE AUTHORITY OF MY KINGLY AND PRIESTLY POSITION WITH GOD MY FATHER (Rev. 1: 6), I BOLDLY DRIVE THESE DECREES, DECLARATIONS, AND RESOLUTIONS AS IRRESISTIBLE STAKES IN THE GROUND; they are established and settled in the earth by the words that I speak (Prov. 18: 21); the Triune God of Heaven affirms their establishment; Satan's threats and menaces against them are reduced to rubble and ruin, and I am confident and persuaded that the light shines upon my ways (Job 22: 28).

In the unbeatable, vanquishing, and winning name of God, my Father, Jesus, my Savior, and the Holy Ghost, my Sustainer! Blessed Godhead, Three-in-One!

AND IT IS SO!

Day 162

FORASMUCH as this is the day which the Lord hath made, I will rejoice and be glad in it (Psa.118:24); and, by His amazing grace and goodness, He has allowed me to live, move, and have my being in Him (Acts 17: 28); and

WHEREAS, I live in the earth by the divine counsel and purposes of God (Rom. 11: 34; Eph. 1: 11); therefore, adoration toward God swells within, and praise to Him without, as I consider the excellence of my Sovereign Father, and all that He has done, and is doing in me; and

WHEREAS, I feel like David when he praised God, and ascribed "the greatness, and the power, and the glory, and the victory, and the majesty" (1 Chron. 29: 11) unto the God of Israel; and

WHEREAS, as a representative of the Body of Christ, I have joy unspeakable as God mobilizes, motivates, and manifests His glory and power through me, a lively stone called by Him in the earth; and

WHEREAS, I am a dedicated, determined, and dutiful child of God with a life-changing and heart-transforming message about Jesus, who gave His life as a ransom for my sins (Jn. 3: 16; 1 Jn. 2: 2).

I DECREE AND DECLARE this Day 162 that

- I am not in the earth to gratify and satisfy my sinful nature; instead, I have been rescued and redeemed by the blood of Jesus; I will glorify and magnify the Lord, and Him only shall I serve (Lu. 4: 8)

- my old desires, disposition, and directions have been amazingly and graciously altered and changed (Eph. 4: 22, 23), and I will move with God in the earth as a new person, created in His righteousness and true holiness (Eph. 4: 24)

- I am not the Devil's dupe; I conquer and overcome his hostility and opposition against me, and by the power of the Holy Ghost, who lives in me, I triumphantly wage war in the Spirit against him from my third-Heaven position of power in Christ, and he (the Devil) has no ground, opportunity, or place in me (Eph. 4: 27)

- I am in the earth to fulfill my God-ordained assignment as salt and light (Matt. 5: 13-16), and I will not die until I have walked all the way with Him, witnessed every day about Him (Rev. 12: 11), worked diligently for Him (Jn. 9: 4), and won overwhelmingly through Him (Rom. 8: 37)

- I will not be defeated, denied, or deterred, but, because I am God's child on the move in the earth, I set the world ablaze with the Gospel, and turn it right side up for righteousness sake

BE IT THEREFORE RESOLVED by me this day that

- I remain adamant, uncompromising, and unwavering in my devotion to God, and in nothing terrified by my adversaries (Phil. 1: 28)

- I pledge my allegiance and loyalty to the tenets, testimonies, and truths of God's holy Word, and I have His guarantee of total victory over the world, the flesh and the Devil (1 Jn. 4: 4)

BY VIRTUE OF MY POSITION AND STANDING AS A KING AND PRIEST UNTO MY GOD AND FATHER (Rev. 1: 6), I HAMMER THESE PROPHETIC DECREES, DECLARATIONS, AND RESOLUTIONS AS MEMORIALS IN THE GROUND; they are established and settled by the fruit of my lips (Prov. 18: 21); there is no doubt that they are fully backed and braced by the Godhead of Heaven; the death knell resounds loudly of the destruction and doom of satanic words and works against them, and I am kept in the earth by the light that shines upon my ways (Job 22: 28).

In the Eminent, Esteemed, and Excellent name of the Father, Son, and Holy Ghost! Blessed Trinity! Three-in-One!

AND IT IS SO!

Day 163

A DECLARATION ACKNOWLEDGING YOUNG PEOPLE

FORASMUCH as the Lord our God Omnipotent reigns, and that He has extended grace and mercy toward me to raise me from overnight rest to experience life for another day; and

WHEREAS, today I give intentional, intense and unceasing praise to God for the blessing of being called out of darkness into His marvelous light because of Jesus (1 Pet. 2: 9); and

WHEREAS, I have a reason for the passion I have to "GO" into the earth and reach the lost with the life-changing and transforming message of Jesus Christ, the Savior of the world, and that is, I want others to know there is something mighty sweet about the Lord, and the change He brings to a life (like He did to mine) is worth telling everyone I see about Him; and

WHEREAS, great necessity is laid upon me to preach and proclaim the message of Jesus to ALL men everywhere (1 Cor. 9: 16), with no age, gender, class, race, or social standing a barrier or blockage to the everlasting love of Jesus reaching their hearts (Jn. 3: 16); and

WHEREAS, this is the season for me to be on the move in the earth (Matt. 28: 19, 20); all ages of God's people include the youth, whom I acknowledge, celebrate and honor today, and who are an integral part of God's master plan for His Church in the earth to reach and reap for the Kingdom (Matt. 9: 38).

I DECREE AND DECLARE this Day 163 that

- I call forth a strong and vibrant cadre and company of youthful firebrands for Christ who will be empowered and equipped to engage the harvest of young people in the global village, and they will ensure that no youth is excluded and left behind

- I prophesy a Holy Ghost awakening, quickening and revival among young people across the four corners of the globe, and that the Present Next Generation of young people will be the catalysts of Holy Ghost anointing that will prompt a supernatural convergence of the needs of young people and God's transforming power, and that His power will bring drastic change and deliverance to their lives for the glory of God

- I rebuke and rebut heathenism, heresy, idolatry, and every devilish doctrine (1 Tim. 4: 1) and dogma that parades and purports to be genuine, but is perverse and putrefying to the eternal soul of man - the blood of Jesus prevails!

- the present generation of young people will march to the drumbeat, and under the banner of Jesus Christ in the earth, and their godly impact and influence will astonish and cause awe in the hearts of others to the saving of their souls (Deut. 2: 25)

- the present generation of young people will live balanced godly lives, walk boldly and bravely for Jesus in the earth; they will be beams of hope to their peers, and, despite their youthfulness (1 Tim. 4: 12), they will be the bastions and beacons of Christlike steadfastness in a world that is chaotic, confusing and corrupting at its core (Phil. 2: 15).

BE IT THEREFORE RESOLVED by me this day that

- I remain determined and dutiful in my Gospel engagement with the lost souls of man, and, come what may, I will not be stopped by any opposing wile and work of Satan from reaching them for the Savior

- I fix and focus my gaze on the Most High, and I attune my spiritual ears to hear what the Spirit says to the Church in the global village (Matt. 11: 15; Rev. 2: 29)

BY THE AUTHORITY VESTED IN ME AS A KING AND PRIEST UNTO GOD (Rev. 1: 6), I AUDACIOUSLY DRIVE THESE PROPHETIC DECREES, DECLARATIONS, AND RESOLUTIONS AS LANDMARK STAKES DEEPLY ROOTED IN THE GROUND; by the fruit of my lips (Prov. 18: 21), they are established and set; the Triune God validates and verifies them; demonic, evil taunts and threats against them boomerang back to the sender for their demise and total destruction, and I confidently abide in the light that shines upon my ways (Job 22: 28).

In the stable, strong, and sturdy name of the Father, Son, and Holy Ghost! Blessed Trinity!

AND IT IS SO!

Day 164

FORASMUCH as God my Father has blessed me to arise in the land of the living one more day, with the use of me senses, a sound mind, and the activity of my limbs; and

WHEREAS, it is a good thing to glorify the Lord, and for my lips to utter high praise unto the Rock of my salvation (Psa. 89: 26), and to lift my heart and hands unto the Savior in honor and thanksgiving (1 Tim. 2: 8); and

WHEREAS, I arise today acknowledging the steadfast faithfulness and love of God for how He has preserved my life, and the way He has manifested His almighty power in me can only be explained as the supernatural power of God at work in my being; and

WHEREAS, I have a burden for the harvest of lost souls in the global village, and God is intentional concerning His willingness that none should perish, but that all men should be saved, and to come unto the knowledge of the truth (1 Tim. 2: 4), and His plan is that I bear precious seed, and to come again with rejoicing bringing the sheaves with me (Psa. 126: 6);

and

WHEREAS, I cast my focus on the harvest; that is, to actively engage in winning lost souls in the earth at any cost, and obeying the Master's mandate to "GO" (Matt. 28: 19, 20).

I DECREE AND DECLARE this Day 164 that

- my ministry mandate and mission to the fields that are white unto harvest (Jn. 4: 35) has primacy and priority; therefore, I put on and buckle up my shoes, knowing that "beautiful are the feet of them that preach the gospel of peace, and bring glad tidings of good things" (Rom. 10: 15)

- knowing the terror of the Lord, I persuade men (2 Cor. 5: 11), and I "go out into the highways and hedges and compel the unsaved to come in, that His house may be filled (Lu. 14: 23)

- I renounce and repel every diabolical work in the earth that is designed to stop and thwart the proclamation of the Gospel of Jesus Christ, and every hindrance to the message of salvation is disarmed by the power of Jesus' blood

- as the harvest is ripe, but the laborers are few (Matt. 9: 37), I make up the few, and I stand up, step up, show up, and speak up in the field, so that I can reap the harvest God has promised (Psa. 126: 6)

- I will not be slack, sleepy, or slothful concerning the harvest; instead, I do occupy until Jesus comes (Lu. 19: 13), activate myself for maximum ministry effectiveness, and exercise diligence and duty to rescue the perishing, and to care for those going headlong to a Christ-less eternity.

BE IT THEREFORE RESOLVED by me this day that

- I arm myself with a ready mind, a strong resilience, a submitted spirit, and willing hands to labour "for the meat which endureth unto everlasting life" (Jn. 6: 27)

- we remain dedicated, devoted and diligent to Jesus' charge and commission to us to "GO" in the harvest field; the hour is late; His work demands haste

BY THE AUTHORITY OF MY CONNECTION WITH THE KING, I BOLDLY DRIVE THESE DECREES, DECLARATIONS, AND RESOLUTIONS AS HARVEST-FIELD STAKES IN THE GROUND; I speak establishment of them by the fruit of my lips (Prov. 18: 21); Heaven affirms and approves them; Satan's assaults and attacks against them are blocked and banished, and as a laborer in the harvest, I am confident that the light continues to shine upon my ways (Job 22: 28).

In the sanctifying, satisfying, and saving name of the Father, Son, and Holy Ghost! Blessed Godhead, Three-In-One!

AND IT IS SO!

Day 165

FORASMUCH as it is by the amazing grace, mercy and lovingkindness of MY Heavenly Father that I opened my eyes today, breathed fresh air, and have the full activity of my limbs; and

WHEREAS, I have unbridled joy when I consider the miraculous, wonder-working power of God that He has manifested in my life during my journey in the earth as a Christian; and

WHEREAS, I am humbled to be in the presence of God today in holy and sweet communion for morning manna and "meditation", which the Psalmist said "shall be sweet: I will be glad in the Lord" (104: 34); and

WHEREAS, God is moving by His power and Spirit in my life; a revival of the "supernatural God-kind" has swept over my being; a holy anticipation and expectation permeate and pervade my spirit, and I am passionate about the harvest, which Jesus said "is plenteous, but the laborers are few" (Matt. 9: 35-38); and

WHEREAS, I hear the call and the cry of the hapless, the helpless, and the hopeless - the harvest, and I "GO", knowing that Jesus is Lord of the harvest (Matt. 9: 38), and I am submitted and surrendered to engage in winning the harvest, which is ripe and white for reaping (Jn. 4: 35).

I DECREE AND DECLARE this Day 165 that

- the ripe, waiting harvest is precious, yet perishing; therefore, I move hastily, hurriedly, and without delay, and, by the power of the Gospel of Jesus Christ, I pluck and pull souls from eternal damnation and danger, and into the safe harbor of the Savior's everlasting care

- "IT STARTS WITH ME" is my pledge and promise to the Savior as I occupy in harvest field, and what I hear, know, or see, will not stymie or stop me from full occupation in the Kingdom mandate in the earth

- diabolical threats and evil menaces that I encounter in in the harvest will prompt the supernatural, and Holy Ghost might and power will propel and push me beyond what appears to be the terrifying and terrorizing into the realm of the Spirit where God prepares a table before me in the presence of my enemies (Psa. 23: 5)

- by God's grace, I am well able to fully fulfill my Kingdom assignment in the harvest field, and all the ingredients of "mission possible" for impact and influence in the global village are accessible to me because "my help comes from the Lord" (Psa. 121: 2)

- I will not argue, bicker, complain, debate, or engage in criticism, negativism, or pessimism in the harvest field; instead, prayer, praise, worship, and the Word of God are my chosen and preferred weapons of warfare that repel and reject carnal schemes and systems designed to derail and deter me from impact and influence in the harvest.

BE IT THEREFORE RESOLVED by me this day that

- I remain totally dependent and reliant upon the Father's full giving of compassion and love for the lost as I fully engage in the harvest

- I outrightly disengage myself from ideas, ideals and thought patterns that will cause me to wane, weaken and wilt as I labor in the fields of harvest

BY THE AUTHORITY VESTED IN ME AS A LABORER AND BOND SERVANT IN THE LORD'S HARVEST, I DRIVE THESE PROPHETIC DECREES, DECLARATIONS, AND RESOLUTIONS AS HARVEST STAKES IN THE GROUND; I believe in them, and, by the fruit of my lips (Prov. 18: 21), they are established and settled in my life; the Triune Godhead of Heaven seals and stamps them "approved"; satanic interferences and interruptions are intercepted and imploded by their own fuel, and I will labor in the field of harvest because of the light that shines upon my ways (Job 22: 28).

In the regathering, repairing and resurrecting name of the Father, Son, and Holy Ghost! Blessed Godhead, Three-In-One!

AND IT IS SO!

Day 166

FORASMUCH as "it is a good thing to give thanks unto the Lord, and to sing praises unto His name, and to shew forth His lovingkindness in the morning, and His faithfulness every night" (Psa. 92: 1, 2); and

WHEREAS, the fact that God, by His grace and mercy, has allowed me to wake up in the land of the living for another day, evokes gladness and joy within, and prompts me to glorify and magnify His high and holy name; and

WHEREAS, I choose to lavish high praise and worship to God for the joy and privilege of redeeming and regenerating me from the mire and muck of sin, and transforming me from darkness to His light; and

WHEREAS, in the Lord, I have a safe harbor and haven from alarm and harm (Prov. 18: 10), and I have a deep yearning and zeal for more of Him during difficult and sometimes distressing days of my life; and

WHEREAS, the mandate and mission from God to me is to be an epicenter of spiritual growth and transformation by the Word of God, and not a platform that promotes selfish personal agendas and designs; and

WHEREAS, it is my choice to be actively engaged in the harvest; a focus that is central to winning lost souls for the Kingdom of God in the earth: "...he that winneth souls is wise" (Prov. 11: 30).

I DECREE AND DECLARE this Day 166 that

- my activation and engagement in the harvest is my personal choice, and I take responsibility for having the correct approach and attitude to God's mandate and mission to His Church in the global village

- the Gospel of Jesus Christ is my mantra; the unconditional and unfailing love of Jesus Christ is my message; the cross of Jesus Christ is my motivation, and redemption through Jesus Christ moves me to labor in the harvest

- I rebuke, rebut, and reject the plots and ploys of Satan's evil systems in the earth, myriads of angelic hosts encamp about me, and they bar and block diabolical schemes from prevailing and prospering over me (Isa. 54: 17)

- reaching and reaping the harvest is central to my existence and function in the global village, and I take every opportunity that God gives me to stand up and speak up for the causes of Christ to those whose lives are darkened by sin; those demeaned by others, the poor who are despised and displaced by society, and the disconsolate who lament in grief and pain

- the harvest moves me to "GO"; Jesus' message of love propels me to share with all (Jn. 3: 16), and I am provoked to engage in a mission possible that guarantees triumph and total victory for the Kingdom (Matt. 28: 20; 1 Jn. 5: 4).

BE IT THEREFORE RESOLVED by me this day that

- I remain a devoted laborer in the harvest, reaping time is coming, and I will return rejoicing, bringing the sheaves with me (Psa. 126: 6)

- I stand committed, dedicated, engaged and fervent in the harvest field occupation, and by the guarantee of God, I WIN FOR THE KING! (Dan. 12: 3; 1 Cor. 15: 57)!

BY THE AUTHORITY VESTED IN ME AS THE KING'S REPRESENTATIVE IN THE EARTH, I DRIVE THESE DECREES, DECLARATIONS, AND RESOLUTIONS AS STAKES IN THE GROUND; they are established by the words that I speak (Prov. 18: 21); they have the agreement and assent of Heaven's holy order; satanic devices and designs against them are derailed, disturbed and doomed, and I occupy in the harvest under the light that shines upon my ways (Job 22: 28).

In the abounding and resounding name of the Father, Son, and Holy Ghost! Blessed Godhead, Three-In-One!

AND IT IS SO

Day 167

FORASMUCH as the good and gracious hand of God has touched me to arise and be alive today; He lovingly allowed me to breathe fresh air, and by His finger of care, He blessed me to have the activity of my limbs, and the soundness of my mind (Acts 17: 28); and

WHEREAS, "Who is like unto the Lord our God, who dwells on high and looks low in the earth, who raises the poor out of the dust, and lifts the needy out of the dunghill, and makes the barren woman to keep house, and to be a joyful mother of children?" (Psa. 113: 5-9); and

WHEREAS, God has no equal; He consults with no one; He has no rival (Isa. 40: 13, 14); He is God all by Himself (Psa. 86: 10); and

WHEREAS, I boast in the Lord (Psa. 34: 2; 1 Cor. 1: 31) for the marvelous and wonderful things that He has done in my life; and

WHEREAS, I am so joyful and jubilant about what the Lord has done, that I have a passion to win the harvest of lost souls in cities and villages to Jesus to experience salvation and transformation (Matt. 9: 35-38).

I DECREE AND DECLARE this Day 167 that

- I am not indifferent or indolent about the field that are already white unto harvest (Jn. 4: 35); instead, I am actively occupied, anointed to be effective, and have the ornament of Jesus' love to reach and reap the harvest for the Kingdom of God

- I will not be disinterested, distracted, or disturbed from my duty in the harvest engagement; the day is at hand, time is winding down, Jesus' appearance in the sky for His Bride is imminent; so, I move hastily and hurriedly to the fields that are already white (Jn. 4: 35) to populate the Kingdom of Heaven

- by Holy Ghost anointing and authority, I decapitate, strangulate, and suffocate every work and wile of the devil against me in the harvest; he cannot, and will not, prevail or prosper; I have no fear; God has his number, and he (the Devil) knows "he hath but a short time" (Rev. 12: 12)

- as I occupy in the harvest, there is wonder-working breakthrough, deliverance, healing, liberty, miracles, triumph, and undeniable victory for the waning ones, the weak, the weary, the wilting, the worn out, and the worried: "the yoke shall be destroyed because of the anointing" (Isa. 10: 27) that envelopes me as a harvest laborer

- the need is urgent, the hour is late, there is no time to sleep (Prov. 10: 5); the fields are ripe and white unto harvest (Jn. 4: 35); therefore, I willingly "GO" into the harvest without delay to preach, teach, reach, and reap a bountiful harvest for Jesus.

BE IT THEREFORE RESOLVED by me this day that

- I remain adaptable, adjustable, and amenable in my spirit to the will of God as a laborer in the harvest for the glory and honor of His Kingdom in the earth

- I refuse and reject the applause and approval of man as I labor in the harvest field; I will please my Father ONLY for whom I labor

BY THE ABILITY AND AUTHORITY THAT THE HOLY GHOST ALLOWS, I DRIVE THESE PROPHETIC DECREES, DECLARATIONS, AND RESOLUTIONS AS HARVEST MARKERS AND STAKES IN THE GROUND; they are established and settled by the fruit of my lips (Prov. 18: 21); the seal and signage of Heaven are upon them; satanic interruptions against them are intercepted and incarcerated, and as a harvest laborer, I am confident that the light shines upon my ways (Job 22: 28).

In the limitless, matchless, and peerless name of the Father, Son, and Holy Ghost! Triune Godhead! Blessed Trinity!

AND IT IS SO!

Day 168

FORASMUCH as the Lord God Almighty, by His tender, yet strong arm, has awakened me to the light of a new day; He allowed me to breathe, and touched me to function physically, and to have a sound mind (Acts 17: 28); and

WHEREAS, my Sovereign Father has granted me the blessing of daily fellowship in His holy presence - what fulness of joy and pleasures I enjoy with Him that He has willed for evermore (Psa. 16: 11); and

WHEREAS, the marvelous handiwork of God in my life prompts and provokes me to exalt and extol Him for the wonders of His grace, and, despite my waywardness, weaknesses, and sometimes my wretchedness, He gives me continuous blessings and wise bestowments that remind me of His compassion, mercy, and good thoughts toward me (Jer. 29: 11); and

WHEREAS, there is a pressing need for loyal laborers of love in the harvest, which is plenteous and already white for reaping

(Matt. 9: 35-38; Jn. 4: 35), and that such laborers will diligently and hastily engage and occupy to reach and reap the promised harvest in the earth; and

WHEREAS, this is the clarion call and commission of the Lord to me; I will lift up my eyes and look on the fields (Jn. 4: 35), to the hedges and highways (Lu. 14: 23), in cities and villages (Matt. 9: 35), and every place where mankind is, so that I can exclaim and proclaim the Gospel message of hope and life that Jesus gives (Jn. 14: 6);

I DECREE AND DECLARE this Day 168 that

- I will not detract, detour, deviate from, or dilute the whole counsel of God (Acts 20: 27) that Jesus came to call sinners to repentance (Lu. 5: 32)

- I spread and stretch wide the Gospel net, and I call forth those ravaged and wrecked by sin, and those damaged and devastated by brokenness and burdens, into the ark of safety and security that Jesus offers

- despite setbacks, the sinister designs of Satan, and traps and tricks of demonic subtlety, my labor in the harvest field brings forth fruit, which shall remain (Jn. 15: 16)

- I will not be afraid or alarmed, fearful, or fretful, terrified or terrorized in the harvest, for "they that be with me are more than they that be with them" (2 Ki. 6: 16); and "greater is He that is in me, than he that is in the world" (1 Jn. 4: 4)

- laboring in the harvest is not for the faint of heart; it will get rough and rugged at times; the hills at times will be hard to climb; hostile enemy fire will buffet me, but, the fight is firmly fixed - I WAR, WORK, AND WIN!

BE IT THEREFORE RESOLVED by me this day that

- I will keep my spiritual ears attuned to the voice of God as I labor in the harvest, and I keep my heart syncopated with the heart of God for the harvest in the earth

- I will remain God's hands extended in the harvest; His feet on the move with tidings of good things (Rom. 10: 15), and, by the help of the Holy Spirit, His voice in the earth that calls the harvest to repentance and redemption through Jesus

BY THE BLOOD OF THE LAMB, AND THE CALL OF LOVE AND MERCY FROM CALVARY, I DRIVE THESE PROPHETIC DECREES, DECLARATIONS, AND RESOLUTIONS AS STAKES IN THE GROUND; they are established and settled in the earth by the words that I speak (Prov. 18: 21); the Triune Godhead of Heaven graces and guarantees their fulfillment; satanic devices and designs against them are blown off course by the wind of the Spirit, and I confidently labor under the light that shines upon ways (Job 22: 28).

In the governing, guarding, and guiding name of the Father, Son, and Holy Ghost! Blessed Trinity!

AND IT IS SO!

Day 169

FORASMUCH as it was the Father's pleasure and prerogative to watch over me throughout the night, to breathe upon me to arise from rest today, and to touch me with His hand of grace and mercy to have the blessing of life in the earth; and

WHEREAS, today is a day of thanksgiving and praise to God for His awesome and mighty acts, and for His excellent greatness toward me (Psa. 150: 2); and

WHEREAS, I have absolute joy in knowing that by the grace and help of Almighty God, I have godly impact and influence for Him in the global village: my witness and record of labor is in Heaven (Job 16: 19); and

WHEREAS, having been blessed, challenged, and edified by the life-giving, quickening Word of God (Heb. 4: 12), I willingly say, "...send me" (Isa 6: 8); and

WHEREAS, my mind is made up, my heart are fixed, my shoes are buckled, and my spirits is ready to "look to the fields, for they are white already to harvest", and "GO" (Jn. 4: 35; Matt. 28: 19, 20).

I DECREE AND DECLARE this Day 169 that

- as God will have mercy on whom He will have mercy, and compassion on whom He will have compassion (Rom. 9: 15), I lay aside my mindsets, paradigms, and thoughts of bias and stereotyping toward the harvest field in the earth, and I open myself to ministry to the "whosoever"

- I submit to the sanctifying work of the Holy Spirit who cleanses and purifies me for usefulness in the harvest, knowing that clean vessels are God's requirement in the fields of labor (Isa. 52: 11; 1 Thess. 4: 7)

- the Devil has no say in this matter; the Lord rebukes him, the blood of Jesus prevails against his pernicious ways, and his evil assignments and weapons that he forms are nullified and void of effect upon my labor in the harvest (Isa. 54: 17)

- as a laborer in the harvest vineyard, I have great delight in doing the Father's will; I sow seeds with joy, I weep in prayerful intercession and heartfelt compassion for the harvest, and I have God's promise that I will come again with rejoicing, bringing the sheaves with me (Psa. 126: 6)

- I labor in the harvest for the Master, not for the masses; I preach and teach to reap the harvest, and not for earthly reward, and, when I suffer during my labor, I will do so knowing that I will reign with Him (2 Tim. 2: 12).

BE IT THEREFORE RESOLVED by me this day that

- I remain keenly aware of my place and position in the harvest - one plants, another waters, but God gives the increase (1 Cor. 3: 6-9)

- I will not seek to box in or limit God during my labor in the harvest; He can do anything with and for anyone whom He chooses (Lu. 1: 37; Rom. 9: 15)

BY VIRTUE OF MY RIGHT STANDING WITH GOD AS A KING AND PRIEST UNTO HIM (Rev. 1: 6), I DRIVE THESE DECREES, DECLARATIONS, AND RESOLUTIONS AS MEMORABLE STAKES IN THE GROUND; they are established by the fruit of my lips (Prov. 18: 21); Heaven embraces and endorses their fulfillment and fruitfulness; demonic designs against them fall flat in failure and futility, and I labor with confidence that the light shines upon my ways (Job 22: 28).

In the beautiful, blessed, and benevolent name of the Father, Son, and Holy Ghost! Blessed Trinity!

AND IT IS SO!

Day 170

FORASMUCH as it was the power and Sovereignty of God that caused me to arise today; He breathed upon me, He lifted me, and has given me life and liberty; and

WHEREAS, I proclaim the glory and majesty of the Lord, and I have holy joy at the remembrance of His name in my life as I have sweet fellowship, prayer, give praise, worship Him, and receive His holy presence into my spirit; and

WHEREAS, a powerful revival of righteousness and manifestation of the glory of the Lord has hit the globe (Hab. 2: 14), and I have the honor to be actively engaged in ministry in the earth by the gracious hand of God upon me; and

WHEREAS, miracles, signs and wonders have manifested in the lives of numerous persons around the world; they have not been sensational occurrences of emotion and hype; rather, they have confirmed the power of the message of Jesus, and His ability to deliver, heal, liberate, and save from the enslavement of sin; and

WHEREAS, being used by God to make inroads for Him in the lives of others in the global village, and to reap the harvest for the Kingdom gives me unspeakable joy and satisfaction.

I DECREE AND DECLARE this Day 170 that

- the strong and sustaining hand of the Lord rests upon me; I have a goodly heritage (Psa. 16: 6), and through them, Holy Ghost power and might will continue to be manifested in market place ministry in the global village

- an end-time anointing and unction of spiritual gifting and grace envelopes my life, and as I submit and subject myself to godly leadership and wisdom, my ability to discern, hear and know the voice of God will become keener and sharper as I develop and grow (1 Sam. 3: 1-10)

- I am a nightmare to the kingdom of Satan; and by the power of the Holy Ghost working in and through me, my impact for Jesus will cause a shaking and a stirring among the lost, who will fall to their knees in sorrow for sin and repentance (Acts 17: 30)

- uncommon and unprecedented boldness and courage drapes me for my God-given assignments in the earth, and I will stand up, and speak up candidly, clearly, and concisely for Jesus wherever I go (Acts 4: 20)

- by God's enablement and grace, I will carry forth the Gospel message everywhere I go, and the mantle of future leadership in the Kingdom will not be lacking or lost (1 Tim. 4: 12)

BE IT THEREFORE RESOLVED by me this day that

- I remain still and surrendered to the plans and purposes of God for my life, and to His sanctifying Word to me (Jn. 17: 17)

- I purpose to willingly obey the voice and Word of God (Isa. 1: 19); to walk in His statutes (1 Jn. 2: 6), and to give testimony and witness to His power and presence in my life (1 Pet. 3: 15)

BY THE AUTHORITY OF MY POSITION AS THE REDEEMED OF THE LORD (Psa. 107: 2), I DRIVE THESE PROPHETIC DECREES, DECLARATIONS, AND RESOLUTIONS AS STAKES IN THE GROUND; they are firmly established and settled in my life by the fruit of my lips (Prov. 18: 21); the Triune Godhead of Heaven validates and verifies them; the power of the Spirit of God causes confusion and a conundrum to the works and ways of Satan against them, and I confidently abide in the light that shines upon my ways (Job 22: 28).

In the never-faltering, never-failing, ever-faithful name of the Father, Son, and Holy Ghost! God in three Persons, blessed Trinity!

AMEN!

Day 171

FORASMUCH as it has pleased God my Father to raise me up from overnight rest today, and by His grace and mercy, He granted me the blessing of life, and the joy of seeing His goodness in the land of the living (Psa. 27: 13); and

WHEREAS, I cannot explain the sheer joy I have because of the marvelous wonders of God's might and power upon me during my life's journey; His grace and mercy has brought me through; and

WHEREAS, to approach and dwell in the presence of God for daily bread and meditation can only be described as "the Lord's doings" (Psa. 118: 23); when I think of the goodness of Jesus in my life, my heart and soul shouts hallelujah, praise God for saving me; the mire I was lifted out of was deep and dirty, but Jesus looked beyond my faults and saw my need for cleansing and washing in His precious blood; and

WHEREAS, I have a Kingdom assignment; the possibilities and potential abound as I labor in the global village with the assurance that He "is able to do exceeding abundantly above all that I ask of think" (Eph. 3: 20); and

WHEREAS, the Church of the Lord Jesus Christ on the move in the earth; I am excitedly engaged in labor in the harvest, and I am ablaze by the fire of God from Heaven.

I DECREE AND DECLARE this Day 171 that

- my ONLY desire and passion is for the fire that God sends down, and His fire consumes every false altar, idolatrous thing and oblation that has the scent of carnality and humanity that dishonors and displeases Almighty God

- God, "a consuming fire" (Heb. 12: 29), by His might and power, consumes and destroys every enemy scheme and system that is designed and formed to eliminate me, and His fire envelopes and surrounds me at all times

- according to 2 Chron. 7: 3, "ALL" shall see God's fire and glory manifested in the earth, and His fire causes astonishment, awe, and unbridled worship from the depths of my soul that will change the lives of multitudes of people in the earth

- revival fire from the presence of God will alter and cause uncommon and unusual transformation in the global village, and unprecedented moves and surges of Holy Ghost power will bring the unsaved to altars of repentance, redemption, and restoration

- God WILL BE magnified through me in the earth; the majesty and weight of His miraculous power will sweep over cities, hamlets, neighborhoods, towns, and villages, and God's fire will ignite a blaze of glory that will engulf and consume sanctuaries and His people, and there will be amazement among witnesses who see me ablaze for God (Hab. 2: 14).

BE IT THEREFORE RESOLVED by me this day that

- I earnestly retain the mindset and position that nothing but God's fire come down from Heaven will satisfy my desire for more of Him

- I remain on the altar and in His presence, and am submitted to being filled again and again and again with Holy Ghost power and fire for His glory and usefulness in the global village

BY VIRTUE OF MY PRIVILEGED POSITION OF GRACE AS A KING AND PRIEST UNTO GOD (Rev. 1: 6), I DRIVE THESE PROPHETIC DECREES, DECLARATIONS, AND RESOLUTIONS AS FIRE STAKES IN THE GROUND; they are established by the words that I speak (Prov. 18: 21); they have the full backing and weight of Heaven; hostile enemy fire against them are incinerated and torched to dust by God's fire, and the light shines upon my ways (Job 22: 28b).

In the consecrating and consuming name of the Father, Son, and Holy Ghost! Blessed Godhead, Three-in-One!

AND IT IS SO!

Day 172

FORASMUCH as the angel of the Lord encamped round about me throughout the night (Psa. 34: 7-9), by His mercies I am not consumed (Lam. 3: 22), His compassions do not fail (Lam. 3: 22), and the hand of the Lord withheld death from me and allowed me to arise from rest; these blessings and more confirm and testify that He is faithful (2 Tim. 2: 13); and

WHEREAS, I today arise with thanksgiving in my heart that I am called, chosen, and ordained by God in eternity by the counsel of His own will (Eph. 1: 11), I have every reason to rejoice in the greatness of God's might and power in my life - to God be the glory; and

WHEREAS, I am still ecstatic, elated, and excited about the Lord my God as I was when He saved me from the horrors of my sinful life, and I am astonished and in awe of His great power and might; and

WHEREAS, I am fueled by the fire that falls from Heaven (2 Chron. 7: 1); it has ignited a blaze in my soul that is uncontainable and unstoppable, and by it all shall see that it has worked, and still works right now in and through me in the global village; and

WHEREAS, holy fire from Heaven has fully engulfed my life, and a holy burning from the hand of Almighty God is upon me.

I DECREE AND DECLARE this Day 172 that

- the holy and unquenchable flame of God sets me apart and distinct from the world's senses and systems, and I live unapologetically in supernatural ability and authority in the earth because of the impact of the fire

- I do not function according to my human intellect and wisdom (Jam. 3: 15); instead, my life is fueled by the fire that enables me to employ divine intelligence and understanding that brings clarity and sharp focus to daily living which produces the fruit of righteousness and peace (James 3: 17, 18)

- the fire causes me to make the conscious choice to live with credibility, dependability, honesty, and integrity, knowing that God does not accept strange fire (Lev. 10: 1), and I will be known as a Christian who lives by standards that are not stained or sullied by sin's decay and decadence

- this holy and pure fire preserves and protect me, and all that I do for the Kingdom of God is fueled by Heaven's fire, and I reject and resist any and every agency or entity of Satan that is formed to exterminate or extinguish the fire (Isa. 54: 17)

- I am set on fire in the global village, and Holy Ghost fire from Heaven causes amazement and astonishment in the lives of the unredeemed and unrepentant, and they will turn from unrighteousness to righteousness; from darkness to the

Kingdom of God's dear Son (Col. 1: 13), and give witness that the fire purifies.

BE IT THEREFORE RESOLVED by me this day that

- I willingly align myself to the refining effects of God's fire upon my life, so that I can function effectively and with excellence for the Kingdom of God in the earth

- I choose to remain under the firepower that God graces me with, so that the word will have no doubt that I am consumed with, and controlled by, the fire of God comes down from Heaven

BY THE AUTHORITY VESTED IN ME AS A RECIPIENT OF THE FIRE, I DRIVE THESE PROPHETIC DECREES, DECLARATIONS, AND RESOLUTIONS AS IMMOVABLE STAKES IN THE GROUND; they are established and fulfilled by the fruit of my lips (Prov. 18: 21); Heaven embraces and graces them with Divine approval; Heaven's holy fire eradicates and incinerates the ways and works of Satan set against them, and the light shines upon my ways in the earth (Job 22: 28).

In the precious, preeminent, and prevailing name of the Father, Son, and Holy Ghost! Blessed Godhead, Three-in-One!

AND IT IS SO!

Day 173

FORASMUCH as the gracious and loving hand of my Sovereign Heavenly Father has raised me up to see the light of a brand new day with the activity of my limbs, my senses, well-being and life (Acts 17: 28); and

WHEREAS, words are inadequate and insufficient to describe the deep gratitude and thanks that I have toward my merciful Abba (Daddy), who, according to the riches of His grace, has allowed me to approach His holy presence; therefore, I raise my Ebenezer (1 Sam. 7: 12) and a praise: hallelujah to the Lord my God the Almighty reigns; how excellent is His name in all the earth (Psa. 8: 1); and

WHEREAS, as His child ordained to reach the lost in the world, I lavish glory, honor, thanksgiving, and praise unto God for the marvelous things that He has done for me; my journey in the Spirit with Him in the earth has been momentous and monumental to say the least (Psa. 118; 23); and

WHEREAS, I have launched out into the deep for a draught (Lu. 5: 4) and am on the move and fully engaged in the fields of harvest; I am on fire (2 Chron. 7: 1-3), fully engulfed by God's holy fire that evokes my heartfelt, passionate adoration and worship of Him.

I DECREE AND DECLARE this Day 173 that

- I do not, and will not, engage in sensationalism driven by emotion and/or external stimuli; rather, my soul is prostrate in awe and reverential fear before God, and I render my body as living sacrifices to Him (Rom. 12: 1), so that His fire fully permeates and penetrates my daily living

- I will not be satisfied with or search for, other sources of fire that are contrary and strange to God's holy order (Lev. 10: 1, 2); instead, God's fire that comes down from His eternal throne (2 Chron. 7: 3) is the ONLY source acceptable and allowable for me to be on fire in the earth

- holy ardor, sanctified fervor, and righteous intensity drive and envelope me, and God's holy fire emanating from my life will cause the unredeemed to cry out to God in contrition and sorrowful repentance for sin that leads to salvation (2 Cor. 7: 10), and I will remain humble before the face of God

- the demonic and diabolical works of evil have no negative or residual effect or impact upon me; rather, agendas of evil are the fuel that stokes God's fire hotter in me, more impacting, influential, and irresistible, and as a member of Jesus's Church in the earth, I blaze and burn trails of revival and righteousness in every corner and crevice I go

- I stand upon, and drink from the Rock (1 Sam. 2: 2; 2 Sam. 22: 32; Isa. 44: 8; Hab. 1: 12; 1 Cor. 10: 4), I am empowered and equipped by the Holy Ghost to witness in the four corners of the earth that the fire empowers and enables (Acts 1: 8), and God's holy fire keeps me engaged for the Kingdom, and engulfed in holy power.

BE IT THEREFORE RESOLVED by me this day that

- I remain fired up by the holiness of God in my life, and I am committed to being a spiritual climate-changer and legacy-leaver for my eternal King in the earth

- only the glory and honor of God is my agenda and reason for spiritual activation and being on fire in the earth

I DRIVE THESE PROPHETIC DECREES, DECLARATIONS, AND RESOLUTIONS AS SIGNIFICANT STAKES IN THE GROUND; they are established and settled by the fruit of my lips (Prov. 18: 21); the seal and stamp of Heaven's approval is affixed to them; satanic resistance against them is annihilated and obliterated by the intensity of God's holy fire, and I live on fire in the world, and walk in the light that shines upon my ways (Job 22: 28).

In the safe, secure and strong name of the Father, Son, and Holy Ghost! Blessed Godhead, Three-in-One!

AND IT IS SO!

Day 174

FORASMUCH as I am alive and well today by the compassions, grace, and mercy of my loving Heavenly Father; He has allowed me to see His goodness in the land of the living (Psa. 27: 13); and

WHEREAS, this is a great day to praise the Lord, who is worthy of glory, honor and thanksgiving for the wondrous things He has done for me (Psa. 107: 31); and

WHEREAS, I am thankful today that God has graced me to enjoy fellowship and intimacy with Him in the secret place of the Most High (Psa. 91: 1), and to pray, praise and worship His majestic name; and

WHEREAS, my joy is Jesus is the center and core of my existence in the earth; and healing, miracles, signs and wonders manifested by God's hand in my life confirm His Almighty power; and

WHEREAS, I am on fire in the global village; my labor for the King in the earth prompts my passion to do so under the power and might of God's holy fire from His throne (2 Chron. 7: 3).

I DECREE AND DECLARE this Day 174 that

- I am fully engulfed by the holiness of God, and His fire that rains down upon me has total control and sway over all that I do in the earth

- this holy fire is God's, is free of the corrupt things that anti-God systems embrace, and I push back against alien, foreign, and idolatrous fires (Lev. 10: 1, 2) of Satan that he offers as options to God's authentic and holy fire in my life

- God's power sets every congregation, arm of ministry, pulpit, and the five-fold ministry gift in the Body of Christ ablaze with Holy Ghost fire, and the glory and weight of God's presence in the midst of His people causes awe, humility, and reverence of Him (2 Chron. 7: 3)

- as Christian on fire in the earth, I come up short, fall behind, or lack, in nothing; instead, the fire from Heaven is in, on, and works through and with me that guarantees my effectiveness and impact with Gospel seed-planting, and other missional mandates of the Kingdom of God

- the fire in me makes a force to be reckoned with; I am unrelenting with the Great Commission (Matt. 28: 19, 20), impregnable to demonic threats and menaces (Isa. 54: 17), and I have the benefit of the Father, Son, and Holy Ghost as Governor, guard, and guide in my life.

BE IT THEREFORE RESOLVED by me this day that

- I remain passionate about being on fire in the global village, and God's standard of excellence and exemplary labor in ministry is my only choice and desire

- I only seek to be actively engaged in Kingdom pursuits that bring credit and honor to God, allowing His holy fire to fully engulf my life as a servant of the King

BY THE AUTHORITY OF MY POSITION BY GRACE AS A CHILD OF THE KING, I DRIVE THESE PROPHETIC DECREES, DECLARATIONS, AND RESOLUTIONS AS STAKES IN THE GROUND; they are established and fulfilled by the words that I speak (Prov. 18: 21); Heaven watches over them and guarantees their fulfillment in my life; the devil's plans and plots against them are amount to chaos and confusion, and being on fire, I move in step and in sync with the light that shines upon my ways (Job 22: 28).

In the high and holy name of the Father, Son, and Holy Ghost! Blessed Trinity!

AND IT IS SO!

Day 175

FORASMUCH as my gracious and loving Father has blessed me with strength to arise to the light of a new day with the activity of my limbs, a sound mind, and eternal life in Him (Jn. 1: 4); and

WHEREAS, today is a day of gladness and rejoicing in the God of my salvation, who continues to manifest His mighty power in my life; my heart is perfect (fully devoted) toward Him (2 Chr. 16: 9); and

WHEREAS, what blessed, sweet communion I enjoy in the presence of the Lord every day, and this blessedness serves as the catalyst for a triumphant and victorious day in my life; and

WHEREAS, a supernatural move of God's hand and power has taken place in my life; a sweeping revival of Holy Ghost 'dunamis' has been released from on high, and with certainty, God has unleashed torrents of glory upon me; and

WHEREAS, I am fully cloaked and clothed in God's holy fire (2 Chron. 7: 3) for end-time deployment in the Kingdom mandate and mission in the world (Matt. 28: 19, 20), and my anthem is, I am on fire for the Lord!

I DECREE AND DECLARE this Day 175 that

- I turn to the Lord, rend my heart, and not my garments (Joel 2: 13), and I reverently bow myself before Him, praise and worship Him, and declare "He is good, and His mercy endures forever" (2 Chron. 7: 3) as He sends down fire from Heaven (2 Chron. 7: 1) upon me

- calamity, chaos, clutter, nor confusion have a place of prominence in my life; rather, the blazing, burning, holy flame of God's fire is my desire, passionate pursuit, and yearning (Phil. 3: 10)

- I am under the total control and dominance of God's fire, and I function, give, labor, serve, and work for the Master under the firepower of the Holy Ghost - self is slain on the altar (Rom. 12: 1)

- I surrender and yield to the cleansing, purifying, and sanctifying work of God's fire in my life, so that no contaminating or corrupt thing lodges in my spirit that will cause the fire to die out (Lev. 6: 13)

- I am on fire in the earth; God's fire keeps me hedged in, surrounded, and protected from the diabolical ways and works of Satan, whose hostility against me turns on itself and renders it weak and worthless (Isa. 54: 17).

BE IT THEREFORE RESOLVED by me this day that

- I choose the disciplines of focus, steadfastness and vigilance as God guides and leads me to stay on fire in the global village

- I wholly accept and admit that without God's holy fire in and upon me, my life will be empty, fruitless, futile, vain and vexatious

BY VIRTUE OF MY RIGHT STANDING WITH GOD THROUGH CHRIST (Rom. 5: 1), I BOLDLY DRIVE THESE DECREES, DECLARATIONS, AND RESOLUTIONS AS SANCTIFIED STAKES IN THE GROUND; they are established and fulfilled in my life by the fruit of my lips (Prov. 21: 18); the Godhead of Heaven agrees with and authorizes their fulfillment; the evil hordes of hell are rebuked, refused, rejected, and utterly ruined by God's holy fire, and I function effectively in the earth by the power of God's holy fire, and the light that shines upon my ways (Job 22: 28).

In the all-conquering, all-triumphant, all-victorious name of the Father, Son, and Holy Ghost! Blessed Godhead, Three-in-One!

AND IT IS SO!

Day 176

FORASMUCH as my kind Heavenly Father has touched me with His finger of love to awaken from rest overnight with liberty, light, and life in Him (Acts 17: 28); and

WHEREAS, the immensity and intensity of my gratitude and thanksgiving toward God my Father cannot be described or explained; rather, shouts of "glory", "hallelujah", "praise Him", and "thank you Jesus" erupt in my soul, and the fruit of my lips give thanks to His glorious, high, and holy name (Heb. 13: 15); and

WHEREAS, I am honored and humbled to have been called, chosen and commissioned by God to bring change, deliverance, healing, liberty, transformation, and victory to countless people in the global village through the power of the Gospel of Jesus Christ - God's ways are past finding out (Rom. 11: 33); and

WHEREAS, I consciously choose to join myself with the Holy Spirit as He manifests and moves by His power in the earth, and by this fellowship, I experience blessings untold from the bountiful, limitless hand of God; and

WHEREAS, as a member of the Body of Christ, the blood-washed Church in the earth, I am on fire, set ablaze by God's holy fire that He sends down from Heaven upon me (2 Chron. 7: 1-3), that evokes awe and reverence within me to worship at His feet, and that burns within me and engulfs my heart, and it shall "never go out" (Lev. 6: 13).

I DECREE AND DECLARE this Day 176 that

- my intercessions, prayers, and supplications to God result in Him attending to them, taking His resting place in my midst, and sending His holy fire down from Heaven (2 Chron. 6: 40 - 7: 1)

- I provide the sacrifice of myself as I worship God, and His fire consumes all debris, dirt, and dross in me, purifying and sanctifying me to live the life ("walk" - 1 Thess. 5: 5), that of being separate from the world's customs and practices, and set apart unto God's ways

- my heart is on fire with love for the lost (Jn. 3: 16); my hands are on fire and extend to serve the oppressed, the poor, and the widow, that mankind may glorify my Father in Heaven who anoints me through servanthood in the earth

- to maintain credibility and integrity for the Kingdom of God in the earth, I do not tinker, trifle with, or touch, any unclean thing, nor do I engage in any unclean practice that has roots in idolatry, falsehood, or vain oblations – I will be clean to bear the vessels of the Lord (Isa. 52: 11)

- I am the torchbearer of truth, the upholder of godliness and righteousness, and the carrier of God's holy fire that impacts, influences, and causes spiritual revolution and transformation to everyone everywhere.

BE IT THEREFORE RESOLVED by me this day that

- I do not rest or relax on my laurels; instead, I remain activated and anointed by God's holy fire to blaze spirituals trails for the King in the earth

- I make the conscious choice to be on fire, to speak about, and to live in God's holy fire

BY THE AUTHORITY OF MY COVENANT RELATIONSHIP WITH GOD MY HEAVENLY FATHER, I DRIVE THESE DECREES, DECLARATIONS, AND RESOLUTIONS AS STAKES IN THE GROUND; I boldly and confidently speak their establishment and fulfillment in my life (Prov. 18: 21); the Triune Godhead of Heaven grants them holy validation; satanic assaults and attacks on them are stupefied and suffocated, and light shines upon my ways as God's blood-washed, covenant child on fire in the earth (Job 22: 28).

In the hallowed, high and holy name of the Father, Son, and Holy Ghost! Blessed Three-in-One!

AMEN!

Day 177
A DECLARATION FOR YOUNG PEOPLE

FORASMUCH as it is by the Sovereign will of my Heavenly Father that I arose this morning to a blessed and beautiful day, with life and liberty in Him (Acts 17: 28); and

WHEREAS, I celebrate the goodness and mercy of the Lord upon me for the honor of being called and chosen to be a change-agent in the world for Him, and it is gratifying to see the supernatural hand of God being manifested in the earth; and

WHEREAS, it has not, and will not be, by might, nor by power, but by the Spirit of the Lord of hosts (Zech. 4: 6), who dwells in me, and who continues to manifest His glory and power in conspicuous and copious ways through me; and

WHEREAS, the consuming, holy fire of God that comes down from Heaven (2 Chron. 7: 1) permeates and saturates my entire being, and the weight of glory prompts and provokes intense praise and worship unto God through the fruit of my mouth (2 Chron 7: 3; Heb. 13: 15); and

WHEREAS, this saturation of God's fire, glory, and power in the midst of His people includes young people who hunger and yearn passionately for a greater anointing in the global village to affect and influence their peers.

I DECREE AND DECLARE this Day 177 that

- God's holy fire engulfs the Christian youth of our day, and they will stand out and up like Josiah, David, Daniel, and the Hebrew boys - these did not bend or bow to the customs and culture of their day, but were true to the God of their fathers, who left legacies of the fear and reverence of Almighty God in the earth

- the holy fire of God erupts in their souls, and out of their mouths will come forth a resounding proclamation of the glorious Gospel of Jesus Christ, and the fire and unction of the Holy Ghost working through them will be evident and obvious

- as youthful arrows and firebrands for God in the global village, the fire from Heaven will cause young people to be graced with a yoke-destroying anointing that will be the reason by which bondages are broken, lifted off, and destroyed in the lives of those with whom they associate (Isa. 10: 27)

- the consuming fire of God will so drape and envelope young people that armies of them will arise in divine demonstrations of audacity and authority unheard of and unseen in the earth

- every demonic and diabolical trap and trick from hell set against young people will turn in on itself and be rendered a complete failure; God's holy fire brings total destruction and doom to the plans of Satan, and the causes of the Kingdom will prevail in the earth, even through the youth.

BE IT THEREFORE RESOLVED by me this day that

- I will remain yoked to the Spirit of God, and submitted and surrendered to the purifying work of God's holy fire

- I will not comply with, or concede to, the contrary spirit of the age; instead, the fire on the altar of my heart consumes and engulfs me to the point of continuous and unceasing burning for God in the earth

BY THE AUTHORITY GRANTED TO ME BY THE HOLY GHOST, AND AS A CARRIER OF GOD'S HOLY FIRE, I DRIVE THESE PROPHETIC DECREES, DECLARATIONS, AND RESOLUTIONS AS FIRE STAKES IN THE GROUND; they are set alight and established by the fruit of my lips (Prov. 18: 21); Heaven's holy court sanctions and seals them; satanic insurrections against them are paralyzed and pulverized, and young people will function with fire in the earth, with the light shining upon their ways (Job 22: 28).

In the uncompromising, unshakeable, and unyielding name of the Father, Son, and Holy Ghost! Blessed Godhead, Three-in-One!

AND IT IS SO!

Day 178

FORASMUCH as the angel of the Lord encamped round about me throughout the night, and kept harm and hurt from me (Psa. 34: 7), and then, the good and gracious hand of my Father touched me to see another day in the land of the living (Psa. 27: 13); and

WHEREAS, I acknowledge the Sovereignty and Supremacy of God my Father for journeying and tabernacling with me as His child in the earth, and I praise and thank God for the momentous and moving times I have experienced in His presence; and

WHEREAS, when I look back and reflect over my life, and think things over; I can truly say that I have been blessed; I have a testimony, and, after all the things I have been through, I still have Jesus and His unspeakable joy in my soul; and

WHEREAS, life has had its hard days, it's horrible moments, and its hurtful events, and these have left marks and scars, and ashes of grief like the bitterness of gall in my innermost being, and only God really knew and saw the impact upon me; and

WHEREAS, despite the depth of the mistreatment, the intensity of grief, and the deep scars of abuse and betrayal, God gave me grace to get out of the ashes to adorn the crown of beauty (Isa. 61: 3); yes, out of the ashes I arose and still do rise.

I DECREE AND DECLARE this Day 178 that

- because of the grace and mercy of God upon me, I am lifted from the awfulness of the ashes to the awesomeness of the ornament of beauty

- although I may not always see it, feel it, or even understand it, I know without a doubt that God is watching me, He is with me, in me, and for me (Rom. 8: 31)

- I will not stay stuck in the ashes of drama, grief, pain, or shame; instead, I am healed and whole in body, mind and soul, mourning is over (Psa. 30: 5), and being fully renewed and restored from the ash heap, God pours the oil of gladness all over me (Isa. 61: 3)

- I will not cave in or under from the lies of Satan (Jn. 8: 44) concerning the ashes of my life, I believe the report of the Lord, who elevates and lifts me to celebrate rather than commiserate, magnify Him rather than murmur, rejoice in victory rather than recoil like a victim, and walk in victory rather than wallow in defeat

- out of the pile of the ashes, this is my anthem of praise, our hymn of worship, and our song of jubilation: "Go ahead, drive the nails in my hands; laugh at me where you stand; go ahead, and say I'm done, BUT I shall rise out of the ashes to LOVE again, to LAUGH again, and to LIVE again (Psa. 118: 17)

BE IT THEREFORE RESOLVED by me this day that

- I refuse to go back to the ash heap of grief and pain; I choose to remain free, healed and whole by the liberating power of the Holy Ghost

- I will not harbor hatred or hurt; rather, I choose to make that misery a ministry, and that pain a pavilion of peace, and God gets the credit for helping me to rise out of the ashes

THE PRECIOUS BLOOD OF JESUS MY SAVIOR HAS LIFTED AND LANDED ME SAFE AND SECURE IN HIM, AND BY HIS ENABLEMENT, I DRIVE THESE PROPHETIC DECREES, DECLARATIONS, AND RESOLUTIONS AS STAKES IN THE GROUND; my words give impetus and life to their establishment in the earth (Prov. 13: 2); Heaven's holy court sanctions and stamps them as sealed and settled; Satan's terror and tyranny against them are disabled, disarmed, and dismembered, and the light that dispels the darkness shines upon my ways (Job 22: 28).

In the fabulous, glorious, and marvelous name of the Father, Son, and Holy Ghost! Blessed Trinity, three-in-One!

AND IT IS SO!

Day 179

FORASMUCH as my loving and kind Father has blessed me to arise this morning to see the light of a brand new day, and God's mighty hand extended has touched my body to breathe fresh air to live, move and have my being (Acts 17: 28); and

WHEREAS, I give high honor and praise to God for the wonder of His goodness and grace toward me His chosen child; and

WHEREAS, the powerful hand of my Omnipotent Father raised me out of the ashes of my life in exchange for an ornament of beauty, the oil of gladness for mourning, and the garment of praise instead of despair; and

WHEREAS, throughout the Scriptures, ashes are symbolic of grief and repentance - a substance, like dust, to which my body will return (Gen. 18: 27; Job 30: 19); and

WHEREAS, my life has had its dark, difficult, and distressing days; grief and pain have been real, and, though knocked about and sometimes knocked down, from the ashes I triumphantly arose.

I DECREE AND DECLARE this Day 179 that

- although battered and bruised, sometimes weary and windswept, a miracle and a wonder happened; from the ashes I arose

- although the devil attempted to imprison me with thoughts and reminders of the devastation, sorrow and terror of grief and pain, the Spirit of God reversed the impact, I rose out of the ashes and experienced the fires of joy and jubilation - God turned my captivity (Eph. 4: 7-10)

- despite what statistics may say, what DNA may suggest, what history tries to repeat with me, God raised me up from the ashes and a fully blooming and beautiful rose emerged for all to see

- I choose to see setbacks as set ups for a comeback, and, because I arose out of the ashes, songs of triumph and victory swell within me, and gush forth like a torrent of cool, fresh water (Eph. 5: 19)

- I rose up and out of the ashes, and will not settle or stay there; they speak of better things for me, and, thanks to Jesus, there will be resurrection, celebration and jubilation

BE IT THEREFORE RESOLVED by me this day that

- I refuse to come apart at the seams because of the hurt and horror that reduced me to ashes; instead, I choose to trust God in the process, because I am coming out of and up from the ashes

- I resist the option to moan and murmur over the grievous circumstances of my life; rather, I choose to raise a praise and worship as I arise out of the ashes

BY VIRTUE OF MY POSITION OF BEING RAISED OUT OF THE ASHES BECAUSE OF MY COVENANT CONNECTION WITH MY HEAVENLY FATHER, I DRIVE THESE DECREES, DECLARATIONS, AND RESOLUTIONS AS STAKES IN THE GROUND; I believe in them, and speak their establishment in my life by the fruit of my lips (Prov. 18 21); the Divine Godhead of Heaven backs and blesses them; the enemy's intimidation and threats are negated and nullified, and the light shines upon my ways as I arise out of the ashes (Job 22: 28).

In the liberating, livening, and lovely name of the Father, Son, and Holy Ghost! Blessed Triune Godhead! Three-in-One!

AND IT IS SO!

Day 180

FORASMUCH as my soul sings "How Great Thou Art" in deep, heartfelt gratitude to God for allowing me to be alive today, and to enjoy the benefits and blessings of a full and free salvation because of Jesus my Redeemer and Savior; and

WHEREAS, I praise God for the honor and joy of feasting on daily bread and morning manna from His banqueting house, and his banner over me is love (S of S 2: 4); and

WHEREAS, I continue to be amazed at how good God has been and is to me; I am stirred in my soul to praise and worship Him intentionally and intensely for the miracles, signs and wonders in my life, and the personal breakthrough, deliverance, freedom from bondage, healing, and victory prompts shouts of "glory to God", and "hallelujah" to my faithful Heavenly Father; and

WHEREAS, my Father's good and gracious hand in and upon my life is the reason for my praise to Him; by Holy Ghost power, the same power that raised up Jesus Christ from the dead (Rom.

8: 11), I have been lifted up out of deep hurt, pain, and sorrow, to experience the delight and joy of resurrection from the ashes; and

WHEREAS, God specializes in reversing the effects of difficult, hard, tough, and rocky circumstances of life that people encounter, and, as amazing as He is, He has lifted me from the heartache and hurt that reduced me to a proverbial pile of rejected rubble; yet, He lifted me UP OUT OF the Ashes to bloom as a rose.

1 DECREE AND DECLARE this Day 180 that

- God lifted me "UP"; my status is miraculously changed, and the critics, doubters, and naysayers will be in astonishment and awe at my out-of-the-ashes beauty

- I reject the speech of the defeatist and pessimist that stabs at me with vain babbling; the Master has lifted me "up" to the place where eagles fly and soar

- the pain of my past is over; lamenting, mourning and weeping over what/why has ended; there is no death in the pot; God's mercy and a manifested miracle has come my way, and I have a new address - UP OUT OF the ashes

- I am no longer choked up, cooped up, and cracked up by it, that, or them; rather, because God cherished and chose me, I boldly announce that I live in the "Son" light of Him who lifted me "UP" and "OUT" to sing melodies of Heaven

- satanic intimidation and irritation have no effect upon me because God has raised me UP out of the ashes, and I have beauty for ashes, the oil of joy for mourning, and the garment of praise for the spirit of heaviness, and I am a nightmare to the Devil.

BE IT THEREFORE RESOLVED by me this day that

- I remain close to, and cuddled by the Savior, who, by His blood-covenant with me, has lifted me up and out of the ashes to a life of joy, peace, and victory

- I remain fully aware that, if it had not been for the Lord on my side, being lifted UP out of the ashes would be nothing but a dream

BY THE AUTHORITY THAT JESUS' BLOOD COVENANT PROVIDES ME, HAVING BEEN LIFTED UP AND OUT OF THE ASHES, I DRIVE THESE PROPHETIC DECREES, DECLARATIONS, AND RESOLUTIONS AS MEMORIALS AND STAKES IN THE GROUND; I believe in their establishment and fulfillment in the earth, and by the fruit of my lips (Prov. 18: 21), they are fully backed, blessed and braced by the Triune Godhead of Heaven; the Devil is clueless and confused about them, and the Son light shines upon me, having been lifted UP and OUT of the ashes (Job 22:28; Isa. 61: 3).

In the eminent, exalted, and excellent name of the Father, Son, and Holy Ghost! Blessed Godhead, Three-in-One!

AND IT IS SO!

Day 181

FORASMUCH as it is a great day to rejoice and give praise to my Sovereign Father for bestowing the gift of life upon me today, and to Jesus Christ for granting me the honor of being called "...kings and priests unto God and His Father..." (Rev. 1: 6); and

WHEREAS, I am joyful and jubilant for the privilege of approaching the holy presence of God with confidence because of His matchless grace, and to meditate daily and receive morning manna from Him is the highlight of a victorious day; and

WHEREAS, God Almighty has manifested His power in my life in so many ways, and the splendor and weight of the outpouring of His glory in my life prompts songs of adoration, exaltation and praise to God; and

WHEREAS, I have the honor of living in the global village to represent God my King and His Kingdom, and to be called an "ambassador for Christ" (2 Cor. 5: 20) bestows a special opportunity by grace to me to make Gospel inroads in the earth on behalf of my Sovereign Father; and

WHEREAS, I focus today upon the Bible account of the outpouring of Pentecostal fire upon the 120 disciples who obeyed Jesus' command to "wait for the promise of the Father" (Acts 1: 4), the Holy Spirit who would be our Comforter and Guide, and that this promise is to "as many as the Lord our God shall call" (Acts 2: 39).

I DECREE AND DECLARE this Day 181 that

- I call forth the power of the Holy Ghost in me afresh, and copious manifestations of supernatural suddenness, sounds, speech, and scenes will cloak and drape me as I function for the Master in the global village, and by these, the lost and unsaved will be convinced and convicted of sin, and turn to the Savior for salvation, and encounter a never-forgotten "This is That" experience (Acts 2: 21, 41)

- I shall see the Bible affirmed and confirmed by the outpouring of the Holy Ghost upon sons, daughters, young men, old men, and on servants and handmaidens Joel 2: 28, 29), all manifestations that testify of Jesus and His saving power in the earth (Jn. 15: 26)

- my willing engagement and occupation in the Kingdom mandate and mission to the Church in the earth has primacy to me (Matt. 28: 19, 20), and as a called-out child of God, I will be ablaze and burn for Him by the power of the Holy Ghost everywhere I go (Acts 17: 6)

- I will not be silent, silenced or stymied by the works of evil, and satanic insurrection, interference, and intimidation against me fuels Holy Ghost fire within me, and "this" Gospel I declare "is that" which will expand and extend to the far corners of the earth despite many adversaries (1 Cor. 16: 9)

- God's plans and purposes for my life in the earth will be completely finished and fulfilled in and through me (Jer. 29: 11; Dan. 11: 32b), and the rich spiritual fertility and fruit I bear will perpetuate legacies of honor for the Kingdom of God.

BE IT THEREFORE RESOLVED by me this day that

- I remain alert, alive, and vigilant for the sake of the effectiveness and influence of the Kingdom of God in the earth

- this Gospel of Jesus that I live and preach is what the world needs, and I take personal responsibility to spread the Good News everywhere I go

BY THE AUTHORITY AND PRIVILEGE GRANTED TO ME BY MY COVENANT WITH THE FATHER, I BOLDLY DRIVE THESE DECREES, DECLARATIONS, AND RESOLUTIONS AS IMMOVABLE STAKES IN THE GROUND; they are established and settled in the earth by the fruit of my lips (Prov. 13: 2a; 18: 21); the Godhead of Heaven grants and guarantees their establishment; the evil one is baffled and befuddled because of them, and I confidently proclaim, "this is that", and the light to shines upon my ways (Job 22: 28).

In the Eternal, Faithful, and Governing name of the Father, Son, and Holy Ghost! Blessed Godhead, Three-in-One!

AND IT IS SO!

Day 182

FORASMUCH as my Heavenly Father has lovingly allowed me to breathe and live, move, and have my being (Acts 17: 28), and to see the light of another day, and to be touched by God to arise from overnight rest again all affirm and verify His faithfulness to me; and

WHEREAS, I am amazed and in awe of God's Almighty hand of power demonstrated in my life, and to have Him stay with, and sustain me on my spiritual journey in the earth as His child prompts praise and thanksgiving to Him from the fruit of my lips (Heb. 13: 15); and

WHEREAS, I am excited and expectant about the glory of God being manifested in my life today, and this anticipation I have in my spirit about God's ability to fix things in my life can be summed up in three words: BUT GOD CAN!; and

WHEREAS, my thoughts of the day surround the text Isa. 61: 1-3, a poignant and significant one that affirms the dynamism and tremendous power of the Spirit of God, and His unequalled ability to supernaturally lift someone out of a spiritual prison with resurrection power from the depths of despair, pain and sorrow to a life of gladness, joy, and beauty as an ornament; and

WHEREAS, I have been resurrected "out of the ashes", and it is abundantly clear that I am "OUT", and have been repositioned and reset into a large room of astonishing breakthrough, liberty, and triumph: "OUT" of agonizing defeat into the arms of sweet deliverance and victory found in Jesus!

I DECREE AND DECLARE this Day 182 that

- the **A**shes are swept away, adieu, bye-bye, and melodies of Heaven gush forth from my spirits into the atmosphere

- the **S**hame and sorrow have been traded for peace and pleasure, and songs in the night are now amplified instead of sighing

- the **H**oly Ghost has reversed and turned my captivity; my hearts' altar burns blue-hot with petitions, praises, and fervent prayers unto God (Lev. 6: 13; Jam. 5: 16)

- the **E**xciting news of my resurrection "OUT of the Ashes" is that they have now become my message and mission to the masses: "OUT of the Ashes" to "Beauty for Ashes" (Isa. 61: 3)

- the **S**anctifying work of the Spirit continues in me, and I affirm, assert, and attest that I am "OUT of the Ashes", never again to moan, mourn or murmur over what was or has been.

BE IT THEREFORE RESOLVED by me this day that

- I remain "OUT of the Ashes", with no desire to return; the crown and ornament of "beauty for ashes" feels and looks too good to let go and lose

- "OUT of the Ashes" I rise is my theme, never again will I hide in the darkness

BY DIVINE AUTHORITY AND ENABLEMENT, I DRIVE THESE PROPHETIC DECREES, DECLARATIONS, AND RESOLUTIONS AS STAKES OF BEAUTY IN THE GROUND; I believe in them, and they are established and settled by the fruit of my lips (Prov. 13: 2; 18: 21); the Godhead of Heaven backs and blesses them; the assaults and attacks of Satan against them are defeated and doomed, and the light shines upon my ways (Job 22: 28) - the Spirit has resurrected me "OUT of the Ashes".

In the beautifying and benevolent name of the Father, Son, and Holy Ghost! Blessed Trinity!

AND IT IS SO!

Day 183

FORASMUCH as the grace and lovingkindness of my Heavenly Father was extended to me to arise today from overnight rest, and He has granted me the blessing of life and liberty in Him (Acts 17: 28); and

WHEREAS, I reflect upon the goodness and greatness of God upon me, and I am forever grateful and thankful to Him for the wonder of His mighty acts in my life during my journey with Him in the earth; and

WHEREAS, as Jesus taught, "For thine is the Kingdom, and the power, and the glory forever" (Matt. 6: 13), and I ascribe worship to the King Immortal; and

WHEREAS, He deserves glory and honor and worship for manifesting His Almighty power in my life after raising me "Out of the Ashes", and He exchanged them for the ornament of beauty (Isa. 61: 3); and

WHEREAS, the Lord's work of lifting me "Out of the Ashes" is a miracle; life had me defeated, dejected and depleted; the grief and pain of abandonment; abuse of all kinds, and the anxiety of it all reduced me to rock bottom; but "Out of the Ashes" I arose to shout, sing and smile again.

I DECREE AND DECLARE this Day 183 that

- I speak words of celebration: I am "Out of the Ashes", never to go back there (Gal. 4: 9), and moving on **B**eautified and bold

- I affirm and assert with exclamation, I am "Out of the Ashes" **E**mpowered and enriched - stronger, wiser, so much better, and not bitter

- without fear or intimidation, this is my proclamation, I am "Out of the Ashes", freshly **A**nointed and fully authorized, and the hordes and hounds of hell are powerless to stop me (Isa. 54: 17)

- I wave goodbye to degradation – I am not going under in shame, but "Out of the Ashes" with **U**nction to function (1 Jn. 2: 20)

- I make this brave declaration: I am "Out of the Ashes"; my test is now a **T**estimony, and **Y**esterday's grief and sorrow is a distant memory: "Out" with **B-E-A-U-T-Y** for Ashes Fulfilled - FULL and FILLED!

BE IT THEREFORE RESOLVED by me this day that

- I will firmly hold onto God, who turned my ashes into beauty, oiled me with joy, and clothed me with the garment of praise (Isa. 61: 3)

- I will unashamedly tell the world: God lifted me "Out of the Ashes", crowned me with beauty, and I remain FULFILLED!

BY VIRTUE OF MY NEW-FOUND PLACE "OUT OF THE ASHES", I GLADLY AND GLEEFULLY DRIVE

THESE PROPHETIC DECREES, DECLARATIONS, AND RESOLUTIONS AS LANDMARKS AND STAKES IN THE GROUND; they are established and settled in the earth by the fruit of my lips (Prov. 13: 2; 18: 21); the Unified Godhead of Heaven grants them holy assent; diabolical devices set against them are done and dusted, and "Out of the Ashes" the light shines upon my ways (Job 22: 28).

In the terrific and titanic name of the Father, Son, and Holy Ghost! Blessed Godhead, Three-in-One!

AND IT IS SO!

Day 184

A DECLARATION FOR YOUNG PEOPLE

FORASMUCH as it is by the compassion, faithfulness, mercy, and Sovereign will of God that I am able to breathe fresh air today, and to enjoy the benefits of life in Him through Christ (Acts 17: 28); and

WHEREAS, I am in awe OF God, and ascribe all glory, honor and majesty to Him for tabernacling with me during my spiritual journey; His grace and mercy have brought me through; and

WHEREAS, it thrills my soul to muse on the fact that I am "Out of the Ashes" based on Isa. 61: 1-3, a text that describes the power and promise of God's Spirit to resurrect and reposition His people from the ashes of despair to the ornament of beauty (Isa. 61: 3), a place of freedom from chains, liberty from bondage, and victory from the jaws of defeat; this is my testimony and witness; and

WHEREAS, due to no fault of their own in many cases, even young people are subjected to grief, pain and sorrow, and have endured the shattering ashes of life; and

WHEREAS, young people, the next generation of God's children in the earth, are not excluded from the mighty deliverance that the Holy Spirit gives, and they, too, are testimonies of those who rise "Out of the Ashes".

I DECREE AND DECLARE this Day 184 that

- young people, like arrows in the quiver of a mighty man (Psa. 127: 4, 5), will not be blown off course or diverted from their God-ordained purpose, and, despite the heartache and hurt, they will rise "Out of the Ashes" and realize the visions God has promised to give them (Joel 2: 28; Acts 2: 17)

- freedom, healing, rebuilding and restoration will crown their lives, and their beauty "Out of the Ashes" will exude an aroma and a fragrance that draws their friends and peers to the deliverance that God gives to anyone who calls on Him in repentance

- I rebuke and reject the spirits that seek to linger and lodge in the lives of young people like anger, bitterness, hatred, vengeance and vexation that are devilish and diabolical, and I loose the forgiveness, love and reconciliation of God that seals their healing and wholeness

- the sediments and residue of pain and sorrow in their lives are negated and nullified, and by the power of the Spirit, they emerge and rise "Out of the Ashes" to move onward and upward for the glory and honor of God

- the youth will rise "Out of the Ashes"; they will be gifted, graced, guarded and guided by the angel of the Lord, and the beauty for ashes, the oil of joy for mourning, and the garment of praise for the spirit of heaviness drapes and drenches their lives..

BE IT THEREFORE RESOLVED by me this day that

- I remain on the prayer-wall for young people, and will endeavor to establish godly and righteous legacies for them in the earth (Prov. 13: 22)

- I aim to develop, teach, and train young people in the ways of the Lord, and facilitate a caring and nurturing environment for them that keeps them safe and secure in the zone of no condemnation (Rom. 8: 1)

BY VIRTUE OF MY PRIVILEGED POSITION BY GRACE AND MERCY, I DRIVE THESE PROPHETIC DECREES, DECLARATIONS, AND RESOLUTIONS AS STAKES IN THE GROUND; they are established and settled by the fruit of my lips (Prov. 13: 2; 18: 21); Heaven backs and blesses them as fruitful and fulfilled; the Devil's animosity and assaults against them are twice dead, and the light of Jesus shines upon the youth and their ways (Job 22: 28).

In the liberating and life-giving name of the Father, Son, and Holy Ghost! Blessed Trinity!

AND IT IS SO!

Day 185

FORASMUCH my Heavenly Father has once again demonstrated His pleasure and unfailing love by preserving me throughout the night, causing death to behave itself, and allowing me to rise to the light of a new day with the full activity of my limbs, and a sound mind; and

WHEREAS, the Lord is worthy of all glory, honor, majesty, and praise for the limitless measure of His grace and mercy, and the marvelous and wonderful works of His hand upon my life; and

WHEREAS, it is my absolute delight and joy to have access to God daily by prayer, praise and worship, and His holy Word, and it is easy for me to exclaim and proclaim His greatness in my life to everyone I see; and

WHEREAS, I am unashamed to have a distinctiveness in my life as a result of the supernatural outpouring of Holy Ghost power upon me, nor am I ashamed to testify that by being filled with the Holy Ghost, I speak in an unknown tongue as the Spirit gives me utterance (Acts 2: 1-4), the initial evidence of being filled, but also the enablement to be an effective witness for the Lord in the earth (Acts 1: 8); and

WHEREAS, this manifestation of holy power upon my life was and is an amazing and awesome encounter with God, and to noise this abroad of what the Spirit had done gives me satisfaction beyond words.

I DECREE AND DECLARE this Day 185 that

- this dynamic, holy power is still being manifested in the earth, and by the Holy Ghost who dwells in me, I shall do exploits for God in the global village (Dan. 11: 32)

- this is not an apparition, hallucination, figment of my imagination, or an illusion; Holy Ghost power has come upon me, lives in me, and I am not the same, and I function and serve with authority in the Kingdom by the same power that raised Jesus Christ from the dead (Rom. 8: 11)

- demons of the darkness, evil enterprises, and satanic fiends and foes are all subject to the power of the Holy Ghost, and "this is that" which will hold evil at bay, blocked from having hellish impact upon the work of the Kingdom in the earth (Isa. 54: 17)

- "this is that" encounters and experiences will continue as the power of the Spirit sweeps all across the world, and a Holy Ghost revival and re-awakening will be noised abroad today as it was in the 1st Century Church (Acts 2: 6, 39)

- the 21st Century Church, under the canopy and covering of Holy Ghost firepower in the earth, will not be silenced or stopped; instead, new doors, blazing trails, and frontiers of the Gospel of Jesus Christ in the earth will swing wide open, and God's army in the earth, the Church of the Lord Jesus Christ, will march along and move forward for the King, winning souls as she obeys Jesus's command to "GO" (Matt. 28: 19, 20).

BE IT THEREFORE RESOLVED by me this day that

- I will not back down or back up from Jesus's Great Commission mandate in the earth; instead, I remain attuned to the voice of the Spirit with devotion, diligence, and duty

- I remain steady, steely, and sturdy for the King and His cause, and, as a tree of righteousness, I lead others to Him (Dan. 12: 3)

BY THE AUTHORITY OF THE HOLY GHOST WHO LIVES IN ME, I AUDACIOUSLY DRIVE THESE PROPHETIC DECREES, DECLARATIONS, AND RESOLUTIONS AS STAKES IN THE GROUND; they are established and settled in the earth by the words that I speak (Prov. 13: 2; 18: 21); the seal and stamp of Heaven graces them; the Devil's schemes against them are rendered impotent and incapacitated, and the light shines upon my ways in light of a "this is that" encounter with God (Job 22: 28).

In the amazing, astonishing, and astounding name of the Father, Son, and Holy Ghost! Triune Godhead, Three-in-One!

AND IT IS SO!

Day 186

FORASMUCH as God, by His Providence, Sovereignty and wisdom, has showered His grace and mercy upon me one more time to awaken me from overnight rest; He touched my body with strength for another day, and given me a strong desire to live for, love, and serve Him with my heart, soul, and mind (Matt. 22: 37); and

WHEREAS, I do not live for, love, and serve Him because of what He can do and has done for me; rather, I serve Him because of who He is: my Deliverer and Lord, and that He loved me enough to send His Son to be the atoning sacrifice for me (1 Jn. 4: 10); and

WHEREAS, I am in awe at the wonder of it all - that God has called, chosen and commissioned me as His child in the earth to have effect and impact for Him; and

WHEREAS, the best is yet to come for me from the Lord; there shall be a performance (completion, perfection, and verification) of those things that the Lord has promised (Luke 1: 45); and

WHEREAS, according to the biblical text, "This is That" which Joel prophesied in Joel 2: 28, was fulfilled in Acts 2: 1-4, and will continue to be fulfilled (Acts 2: 39) as long as the earth remains under the Dispensation of God's grace.

I DECREE AND DECLARE this Day 186 that

- I am the righteousness of God through Christ Jesus; the world does not own me; I belong to God; "This is That" salvation that Jesus secured for me at Calvary (1 Pet. 2: 24), and I will talk and walk in His light in the earth

- I am Holy Ghost filled and fire baptized; "This is That", and Pentecostal power and unction is resident within me, and by Holy Ghost influence, I take territory and turf in the earth for the King and His Kingdom

- I exercise my authority, and command that the regions and realms of the darkness of this world come under subjection to the power of the Holy Ghost; "This is That", and I cast down and tear down every argument and presumptuous thing that exalts itself against the knowledge of God (2 Cor. 10: 5)

- I will see the honor of Almighty God manifested in the earth through miracles, signs and wonders, and His glory and power ("This is That") will blanket the earth as the waters cover the sea (Hab. 2: 14)

- "This is That" which God has promised me as His representative in the earth, and if "this" is not "that", I shall grasp and grip "this" with every ounce of fortitude I have until "hat" comes.

BE IT THEREFORE RESOLVED by me this day that

- I remain strong in my determination to bring credit, glory and honor to God in the global village by living intentionally and purposely for Him and the causes of the Kingdom

- I will be decisive about, deliberate, and fully devoted to my walk with God in the earth, and nothing but credibility, dependability, and excellence for the Lord of glory will suffice

BY VIRTUE OF MY STANDING IN CHRIST AS HIS RIGHTEOUS VESSEL, I DRIVE THESE PROPHETIC DECREES, DECLARATIONS, AND RESOLUTIONS AS STAKES IN THE GROUND; they are established and settled in the earth by the fruit of my lips (Prov. 13: 2; 18: 21); they have the authorized signature of Heaven's holy court; satanic schemes and systems against them are immobilized and paralyzed, and I am confident, having had a "This is That" encounter with God, that the light shall shine upon my ways (Job 22: 28).

In the Sovereign, Sufficient, and Supreme name of the Father, the Son, and the Holy Ghost! Blessed Godhead, Three-in-One!

AND IT IS SO!

Day 187

FORASMUCH as my good, gracious, kind, and loving Heavenly Father has blessed and given me the privilege to be in the land of the living today, and to experience the peace that passeth understanding (Rom; 5: 1; Phil. 4: 7) as a benefit of being called His child; and

WHEREAS, I give high honor, and offers heartfelt sacrifices of praise to God (Heb. 13: 15) for giving me the joy of fellowship with Him in His holy presence - what fellowship divine at the Master's table!; and

WHEREAS, God's holy power is moving right now in the earth bringing healing, restoration, and transformation to the lives of so many people by the power of His Spirit; and

WHEREAS, the presence of the Lord is with me; I can feel and sense Him in the atmosphere; I can feel and sense Him in my soul, and these validate and verify that a great outpouring of Holy Ghost power, prophesied by Joel (2: 28), has happened in my life; I am a recipient of this holy move, and, despite difficult and despairing days, God is as close as the mention of His name; and

WHEREAS, there is no doubt whatsoever that Holy Ghost power is manifesting in my life, and like the 120 in the Upper Room (Acts 2: 2), a "This is That" (Acts 2: 16, 17) encounter and experience with the Living Lord of glory has permeated and pervaded me!

I DECREE AND DECLARE this Day 187 that

- like Peter and John at the Gate Beautiful (Acts 3: 1-8), I continuously speak the liberating and life-giving Word, "such as I have give I thee"; "This is That" to the lame, the languid, and limp issues in my life, and that they do not have a place of abode in me

- a holy anointing and unction of power envelopes me, and I will not miss the momentous "This is That" demonstration of miracles, signs and wonders God has ordained for me (Acts 5: 12-16)

- as a "This-is-That" vessel of Holy Ghost infusion and power, I fear no man or thing, or work of Satan; instead, I am canopied by the "This-is- That" covering that all such evil interferences and intrusions are banned, barred, and blocked in the name of Jesus

- I will serve and witness in the earth by such a powerful anointing, that corporate executives, civic heads, leaders of national bodies, and members of parliaments will be affected and drawn to a never-before-experienced "This is That" life-transforming encounter with God

- I saturate and soak the atmosphere around me with intense and intentional praise and worship to God; such sacrifices open the portals of Heaven, and His fire and glory descend (2 Chron. 7: 1) with a "This-is-That" blazing and burning.

BE IT THEREFORE RESOLVED by me this day that

- I maintain a sober and vigilant "This is That" mindset about the things of the Spirit, and remain convinced that God's power can do anything but fail

- I remain anchored and unmoved from my rock-solid position in the faith, unshaken from my "This is That" standing in Christ

BY HOLY GHOST ABILITY AND AUTHORITY, I DRIVE THESE DECREES, DECLARATIONS, AND RESOLUTIONS AS IRREVOCABLE STAKES IN THE GROUND; they are established and settled by the words I speak (Prov. 13: 2; 18: 21); they are ratified and resourced by the order and protocol of Heaven; satanic insurgents and insurrections are locked out and locked up, and the light shines upon my ways (Job 22: 28) having encountered a "This is That" moment with the Master.

In the life-transforming, mind-regulating name of the Father, Son, and Holy Ghost! Blessed Godhead, Three-in-One!

AND IT IS SO!

Day 188

FORASMUCH as the Lord God Omnipotent reigneth, the angel of the Lord kept watch over me throughout the night as I rested and slept in peace and safety (Psa. 34: 7), and His tender hand touched me to arise to the dawning of a new day with life and limbs (Acts 17: 28); and

WHEREAS, I am amazed and awestruck at the wonder of it all; to muse, ponder, and think that God loves me unconditionally and limitlessly, and that, despite my weaknesses and wretchedness, His unfailing love reached me where I was - eternally lost, undone, without Him and hope, and rescued me from eternal damnation and death; and

WHEREAS, I offer sacrifices of joy and thanksgiving to Almighty God for His never-failing, unending grace and mercy toward me, and for empowering and enabling me to represent His Kingdom in the earth - I am so glad to be a part of the Kingdom; and

WHEREAS, the awe-inspiring, mind-boggling, and sometimes overwhelming accounts of God's Omnipotence and miraculous hand upon my life amount to a resounding "This is the Lord's doing; it is marvelous in my eyes" (Psa. 118: 23); and

WHEREAS, undoubtedly, Heaven has come down, glory fills my soul, Holy Ghost fire and power has enveloped me with a mighty revival that only He could orchestrate.

I DECREE AND DECLARE this Day 188 that

- the firepower of the Holy Ghost graces me with a freshness, liveliness, and richness that impacts and influences the atmosphere around me; and ALL who are hostile and stubborn to the reach of the Gospel is shaken and shifted into submission to a "This is That" encounter with Him

- Holy Ghost power is no trite or trivial matter; such power is not to be tinkered or trifled with; He will level the mountain for me; He will lift me out of Lodebar (no pasture - 2 Sam. 9: 3-5); He will make my Valley of Baca (weeping) a well (Psa. 84: 6), and will take the heat out of the fiery furnace (Dan. 3: 20-25), and "This is That" power will move any obstacle or obstruction for me

- I am created, designed and engineered by God to be highly credible, effective, and productive in the earth (Jer. 29: 11), and Holy Ghost "This is That" moments validate and verify that I am called and chosen in Him before the foundation of the world (Eph. 1: 4, 5)

- "This is That" power who dwells is me outmaneuvers and outwits, overrules and overruns every deceptive design and device of Satan and his evil hordes, and I am ablaze and burning by "This is That" fire that He sends down from Heaven (2 Chron. 7: 1)

- I labor, occupy, serve, witness and work for the King in the global village by the unction of Holy Ghost dynamism, and I WIN because "This is That" is the weapon within me.

BE IT THEREFORE RESOLVED by me this day that

- I remain strong in faith and trust in my Heavenly Father, who is pleased to grant me "This is That" moments that anoint and arm me for Kingdom excellence in the earth

- I rest daily in the Father's full giving of giftedness, goodness, and graciousness, and I willingly choose to allow His power to live in and through me

BY VIRTUE OF THE POSITION INTO WHICH THE HOLY GHOST HAS PLACED ME, I BOLDLY AND BRAVELY DRIVE THESE PROPHETIC DECREES, DECLARATIONS, AND RESOLUTIONS AS STAKES MARKED "THIS IS THAT" IN THE GROUND; I speak their establishment in the earth by the fruit of my lips (Prov. 13: 2; 18: 21); Heaven guarantees their fruitfulness and fulfillment; the works of darkness set against them are scuppered and spoiled, and the light shines upon my ways (Job 22: 28c).

In the wonderful and worthy name of the Father, Son, and Holy Ghost! Blessed Godhead, Three-in-One!

AND IT IS SO!

Day 189

FORASMUCH as God Almighty, my loving Heavenly Father (Abba), has blessed me to be alive today with the activity of my limbs, a sound mind, and a deep desire to live for and serve Him in the earth; and

WHEREAS, with my voice raised in worshipful praise to God, I sing, "High and lifted up in all the earth that's who you are; high and lifted up in all the earth that's who you are; high and lifted up in all the earth that's who you are; Lord I exalt your name; Lord I exalt your name"; and

WHEREAS, as the Psalmist said, "Praise waiteth for Thee, O God, in Zion" (Psa. 65: 1); I am blessed having been chosen and allowed to approach my Heavenly Father (Psa. 65: 4), and

WHEREAS, I joyfully celebrate the presence of the Lord in my life; He is All-Powerful and Mighty, and "His right hand and holy arm hath gotten Him the victory" (Psa. 98: 1); and

WHEREAS, on that unforgettable Day of Pentecost, when the Church of the Lord Jesus Christ was birthed in the earth, Holy

Ghost power descended suddenly upon the one hundred and twenty in the Upper Room, who assembled in one accord in one place, and "This is That" power fell from Heaven, an eruption of glorious power fell upon the people; they were all filled with the Holy Ghost, and began to speak with other tongues as the Spirit gave them utterance (Acts 2: 1-4).

I DECREE AND DECLARE this Day 189 that

- "This is That" power in my life fuses, harmonizes, unifies, and yokes me unto God, and the prevailing potency and power of prayer cloaks me with spiritual stamina and sustenance

- my "This is That" prayer causes the portals of Heaven to open; and a "Niagara" of holy power drenches me in astonishing, astounding and awesome ways

- my "This is That" prayer bans and blocks the evil hand of Satan, and "This is That" prayer and firepower releases God's hand of triumph and victory upon me to overcome, and by Holy Ghost enablement, I overtake all the power of the enemy, and nothing shall by any means hurt me (Luke 10: 19)

- my "This is That" fervent, prevailing prayer releases my deliverance, healing of bodily illnesses and infirmities, liberty from the prison of enslavement to sin, and victory from the jaws of defeat, despair and distress (Rom. 8: 35-37)

- my "This is That" prayer prompts and propels me to intercede and pray on, remain quickened by the Spirit to mobilize and move on, to soldier on, to trust God more, and to dwell under the canopy of Holy Ghost audacity and authority in the earth.

BE IT THEREFORE RESOLVED by me this day that

- I remain conformed to the image of Christ so that I will walk in Holy Ghost ability and power

- I remain enlivened and enriched, and unified and yoked in heart and mind in Christ, so that by "This is That" power, God's Kingdom advances and expands in the earth

BY THE AUTHORITY OF MY ADOPTION AS A HEIR OF THE FATHER, AND A JOINT-HEIR WITH THE SON (ROM. 8: 17), AND A BELIEVER IN "THIS IS THAT" POWER, I DRIVE THESE PROPHETIC DECREES, DECLARATIONS AND RESOLUTIONS AS PRAYER POWER POSTS IN THE GROUND; they are established and settled by the fruit of my lips (Prov. 13: 2; 18: 21); Heaven backs, blesses, and braces them in the earth; satanic interferences against them are intercepted and incinerated, and the light shines upon my ways (Job 22: 28) by "This is That" prayer and firepower.

In the unequalled and unrivaled name of the Father, Son, and Holy Ghost! Blessed Triune Godhead, Three-in-One!

AND IT IS SO!

Day 190

FORASMUCH as it was the Father's pleasure and providence that allowed me to rest and sleep in peace and safety throughout the night, and then, by His faithfulness and lovingkindness, He touched me to arise to the light of a new day with the use of my faculties and a sound mind (Acts 17: 28); and

WHEREAS, if He keeps on blessing and blessing; if He keeps on pouring it on; if His love gets richer and richer; if he keeps on giving a song; if my cup gets fuller and fuller, and my prayers keep on getting through; if it keeps getting better and better Oh Lord, I don't know what I'm gonna do (Gaither); and

WHEREAS, I arise today with total confidence that God remains with me as I follow the cloud of His glory and power in my life; and

WHEREAS, the dynamic power of Pentecost is never a topic out of date or season; it is the DNA of the Lord's Church in the earth, and the text in Acts 2: 16, 17 is the classic New Testament template for the 21st Century Church to function in as I engage in the Great Commission in the earth (Matt. 28: 18 - 20); and

WHEREAS, the Pentecostal outpouring is the promise of the Father to the 120 gathered in the Upper Room (Acts 1: 8), and, as Peter so boldly proclaimed (Acts 2: 16, 17), "This is That" which Joel prophesied (Joel 2: 28, 29), and "This is That" manifestation and move of God that has enabled and empowered the Church to be effective and impactful in the global village.

I DECREE AND DECLARE Day 190 that

- as the days of my life progress in the earth by God's grace and will, Holy Ghost indwelling and power adds strength to my years, and I refuse to fall and faint under the pressures of life that come my way because of the Lord's enablement

- I will leave lasting spiritual landmarks and legacies to the those whom I impact and influence in the earth, and the wisdom God downloads to me by His voice and His Word I will pass on

- by God's grace, I will be known in the earth as a tree of righteousness, and the planting of the Lord (Isa. 61: 3), and there will be peace within my walls, and prosperity within my palaces (Psa. 122: 7)

- God is my battle axe and weapon of war (Jer. 51: 20), and through Him, I do not lose step or tempo with the movement of Holy Ghost power, and I will be one used mightily by God to destroy and pull down strongholds of darkness in the earth

- "This is That" enablement graces and guides me, and the resounding anthem, epithet, and theme of my life will be as the Psalmist declared, "...this is the Lord's doing; it is marvelous in our eyes" (Psa. 118: 23).

BE IT THEREFORE RESOLVED by me this day that

- I remain devoted to the call and charge of the Lord upon my life to influence others for the cause of the Kingdom in the earth

- I will not allow known or perceived hindrances to thwart my desire, determination or drive for maximum usefulness and value in my God-given Kingdom assignments

BY THE AUTHORITY OF THE HOLY GHOST, I BOLDLY DRIVE THESE PROPHETIC DECREES, DECLARATIONS, AND RESOLUTIONS AS STAKES IN THE GROUND; they are established by the fruit of my lips (Prov. 13: 2; 18: 21); the Heavenly Trinity grants their activation; the foes and forces of the dark domain set against them are blown off course by the irresistible wind of the Spirit, and the light shines upon my ways (Job 22: 28).

In the strong name of the Father, Son, and Holy Ghost! Blessed Trinity!

AND IT IS SO!

Day 191

FORASMUCH as my good and gracious Heavenly Father has blessed me to be alive to see another day in the land of the living, and that, through Jesus our Savior, His tender hand has lifted me from shades of night to plains of light; and

WHEREAS, I arise with an intense desire to give high praise to God for the marvelous things that He has done for me during my joyful spiritual journey (Psa. 107: 8); and

WHEREAS, I am a beneficiary of the strong arm of the Lord who is manifesting Himself in my life, and for the outpouring of Holy Ghost fire and power in and upon me; and

WHEREAS, what God has done, and is doing, are accurate fulfillments of Old Testament prophecy (Joel 2: 28, 29), and the one hundred and twenty First Century saints in the Upper Room are the initial recipients of the sudden, rushing mighty wind that filled all the house (Acts 2: 2); and

WHEREAS, as Peter clearly proclaimed, "This-is-That" Pentecostal scenes, speech, and sounds of power fell upon them all, and they were filled with the Holy Ghost (Acts 2: 4); the fresh First Century infusion of dynamism for witnessing to the world, and this promise is to me as well, being called and chosen by God as a channel and a vessel for His honor in the global village (Acts 2: 39).

I DECREE AND DECLARE this Day 191 that

- I rise and take my position in the Lord's army, and by God's power working through me, others will be drawn to salvation and experience the transforming power of Jesus Christ in their lives

- a holy and sanctified delight and desire for the Word of God will increase and surge in my life, and my appetite for the Holy Scriptures will be the catalyst for prosperity and good success in my life (Josh. 1: 8)

- despite the harassments and hassles of satanic warfare, a "This is That" anointing and authority drapes and drenches me, and through the power of the Holy Ghost, I plunder, pull down, and pulverize the encroachments, enslavements, and enticements of the enemy

- my name will be known in the global village as Daniel's was, who had an excellent spirit in him (Dan. 6: 3), as Joseph's was, who refused to sin wickedly against God with Potiphar's wife (Gen. 39: 9), and as Jesus's was, who did the things that pleased His Father (Jn. 8: 29)

- a mantle of power, praise, prayer, and worship envelopes my life, and a strong prophetic unction will come upon me to be a carrier of the glory and glow of Pentecost, and I will be as an arrow in the hand of a sharpshooter to reach and reap the harvest of lost souls in the earth.

BE IT THEREFORE RESOLVED by me this day that

- I will not fall away into folly or foolishness through the seductiveness of worldliness, but will stand up and out for Jesus in the global village

- I remain one whose choices, heart and mindset is to live fully and wholeheartedly for the causes of the kingdom of God in the earth

BY THE AUTHORITY AND POWER OF THE HOLY GHOST, I DRIVE THESE PROPHETIC DECREES, DECLARATIONS, AND RESOLUTIONS AS SPIRITUAL STAKES IN THE GROUND; they are established and settled by the fruit of my lips (Prov. 13: 3, 18: 21); the holy hill of Heaven grants benediction and blessing upon them; demonic distractions and disturbances designed to spoil them are consigned to fire and brimstone, and the radiant light of Jesus shall shine upon my ways (Job 22: 28).

In the Hallowed, High and Honored name of the Father, Son, and Holy Ghost! Blessed Godhead, Three-in-One!

AND IT IS SO!

Day 192

FORASMUCH as my Sovereign God is pleased to allow me to arise from overnight repose and rest today to see the dawning of a new day, and He has given me life, the use of my limbs, and His unending, unfailing love; and

WHEREAS, delight and joy floods my soul as I receive daily bread from the Lord's table, and marvelous and miraculous manifestations of His strong and powerful hand in my life are sometimes difficult to explain; and

WHEREAS, as the songwriter sang, "Something beautiful, something good; all my confusion He understood; all I had to offer Him was brokenness and strife, but he made something beautiful of my life" (Bill Gaither); and

WHEREAS, as a force in God's hand to be reckoned with in the earth, I am on the move by the power and unction of the Holy Ghost, and to back down or back up in retreat on my spiritual journey is out of the question; and

WHEREAS, I am firm and fixed in my stance – retreating is not a choice or an option; I choose to advance and move forward with the help of the Lord.

I DECREE AND DECLARE this Day 192 that

- I will obey the prophetic voice of God through His servants, take the bow, and put my hand upon it (2 Kin. 13: 16), symbolizing my obedience in preparation for advancement, deliverance and ultimate victory

- as arrows in the bow of a sharpshooter, I will only go forward with progress and purpose, elevating in the Spirit, and expanding by the Spirit, as I advance in the earth

- I am advancing, and hostilities from Satan will not stop or stymie me; instead, the arrow from my bow, which speaks of victory, will penetrate and pierce the cruel and oppressive enemy's territory, and I will totally possess it all (2 Kin. 13: 17)

- as I advance to the mark of my deliverance and complete victory, I take my attention, eyes and focus off the carnal man, and I put everything and everyone that will distract or divert me from onward advancement under Jesus' blood, and under my feet

- as I advance to the mark, I will keep my hands in the right hands (2 Kin. 13: 16), which will ensure and guarantee my effectiveness.

BE IT THEREFORE RESOLVED by me this day that

- I choose to be ready to advance according to God's plans and purposes, even if they appear unconventional and unorthodox, and I reject the emptiness and vanity of man's mastery and might

- I refuse to be sidelined or sidetracked from spiritual advancement, and I access all rights and privileges afforded to me by God, who assures my ultimate triumph

BY THE COVENANTAL ASSURANCE OF GOD, I DRIVE THESE PROPHETIC DECREES, DECLARATIONS, AND RESOLUTIONS AS STAKES IN THE GROUND; they are established and set in the earth by the fruit of my mouth (Prov. 13: 2; 18: 21); Heaven's assent and consent secures them; the way, wiles, and works of Satan against them are stalled, stopped and stunned, and I confidently advance under the light that shines upon my ways (Job 22: 28).

In the insurmountable, invincible, and invulnerable name of the Father, Son, and Holy Ghost! Blessed Godhead, Three-in-One!

AND IT IS SO!

Day 193

FORASMUCH as it is the Father's good pleasure and gracious will to awaken me today with my health, peace of mind, and strength (Acts 17: 28) - what a mighty God I serve!; and

WHEREAS, holy anticipation, excitement and expectation fills my soul that I have the privilege to dine at the Master's table today, and to be fed and furnished by His Omnipotent hand; and

WHEREAS, high praise and worship of the Lord in my heart is without doubt the His doing (Psa. 118: 23) when I think of where He has brought me from, intimate fellowship with the Lord gives me joy unspeakable; His Almighty power and providence in my life evokes holy ardor and fervor within me; God in my midst is mighty (Zeph. 3: 17), and His ways past finding out (Rom. 11: 33); and

WHEREAS, I am passionate about the Lord, fully prepared to glorify and honor Him, and to be in His presence gives me fulness of joy and pleasure untold (Psa. 16: 11); and

WHEREAS, I am on a journey in the Spirit, not yielding a step in the hottest fight, but advancing and gaining with Jehovah's help from the realms of light.

I DECREE AND DECLARE this Day 193 that

- I am advancing, activated by Holy Ghost audacity and authority; I am faithful and fearless, with belief and confidence that the good work God has begun in me will be completed and fulfilled (Phil. 1: 6) in the global village

- my journey of advancing is possible through Jesus, and I advance with a purpose, not uncertainly, as one who beats the air, (1 Cor. 9: 26) but I press and progress toward the objective with the attitude and mindset of a warrior who wins

- I advance to the mark and hit the target by the stamina and strength of the Holy Ghost; nothing in my hands I bring, but simply to the cross I cling, and only by the help of the Spirit do I hit the target (Zech. 4: 6)

- as I advance, my elevation and expansion in the Spirit causes satanic irritation and indignation, and, despite harassing and hassling me, the Devil's plots and ploys are foiled and thwarted (Isa. 54: 17), and I hit the target with accuracy and precision, bringing glory and honor to God

- I will advance to the mark and hit the target - that is Christ's guarantee (Phil. 4: 13); however, I will "keep under and bring my body into subjection" (1 Cor. 9: 27), being keenly aware of the requirement for total obedience and observance of all that God commands of me (2 Kin. 13: 19).

BE IT THEREFORE RESOLVED by me this day that

- I remain fully submitted and surrendered to the voice of the Lord as I march on, and to Him only will I hearken and heed

- I refuse and reject alternatives, options and substitutes to advancing according to the plans and purposes of God, and remain fixed and focused on fulfilling my God-given assignment in the earth to march well and hit the target.

BY VIRTUE OF MY POSITION AND PRIVILEGE AS A KING AND PRIEST UNTO GOD MY FATHER (Rev. 1: 6), I BOLDLY DRIVE THESE PROPHETIC DECREES, DECLARATIONS, AND RESOLUTIONS AS STAKES IN THE GROUND; by the fruit of my lips, they are established and settled (Prov. 13: 2; 18: 21); Heaven's holy hill legalizes and legitimizes them; demonic rebellion and resistance against them is reduced to rubble and ruin, and the light shines upon my ways (Job 22: 28) as I advancing toward the mark.

In the name of the Omnipotent, Omnipresent, Omniscient Father, Son, and Holy Ghost! Blessed Trinity!

AND IT IS SO!

Day 194

FORASMUCH as the Lord God has, by breathing into my lungs this morning (Job 33: 4), awakened me to see a new day in the land of the living (Psa. 27: 13); and

WHEREAS, His goodness and mercy has followed me during the days of my life thus far (Psa. 23: 6); my heart is thankful to Him for the wonder of His amazing grace in my life, and I choose to demonstrate my thanks to Him with honor and praise; and

WHEREAS, I am rapturously ecstatic and joyfully delighted to have the honor of approaching God's presence with boldness and humility because of the riches of His grace; and

WHEREAS, what excitement I feel when I encounter God every day; it is a joy worth sharing and telling others about; it is a thrill to experience His presence without feeling condemned (Rom. 8: 1); these foretastes of seeing God face-to-face cause me to discipline and keep myself in His love; and

WHEREAS, it is my daily endeavor to advance toward the mark of the prize of the high calling in Christ Jesus (Phil. 3: 14), and by Holy Ghost anointing and unction, regressing, relenting, or retreating is out of the question for me.

I DECREE AND DECLARE this Day 194 that

- I will be anxious and apprehensive for nothing, but by prayer and supplication, with thanksgiving, advance and progress in the things of God in my life

- I am unapologetically blessed and bountifully progressing with motivation and militance by Holy Ghost power to the mark to hit the target with the arrow of deliverance and victory, which belongs to the Lord (2 Kings 13: 17)

- I committed and courageous (Josh. 1: 6, 7, 9), and, despite the diabolical designs, duress and devices of Satan against me, the blood of Jesus canopies and covers me as I advance, and the cause of the Kingdom of God in the earth (the target) will be completely accomplished and fulfilled in my life (Luke 1: 45; Phil. 1: 6)

- I am determined, diligent and have dominion with my God-ordained assignment and calling in the earth (Psa. 8: 6; Luke 2: 49; 19: 13), and by the touch of His hand upon me (2 Kin. 13: 16), I shoot for victory (2 King. 13: 17) with the guarantee of God that I will hit the target

- I am empowered and equipped by the Holy Ghost (Zech. 4: 6; Acts 1: 8); my hands and heart are fully engaged and enlivened by His enablement (Psa. 18: 29, 34), and I will only advance, go forward, and progress to the mark, and will precisely and purposefully hit the target.

BE IT THEREFORE RESOLVED by me this day that

- I will not be arrogant or haughty, but remain assured and confident in the Lord's ability to brace and grace me to advance and win

- I will not be a forgetful hearer, but remain a willing and obedient doer of all that God instructs me in His Word for blessings (Jam. 1: 25), spiritual impact and influence as one who advances to the mark and hits the target

BY THE ABILITY THAT THE HOLY GHOST GIVES, I BOLDLY AND BRAVELY DRIVE THESE PROPHETIC DECREES, DECLARATIONS, AND RESOLUTIONS AS ANCHORS AND STAKES IN THE GROUND; by the fruit of my lips, they are established and fulfilled (Prov. 13: 2; 18: 21); it is Heaven's pleasure and prerogative to sanction and seal them; Satan's efforts against them are fruitless, futile, and stamped FAILED, and the light shines upon my ways (Job 22: 28) as I advance to the mark and hit the target.

In the All-Wise, Only-Wonderful name of the Father, Son, and Holy Ghost! Blessed Godhead, Three-in-One!

AND IT IS SO!

Day 195

FORASMUCH as the Lord was pleased to awaken me from overnight rest to see the light of a brand new day with a sound mind, the activity of my limbs, and the use of my senses (Acts 17: 28); and

WHEREAS, I am joyful and thankful to God today for the honor and privilege of dwelling in the secret place of His presence, and to humbly bow to His High and Holy name, and

WHEREAS, being in His presence allows me to enjoy seeing Him move in and through my life, and His marvelous and wonderful works in me attest to His power; and Sovereignty: "He has done whatsoever He hath pleased" (Psa. 115: 3); and

WHEREAS, I am born of, and filled with, the Spirit (Jn. 3: 6; Acts 2: 1-4), and am on the move by and through His power in the global village "Advancing to the Mark and Hitting the Target" (2 King 13: 15-17); and

WHEREAS, this is a move ordained and orchestrated by God; the target will be hit, and the kingdoms of this world are become the kingdoms of our Lord, and of His Christ, and He shall reign for ever and ever (Rev. 11: 15).

I DECREE AND DECLARE this Day 195 that

- I advance to the mark with boldness and confidence in the Holy Ghost who lives in me; my hands are in the Master's hands (2 King. 13; 16); the deeds of my flesh are mortified (Rom. 8: 13), and it is only by the Spirit that I will hit the target with accuracy and precision

- my advancement to the mark and hitting the target is not a figment of my imagination, guess work or luck; instead, the full assurance of God's presence with me is the basis of my confidence (Ex. 33: 14); I can (and will) do all things through Christ which strengthens us (Phil. 4: 13)

- I will hit the target and accurately strike at the heart of the agendas and agents of Satan set against my advancement and progress, and the strike I render through God will plunder and plunge his evil schemes and systems into submission and surrender to the Omnipotent One (isa. 54: 17)

- I cancel, rebuke, and strike at the heart of sin sickness, bodily infirmities, and malignancies of every kind, and I call forth the healing hand of Christ, and His precious blood, to be applied to every issue for complete and total victory for the glory of God (Isa. 53: 5)

- I will be assailed, but I advance; I will be buffeted, but I remain blessed; I will be challenged, but will come through more than a conqueror (Rom. 8: 37)

BE IT THEREFORE RESOLVED by me this day that

- I will maintain an advancing, gaining, and progressing mindset, and every negative and pessimistic suggestion designed to derail me is rejected

- I will discipline myself to remain steadfast and unmovable (1 Cor. 9: 27; 15: 58), conforming and being obedient to every command that the Lord gives me (2 Kin. 13: 19)

BY THE AUTHORITY VESTED IN ME BY THE HOLY GHOST, I DRIVE THESE PROPHETIC DECREES, DECLARATIONS, AND RESOLUTIONS AS IRREPLACEABLE STAKES IN THE GROUND; by the fruit of my lips, they are established and settled (Prov. 13: 2; 18: 21); they are graced and guaranteed by the order of Heaven; satanic taunts, tentacles, and threats set against them are dismembered and subject to total destruction, and the light shines upon my ways (Job 22: 28) as I advance to the mark and hit the target.

In the unconquerable, uncontainable and uncontrollable name of the Father, the Son, and Holy Ghost! Blessed Trinity!

AND IT IS SO!

Day 196

FORASMUCH as my good, good Father has bestowed the blessing of life upon me to awaken to the light of another day; the blessing of liberty from sin's bondage because of Jesus, and the unending bounty of love He lavishes upon me; and

WHEREAS, I am more than joyful that God has allowed me to receive daily bread from His table, and to experience His power and presence in my life for another day's journey; and

WHEREAS, the songwriter sang, "O what blessed sweet communion, Jesus is a friend of mine" (Joseph C. Ludgate); this sums up what being in fellowship with the Savior means; and

WHEREAS, the water is troubled; God's holy power is moving this hour; things are getting better; the Lord is on my side, and I have the victory; and

WHEREAS, God's call to me demands audacity, bravery, tenacity and intrepidity (face danger, don't show fear); this is marching and moving time; I do not have the option of being lethargic or lazy; there is a mark to which I am advancing.

I DECREE AND DECLARE this Day 196 that

- I shoot all the arrows of deliverance and victory toward unredeemed souls, rescuing the perishing, and caring for the dying, and I will not be fearful to bear testimony of the power of salvation through Jesus in the global village

- I shoot all the arrows of deliverance against spiritual Aphek (strength, stronghold) in my life, and I do so fearlessly and ferociously in the Holy Ghost, who empowers and equips me with spiritual weapons of mass destruction until the stronghold is fully consumed/destroyed (2 Kings 13: 17)

- every encampment, enslavement, and enticement of Aphek built to eliminate me will turn in on itself, implode, and be totally consumed and demolished, and not one iota of evil from the wicked one will be spared (1 Sam. 15: 18; 2 King. 13: 19) - I will hit the target dead center, and without fail

- as I advance, God will be glorified in the earth, Jesus will be lifted on high, and the Holy Ghost will witness and work in and through me to bring credit, glory, and honor to the Kingdom of God

- I advance to the mark with holy anticipation, belief, and expectancy; there is a target to hit, and I will not be denied, deterred, or detoured until the arrow strikes at the center, the very heart of the target for total breakthrough, deliverance, triumph, and victory over Aphek.

BE IT THEREFORE RESOLVED by me this day that

- I will advance with militance and vigilance, not fearing man, but seeking to please God, who graces me to advance to the mark and hit the target

- I remain in a state of readiness to advance and forge ahead with the momentum of the Spirit, taking every care that I totally adhere to God's call and commission to me

BY THE AUTHORITY OF MY POSITION IN THE SPIRIT, I DRIVE THESE PROPHETIC DECREES, DECLARATIONS, AND RESOLUTIONS AS PILLARS AND STAKES IN THE GROUND; they are established in the earth by the words that I speak (Prov. 13: 2; 18: 21); Heaven's high and holy court grants them approval and assent; the intentions of evil against them are returned to sender marked "death of assignment", and I advance to the mark and hit the target by the light that shines upon my ways (Job 22: 28).

In the immortal, impartial, and imperial name of the Father, Son, and Holy Ghost! Blessed Godhead, Three-in-One!

AND IT IS SO!

Day 197

FORASMUCH as my Heavenly Father has bestowed compassion, His unfailing faithfulness, and great grace upon me to raise me up from overnight rest to live, move, and have my being in Him (Acts 17: 28); and

WHEREAS, I am delighted today to have the privilege, by God's grace, to approach the presence of the most high and Holy God of glory for daily bread from Him; and

WHEREAS, I testify and verify that I am harnessed, held and helped by God in the earth, and that advancing to the mark and hitting the target" (2 Kings 13: 15-17) is my goal; total obedience to the Master is my deliberate choice; I have assurance that the Lord's arrows of deliverance shall secure complete victory over strongholds for me as I follow His commands, and through His enablement, the enemy will be totally destroyed; and

WHEREAS, the battle cry is sounded; the foe is nigh; the standard must be raised high for the Lord, and the call of the Lord is to gird up, stand firm, and advance, resting my cause upon His Holy Word, as I hit the target dead center in triumph; and

WHEREAS, this not the time to lay down my weapons, get weary in the march, or retreat and surrender under the pressure; instead, it's time to rally around the banner, advance, go forward, and shout loud Hosannas to Christ my Captain as I go forward and onward to hit the target.

I DECREE AND DECLARE this Day 197 that

- my mission of advancement is possible; the plans and purposes of Almighty God for me are guaranteed and sure, and I am an irresistible and unstoppable warrior of the Kingdom of God in the earth who will prevail and hit the target

- God holds my hands as I advance and hit the target with the arrow of the His deliverance, and without fail, Aphek (strongholds) will come down in subjection to His Almighty power (2 Cor. 10: 5)

- I am battle-ready, bold and brave; I have Holy Ghost firepower, and I march relentlessly and resiliently to the mark for the ultimate prize of the high calling of God in Christ Jesus (Phil. 3: 14)

- I advance with assurance and confidence; I pray effectually and fervently as I go; I shout and sing joyfully and jubilantly, and every contrivance and cunning craftiness of Satan is crumbled by the power of the wind of the Spirit, as my weapons of warfare hit and strike at the heart of every evil way and work

- yesterday is gone; my past failures and flops are not the end or my undoing; instead, I advance and march forward and onward; I take bow and arrow, and shoot (2 Ki. 13: 17); the war is settled; I WIN, and Aphek is totally destroyed and overcome (v. 17)

BE IT THEREFORE RESOLVED by me this day that

- I refuse to yield a step in the hottest fight from unfriendly enemy fire as I audaciously advance to the mark and hit the target

- I remain submitted and surrendered to the Omnipotence of God as I advance, and will retain the secret of my effectiveness - His holy power and presence in my midst (Zeph. 3: 17)

BY VIRTUE OF MY BLOOD-COVENANT CONNECTION WITH GOD THROUGH CHRIST, I DRIVE THESE DECREES, DECLARATIONS, AND RESOLUTIONS AS STAKES IN THE GROUND; by the fruit of my lips (Prov. 13: 2; 18: 21), they are established and settled; Heaven's pleasure and prerogative seals and secures them; satanic intrusion against them is twice dead, doomed and dusted, and the light shines upon my ways (Job 22: 28) as I advance to the mark and hit the target.

In the sanctifying, saving, and stable name of the Father, So, and Holy Ghost! Blessed Godhead, Three-in-One!

AND IT IS SO!

Day 198

FORASMUCH as the faithfulness, goodness, and lovingkindness of my Sovereign Father kept death away from me during the night, and blessed me to rise to the dawn of a new day with life and limbs because of Him (Acts 17: 28); and

WHEREAS, as the Psalmist sang, "Because thy lovingkindness is better than life, my lips shall praise thee, Thus will I bless thee while I live: I will lift up my hands in thy name" (Psa. 63: 3, 4); and

WHEREAS, I give adoration and adulation to God for His abiding presence with me, and for His unending and unfailing faithfulness to me during my journey with Him in the earth as a Christian; and

WHEREAS, the Lord's power and presence in my life is empowering, life-changing and transforming, as the Holy Spirit continues to manifest Himself in and through me; and

WHEREAS, as a soldier in God's army in the earth, I am advancing, marching, and progressing to the mark and hitting the target based on the biblical text in 2 Kings 13: 15-17.

I DECREE AND DECLARE this Day 198 that

- my advancement is not an emotional, one-hit wonder, run-of-the-mill, try-it-if-you-will experiment; instead, I am an anointed, branded-by-fire, and courageous believer who fearlessly and steadfastly advances and presses toward the mark to hit the target

- I are secure and stable in my belief that God is able "to do exceeding abundantly above all that I ask for think" (Eph. 3: 20), and I am a recipient of His enablement by the power of the Holy Ghost, who dwells richly in me, and who manifests Himself through me in demonstration and power as I hit the target (1 Cor. 2: 4)

- as I advance to the mark, doors of opportunity to proclaim the Gospel swing wide open for me; and, despite adversaries and opposition (1 Cor. 16: 9), the arrows of deliverance and victory strike at the center and heart of satanic resistance, totally cancelling, confounding, and consuming the intents of evil set against me (Isa. 54: 17)

- as I advance to the mark and hit the target, the Holy Ghost gives me Divine downloads that provide valuable insight and intelligence of the heart and mind of God, gracing me with the ability to overcome obstacles and obstructions as I advance and hit the target

- I call forth my God-ordained destiny and purpose (Jer. 29: 11), and I will engage with, and have meaningful and monumental impact and influence over my peers in the global village that draws the unsaved to Jesus, and God gets the glory.

BE IT THEREFORE RESOLVED by me this day that

- I remain reliant upon God, and resilient through the Holy Ghost, as I advance to the mark and hit the target in the earth

- I rest in God my Source, who braces and graces me with the mindset, momentum, and motivation to stay the course of advancement to the mark and hit the target

BY VIRTUE OF MY COVENANT-CONNECTION WITH GOD THROUGH JESUS CHRIST, I BOLDLY DRIVE THESE PROPHETIC DECREES, DECLARATIONS, AND RESOLUTIONS AS STAKES IN THE GROUND; they are established and settled by the fruit of my mouth (Prov. 13: 2; 18: 21); the Triune Godhead of Heaven is pleased to affirm and approve them; diabolical invasions of the dark domain are consigned to eternal calamity, chaos, confusion, and the light shines upon my ways (Job 22: 28) as I relentlessly advance to the mark and hit the target.

In the resilient, resounding, and resourceful name of the Father, Son, and Holy Ghost! Blessed Triune Godhead!

AND IT IS SO!

Day 199

FORASMUCH as it was the Father's pleasure and will to breathe His breath into my body and cause me to rise today to the light of a new day to live for Him, to long after Him, and to love Him more and more; and

WHEREAS, I am honored and humbled to have intimate, secret-place fellowship with God as I journey with Him in the earth as His called and chosen child; and

WHEREAS, to encounter and experience God in my life is abundantly clear and obvious that my transformation is only the handiwork of God (Psa. 118: 23), and the marvelous and miraculous manifestations of His Almighty power and presence in my life affirms and confirms that He makes all things new (Isa. 43: 19); and

WHEREAS, "Elohim is Here", based on Zeph. 3: 17, a text brimming with undiluted truth of the presence of Elohim ("Supreme" or "Mighty One") in my life; and

WHEREAS, Elohim is Creator (Gen. 1: 1), Supreme Judge of the world (Psa. 7: 9), Superior in all His ways (Rom. 11: 33) Sustainer of all life and things (Col. 1: 17), and He is Here! Hallelujah!

I DECREE AND DECLARE this Day 199 that

- like the Daughter of Zion, I sing - the thrilling and trembling burst of joy; I am glad - the calm joyfulness of my soul; I shout - the loud, trumpet-blast of jubilance, and I rejoice - a triumph from deep within that I cannot contain or even explain (Zeph. 3: 14)

- like Israel, I base my joy and jubilation on the fact that my calamity is taken away (v. 15), afflictions and inflictions of the enemy are gone, my sins have been pardoned and purged, and I am no longer in the vice-grip of condemnation (Rom. 5: 11; 8: 1)

- Satan is cast out (v. 15); I may be harassed and hassled by his pernicious ways, but he will harm and hurt me no more, and because Elohim is in my midst, the prince of this world, my chief enemy, is designated thief and trespasser, and he is expelled from my regenerated and renewed nature (Jn. 12: 31; Titus 2: 15)

- God (Elohim) is Here! - in His covenantal place in my midst as the Mighty Lord, Powerful Protector, and Reigning Ruler, and I have no cause or need for alarm or anxiety, or fear or fright of the sight of evil (v. 15; Lu. 12: 32)

- God (Elohim) is Here! – I am not, and will not, be despondent; I will not have drooping, idle hands and/or an ailing, fainting heart (Zeph. 3: 16; 2 Cor. 4: 16); instead, I am made strong, wax valiant in the good fight of faith (Heb. 11: 34; 1 Tim. 6: 12), and God teaches my hands to war (Psa. 144: 1) in the Spirit.

BE IT THEREFORE RESOLVED by me this day that

- I will remain in the joy of Elohim (Zeph. 3: 17) until, like the rising tide, it overflows the banks of my soul and breaks forth into singing and shouts of praise and worship to God

- I will remain satisfied and sustained by the joy of Elohim, who is mighty in my midst, and by this joy that erupts from within like a volcano, mankind are amazed and astounded by Elohim, the Power of powers

BY THE AUTHORITY OF ELOHIM THE MIGHTY ONE IN MY MIDST, I DRIVE THESE PROPHETIC DECREES, DECLARATIONS, AND RESOLUTIONS AS STAKES OF JOY AND JUBILEE IN THE GROUND; they are established in the earth by the fruit of my lips (Prov. 13: 2; 18: 21); Heaven backs and blesses their fulfillment; demons of the darkness who are dead set against them turn in on themselves to their own death and demise, and the light of Elohim shines upon my ways (Job 22: 28) because He Is Here! Hallelujah!

In the Sovereign, Strong, and Supreme name of the Father, Son, and Holy Ghost! God in three Persons, blessed Trinity!

AND IT IS SO!

Day 200

FORASMUCH as my Sovereign Father has, by His compassions, faithfulness and grace (Lam. 3: 22, 23), raised me up and touched me with His hand of love to be alive today in Him (Acts 17: 28); and

WHEREAS, joy floods my soul today, and I honor and praise the Most High for His goodness, greatness and lovingkindness toward me as I journey through life as a pilgrim and a stranger to Heaven; and

WHEREAS, I am drawn by the Holy Ghost into glorious fellowship with the Lord by an insatiable drive and passion for more of Him, and to encounter Him in the fulness of His glory and power is the desire of my heart; and

WHEREAS, God Almighty, who has no counselor, equal, rival or teacher (Isa. 40: 13, 14), is pleased to dwell in me, and as long and as often as He receives the glory (Isa. 42: 8), honor, and worship from me as the ONLY wise God worthy of the same,

He will demonstrate the power of His name in and through me; and

WHEREAS, I make the bold proclamation, "Elohim is Here", and as Creator (Gen. 1: 1), Sustainer, and Upholder of all things (Col. 1: 16, 17), He is pleased to tabernacle in my life, and every fiend and foe is subject to His Almighty power.

I DECREE AND DECLARE this Day 200 that

- the joy of Elohim/Jehovah is not lacking in me; rather, my singing, shouting, gladness, and rejoicing in Him burst and gush forth like an unstoppable fountain from the city of my soul

- the joy of Elohim in me prompts and sustains my joy in Him; I love Him because He first loved me (1 Jn. 4: 19), and I will joy in God through Christ Jesus (Rom. 5: 11), knowing that for Christ's sake, God is pleased with me and is Here!

- the God of Covenant is Here; my rightful King and mighty Savior is Here; I am saved and secured from the guilt and power of sin, from the danger of ignorance and error, from the corruptions and temptations of the world, and from the fear of death and the dominion of the grave (Hos. 13: 14)

- Elohim is Here; He has great joy over my redemption and regeneration from ruin (Zeph. 3: 17; Tit. 3: 5), and my rescue from the oppression and suffering of the enemy by Him speaks to His undoing of all that afflicts me (Zeph. 3: 19)

- Elohim is Here; I am reconditioned, remembered, and repositioned by His power, and I have His guarantee that I am kept and preserved from all fear, guilt, and harm (Zeph. 3: 15)

BE IT THEREFORE RESOLVED by me this day that

- I will remain under the abiding canopy and shadow of the Almighty, and fear and fright are banished from me because Elohim is Here

- I will remain safe and secure in my position of regeneration and restoration, all because my Sustainer, Elohim, is Here

BY VIRTUE OF THE CERTAINTY AND SECURITY I HAVE IN GOD THROUGH CHRIST, AND WITH BOLD ASSERTION, I DRIVE THESE PROPHETIC DECREES, DECLARATIONS, AND RESOLUTIONS AS STAKES IN THE GROUND; they are established and fulfilled by the words that I speak (Prov. 13: 2; 18: 21); the Triune Godhead of Heaven gives benediction and blessing upon them; the hell hounds of evil that conspire against them are thrown into calamitous chaos and confusion, and because Elohim is Here, the light shines upon my ways (Job 22: 28).

In the Omnipotent, Omnipresent, and Omniscient name of Elohim: God the Father, God the Son, and God the Holy Ghost! Blessed Trinity, Three-in-One!

AND IT IS SO!

Day 201

FORASMUCH as I am a beneficiary of God's grace and mercy that allowed me the privilege to wake up this morning with life, limbs, and love for Him (Acts 17: 28); and

WHEREAS, I proclaim, "Then sings my soul my Savior God to Thee, how great thou art, how great thou art; then sing my soul my Savior God to Thee, how great thou art, how great thou art" (Robert J. Morgan); and

WHEREAS my heart is filled and overflowing with praise, thanksgiving and worship to God today for the abundant blessings He has bestowed me, and my fellowship with Him in the Spirit evokes in me joy that is unspeakable, and full of glory; and

WHEREAS, without doubt, great is the Lord God Almighty in my life, and He inhabits the praises that gush forth from me to His amazing (Psa. 22: 3); and

WHEREAS, Elohim is Here; the Lord my God, Creator and Sustainer of all things in my midst, is mighty; He will save, rejoice, rest in His love, and joy over me with singing (Zeph. 3: 17); the bond, guarantee, and sure promise of my gracious, loving Father.

I DECREE AND DECLARE this Day 201 that

- I sing: affliction, condemnation, judgment, and punishment are yesterday's shame; I am discharged and released from the enslavement and hostility of my enemy, and I do not fear: Elohim is Here!

- I shout: the accuser, adversary, annihilator, and antagonist from the dark domain of hell is cast out; he has no authority, place or power over me, and I do not fret: Elohim is Here!

- I am glad: the rush of exaltation, excitement and exuberance gush forth from my being to God in my life, and a wave of God's gladness returns to me as He joys over me, His child (Zeph. 3: 17), who am liberated from bondage and enemy captivity: Elohim is Here!

- I rejoice: God, who is mighty in my midst, is a pain, a nightmare, and a violent terror and tormentor to the enemy of my soul, and my joy and rejoicing in Him is full, overflowing, and running over: Elohim is Here!

- I am totally reinstated and restored in God to the joy of deliverance, to true dignity and honor, and because Elohim is Here, He gives me a name in the earth that is credible, impactful, and influential (Zeph. 3: 20).

BE IT THEREFORE RESOLVED by me this day that

- I rest in the finished work of Christ at Calvary, who secured my deliverance, redemption and salvation by His precious blood

- I choose to remain free from the interferences, interruptions, and insurrections of the evil one; my liberty is possible because Elohim is Here!

BY VIRTUE OF MY CONNECTION WITH GOD THROUGH THE UNBREAKABLE COVENANT HE MADE WITH ME (Psa. 89: 34), I DRIVE THESE PROPHETIC DECREES, DECLARATIONS, AND RESOLUTIONS AS STAKES IN THE GROUND; they are established and settled by the fruit of my lips (Prov. 13: 2; 18: 21); Almighty God, the Son, and Holy Ghost backs and blesses them; the devil's traps and tricks set against them are overcome, overruled and overrun by Elohim, the Power of powers (Rom. 13: 1), and the light shines upon my ways (Job 22: 28) because Elohim is Here!

In the vanquishing and victorious name of the Father, Son, and Holy Ghost! The Blessed Triune Godhead of Heaven!

AND IT IS SO!

Day 202

FORASMUCH as it was because God Almighty touched me with His miraculous hand today, breathed His breath into my body (Job 33: 4), and allowed me to awaken with the use of my senses and a sound mind (Acts 17: 28); and

WHEREAS, had it not been for the Lord who is on my side, when circumstances of life would have swallowed me up; when man rose up against me, their wrath kindled against me, the waters overwhelmed me, and the stream gone over my soul, thanks be to God, who has not given me as a prey to their teeth (Psa. 124: 1-6); and

WHEREAS, I adore and laud God my Father for the wonders of His grace and might in me, through me, and to me; and

WHEREAS, songs of glory, honor, praise and thanksgiving erupt and gush forth from my soul unto the Most High God, who is delighted and pleased to dwell in my life; and

WHEREAS, "Elohim is Here" – He always has, always is, and always will be; and I shout, sing, rejoice and am glad that He has marvelously and miraculously freed, liberated, and released me from the evil one, cast him out, and caused me to see evil again no more (Zeph. 3: 15).

I DECREE AND DECLARE this Day 202 that

- Elohim is Here, and every act of adversity, affliction and anguish against me is undone, broken and dissolved by the might of Elohim (Zeph. 3: 19)

- Elohim is Here, and, rather than halt (fall) from great distress and duress, torment and trouble, I am salvaged and secured by the hand of Omnipotence (v. 19)

- Elohim is Here, and He will avenge and vindicate me; I am not rejected, but accepted into the Beloved, and have a name and a praise in the global village (v. 20)

- Elohim is Here, and those whom Satan uses as agents to scoff at and scorn me become a derision and disdain, are driven out from me, and remembered no more (v. 15)

- Elohim is Here, and He delights, joys, rejoices, and rests in His love for and over me, and He sings over me with enjoyment and pleasure for the breakthrough, freedom, and salvation He has secured for me through Christ (Zeph. 3: 19; Jn. 8: 36)

BE IT THEREFORE RESOLVED by me this day that

- I rest my cares and causes into the hands of Elohim, submitted and surrendered to His Omnipotence and Providence

- I reject every idea, suggestion, or thought of anti-God systems of this world that seek to derail my total reliance upon Elohim, Creator, Sustainer and Upholder of all things

BY VIRTUE OF THE AUTHORITY VESTED IN ME BY ELOHIM, I DRIVE THESE DECREES,

DECLARATIONS, AND RESOLUTIONS AS STAKES IN THE GROUND; they are established by the words that I speak (Prov. 18: 21); Heaven is pleased to back and bless them; Satan's angst against them are apprehended and annihilated, and I live with certainty that the light shines upon my ways (Job 22: 28).

In the Sovereign and Supreme name of the Father, Son, and Holy Ghost! Blessed Trinity, Three-in-One!

AND IT IS SO!

Day 203

FORASMUCH as my Righteous, Sovereign Heavenly Father has extended grace and mercy to me to awaken me from rest to see a day that I have never seen before with the use of my limbs, a sound mind, and a desire to live for Him; and

WHEREAS, my spirit and soul overflows with thanksgiving and worship to God for the great and mighty works of His hand upon my life, and I command my hands, my heart, and my mouth to raise a praise unto the Master; and

WHEREAS, I ascribe and render homage and honor to God for manifesting His glorious power in my life as I have journeyed during my earthly pilgrimage to the land of boundless glory; and

WHEREAS, to meditate and muse over the wondrous works of the Lord in my life causes me to conclude, Elohim is Here: Creator, Sustainer, and Upholder of all things is mighty in me, and He will save (Zeph. 3: 17); and

WHEREAS, it is the delight and desire of my Sovereign God to deliver me from all who bring distress and duress, and who oppress and suppress, and Elohim in my midst will rejoice with joy, and joy over me with singing (Zeph. 3: 17).

I DECREE AND DECLARE this Day 203 that

- I have the answer and antidote to fainting, faltering and fear - the Lord my God in my midst is mighty, just as close as the mention of His name

- Elohim is Here; I have the blessing and benefit of His essential presence and power with me, and the promise of His Providential care is my gift and guarantee that He will never fail me (Psa. 89: 33)

- I am not dismayed or doubtful; instead, Elohim is Here, the Being of beings, Eternal, Immutable, All-Sufficient and Supreme, and He delivers me from the hate and hostility of the Devil; and when I call, Elohim will save me

- by the counsel and covenant of Elohim, I am empowered, equipped, and established, and He gives and graces me with wisdom from above (Jam. 3: 17) that supplies and sustains me during my earthly pilgrimage

- Elohim is Here, and He saves me from sin, Satan, hell and wrath, and every spirit from the domain of darkness is cast away and out from me, never to be seen again forever (Ex. 14: 13).

BE IT THEREFORE RESOLVED by me this day that

- I rest in the ability of Elohim to work wonders for me as I walk, work and witness for Him in the global village

- I remain redeemed and repaired by God Almighty in my midst, and I fix and focus my faith in Him who is here: Elohim!

ELOHIM IS MIGHTY IN MY MIDST, AND BY HIM, I DRIVE THESE PROPHETIC DECREES,

DECLARATIONS, AND RESOLUTIONS AS IMMOVABLE STAKES IN THE GROUND; they are established and fulfilled by the fruit of my lips (Prov. 13: 2; 18: 21); the Triune Godhead of Heaven affirms, endorses and confirms them; the meanness and menaces of hell are mangled and mutilated, and the light of Elohim shines upon my ways (Job 22: 28).

In the eminent, essential and eternal name of the Father, Son, and Holy Ghost! God in three Persons, blessed Trinity!

AND IT IS SO!

Day 204

FORASMUCH as my faithful and merciful Father has watched over me during the night, kept death at bay for me, raised me up to see the light of a brand new day, and graced me with the benefit and blessing of a free and full salvation because of Jesus; and

WHEREAS, gladness, happiness, and joy in the Holy Ghost fills my heart today; I just cannot explain these rivers of joy, except to sing with the hymnologist, "I'm happy today, in Jesus Christ I'm happy today, because He's taken all my sins away, and that's why I'm happy today" (R. J. Stevens); and

WHEREAS, I rejoice that I am a radical, redeemed, and righteous Christian in the earth, and to encounter God every day during personal devotional time with Him is monumental for me; and

WHEREAS, God has me on the proverbial "edge of my seat" in holy anticipation of what He will do next for me, having manifested His awesome presence and power in my life in so many ways keeps me excited and expectant of Him; and

WHEREAS, ELOHIM IS HERE, and He is mighty in my midst (Zeph. 3: 17), and I have felt and witnessed Him touching, transforming, and turning lives for His glory and honor.

I DECREE AND DECLARE this Day 204 that

- Elohim is Here: I am an activated, anointed, and audacious sharp threshing instrument having teeth (Isa. 41: 15); enemy one has been cast and thrust out (Zeph. 3: 15), and my assignment in the earth from the King is fulfilled because Elohim is here!

- Elohim is Here: I am blessed, bold, and brave (Prov. 28: 1), and I have no fear, fret or fright of the maliciousness of evildoers (Psa. 37: 1)

- Elohim is Here: He's my Champion and Chief Cornerstone, and I celebrate, commemorate, and contemplate with high praise the work of breakthrough and deliverance He has wrought in me from the power of the Devil

- Elohim is Here: I am His delight and desire (Zeph. 3: 19), and my deliverance in Him demoralizes every evil entity that seeks to damage and diminish the work of the Almighty in me

- Elohim is Here: the Eminent, Esteemed, Eternal One, and the sacrifices of praise and thanksgiving of His name testifies to my emancipation from the grip of condemnation (Rom. 8: 1).

BE IT THEREFORE RESOLVED by me this day that

- I will remain in the safe and secure hands of Elohim, the Sustainer and Upholder of my life

- I rebuke alarm, anxiety, and apprehension set against me, and I walk in the unction of the Holy Ghost my Leader, Guide and Teacher in the global village

BY THE AUTHORITY OF MY RIGHT STANDING BEFORE GOD IN HEAVEN, I DRIVE THESE DECREES, DECLARATIONS, AND RESOLUTIONS AS SANCTIFIED STAKES IN THE GROUND; Heaven's high and holy order give creative credence to their fulfillment; the hordes of hell are hijacked and humiliated by the power of Elohim, and the light shines upon my ways (Job 22: 28) because Elohim is Here!

In the stable and strong name of the Father, Son, and Holy Ghost! Blessed Godhead, Three-in-One!

AND IT IS SO!

Day 205

FORASMUCH as my kind and loving Heavenly Father has extended grace and mercy to me to awaken me from rest, and to enjoy the blessing to be alive and well; and

WHEREAS, on this brand new day which the Lord has made (Psa. 118: 24), I offer the incense of praise and thanksgiving to God for the unmatched and unparalleled manifestations of His Omnipotence in me, through me, and to me; and

WHEREAS, my soul and spirit are engulfed by holy adoration and affection toward the Lord as I celebrate the awesomeness of His person, power, and presence in my life; and

WHEREAS, living for Jesus in the global village is a spiritually breathtaking and rapturous experience; the blue-hot fire of Pentecost rages in me like a fire out of control, and this blaze in the Holy Ghost keeps me singing and shouting praise into God; and

WHEREAS, Elohim is (still) Here; He's even closer, anointing, blessing, covering, and delighting in me, and singing with joy over my status as an heir of the Father who has received breakthrough and liberty from the effects of evil against me (Zeph. 3: 13, 17).

I DECREE AND DECLARE this Day 205 that

- as one who enthrones Elohim in my life, I reject the notion and practice of iniquity or speaking lies, nor shall deceit be found on my tongue (v. 13)

- Elohim is mighty in my midst, and by His power, I decapitate, dethrone, disarm every scheme and system of satanic origin; the evil one is cast out, reduced to calamity and chaos, and consigned to the pit

- I call forth the power of Elohim to cities, homes, neighborhoods, towns, and villages, and waves of His glory and power cause salvation and deliverance of souls in abundance (Acts 2: 47)

- Elohim is (still) Here, and revival fires break out in unprecedented measure upon congregations and houses of worship, and miracles, signs and wonders rain down in torrential power upon the lives of God's people

- the power of Elohim will shake what can be shaken; Heaven's order and protocol reigns, and Holy Ghost dynamism blankets and canopies the earth for God's glory (Hab. 2: 14).

BE IT THEREFORE RESOLVED by me this day that

- I shelter myself under the governance and guidance of Elohim, shielded by His glory and grace

- I remain submitted and surrendered to Elohim, and by His irresistible power, He activates me to blaze trails and take territory for the Kingdom in the earth

BY THE AUTHORITY OF MY STRONG STANDING IN ELOHIM, I DRIVE THESE PROPHETIC DECREES, DECLARATIONS, AND RESOLUTIONS AS STAKES IN HE GROUND; they are established by the words that I speak (Prov. 13: 2; 18: 21); the Supreme Court of Heaven grants them holy assent; diabolic devices of evil set against them are torched and utterly tormented, and the light shines upon my ways (Job 22: 28c) because Elohim is (still) Here!

In the gratifying, great, and glorious name of the Father, Son, and Holy Ghost! Blessed Triune Godhead!

AND IT IS SO!

Day 206

FORASMUCH as my faithful, kind and loving Heavenly Father has enabled me to arise from rest today with a sound mind, the activity of my limbs, and a desire to live for Him in the earth; and

WHEREAS, this is a good day to give thanks unto the Lord; to call upon His name, to make known His deeds among the people (1 Chron. 16: 8), and to make mention that His name is exalted (Isa. 12: 4); and

WHEREAS, to posture myself with humility in the presence of the Pre-Eminent God; to feast on manna from on high, to taste of the good Word of God and not fall away (Heb. 6: 5), and to see that the Lord is good and gracious (1 Pet. 2: 3), is a privilege of mine that only grace can secure for me; and

WHEREAS, God, Elohim, Creator, Omnipotent One, Power of powers, Sustainer and Upholder of all things (Col. 1: 16) is pleased to dwell and live in me, and to manifest Himself in marvelous and miraculous ways past finding out (Rom. 11: 33); and

WHEREAS, Elohim is Here!, and I am the beneficiary of His Providence and wise bestowments that validate and verify the indisputable fact that He is mighty in my midst, and He will save me, take away judgements, and cast out the enemy before me (Zep. 3: 15-17).

I DECREE AND DECLARE this Day 206 that

- Elohim is here; He ONLY will be known through me in the earth, and not my carnal, unregenerate man, and I dare not puff myself up with pride, which goeth before destruction (Prov. 16: 18), and which God hates (Prov. 6: 17)

- Elohim is mighty in my midst; I will preserve the purity of His holiness in me by living righteously and uprightly in the earth, and as His representative, I will not patronize evil of any sort that will bring disgrace and dishonor to His name

- Elohim is mighty in my midst; the riches and wonder of His grace yields fertility and fruitfulness in and through me, and I function in the earth in the comfort and consolation of His delight and joy in my deliverance and salvation wrought by His Son, Jesus our Savior

- Elohim is here, and I am not disposed to fear or fright, nor do I drop my spirit in despair or despondence; instead, I lift my hands, heart and voice in praise, prayer, and worship, because the joy of the Lord is my strength (Neh. 8: 10)

- Elohim is mighty in my midst; He takes great delight in me and will do me good; Elohim takes me into His approval and favor, and He grants me freedom and liberty from banishment, bondage and brokenness to mount up and magnify Him who dwells mightily and richly in and through me.

BE IT THEREFORE RESOLVED by me this day that

- I remain free from the reproach and repulsiveness of my past, and I remember that Elohim in my midst has cast out and removed the enemy from me forever, who seeks to destroy and kill me (Zeph. 3: 15)

- I will redeem the days and time Elohim grants me in the earth for His good, so that I can effectively bring credit and honor to the Kingdom in the earth as His called-out, chosen one

BY THE AUTHORITY OF MY BLOOD-CONNECTION WITH CHRIST, I DRIVE THESE PROPHETIC DECREES, DECLARATIONS, AND RESOLUTIONS AS STAKES IN THE GROUND; they are firmly established in the earth by the fruit of my mouth (Prov. 13: 2; 18: 21); Heaven acknowledges and endorses their fulfillment; satanic invasions against them are scorched and torched to dust, and the light of Elohim shines upon my ways (Job 22: 28).

In the darling and delightful name of the Father, Son, and Holy Ghost! God in three Persons, Blessed Trinity!

AND IT IS SO!

Day 207

FORASMUCH as this is a great day to praise the Lord; I am alive by His grace, I talk and walk by His enablement, and I am blessed to see a day that I have never seen before, or ever will see again; and

WHEREAS, I am privileged to offer sacrifices of praise and thanksgiving to my faithful and loving Heavenly Father for extending His hand of blessing and favor to me today; and

WHEREAS, adulation, celebration, exaltation and jubilation toward God are fitting words to describe my heartfelt gratitude, and I will not stop praising and worshipping the Lord for the wonder of His doings in my life; and

WHEREAS, Elohim is Here; dear to me, He hears me, and is near to me, and I exclaim, "How Great Thou Art" as I adore and magnify His matchless name.

I DECREE AND DECLARE this Day 207 that

- condemnation, judgment, and punishment for sin are gone from me; I am free and liberated from enemy infiltration, and gladness, joy, rejoicing and singing songs of praise and worship unto the Lord pervade and reverberate the atmosphere about me

- the enemy has been cast out forever by Elohim (Zeph. 3: 15); his pernicious threats and menaces wane and wilt away, and God my Deliverer takes great delight in my freedom from the bondage and enslavement that the Devil can inflicted upon me

- Elohim is Here; He bans, bars, and blocks the afflictions and assaults of Satan against me, and I function in the global village with Holy Ghost anointing, boldness and courage as one who has something and so much to live for

- I am the delight and desire of Elohim; He rests in His love for me as His child (Zeph. 3: 17), and I am held safely, securely and strongly by His hand of Omnipotence

- my confidence, faith and trust is in Elohim, and although His ways are past finding out (Rom. 11: 33), my reliance upon His unfailing faithfulness toward me is without question.

BE IT THEREFORE RESOLVED by me this day that

- I will remain at rest in the unfathomable power of Elohim to do amazing things, and work wonders, for me in the global village

- I will forever return thanks to Elohim, who is mighty in my midst, for manifesting His astonishing and awesome transforming power, and making something beautiful out of my life

BY THE AUTHORITY OF MY PRIVILEGE OF SONSHIP WITH MY HEAVENLY FATHER, I DRIVE THESE PROPHETIC DECREES, DECLARATIONS,

AND RESOLUTIONS AS MAINSTAYS AND STAKES IN THE GROUND; they are established and settled in the earth by the words that I speak (Pro. 13: 2; 18: 21); the holy court of Heaven endorses and embraces them as favored and fruitful; Satan's designs and devices against them are subject to eternal brimstone and fire, and the light shines upon my ways (Job 22: 28). Elohim is Here!

In the Supernal, Superior and Supreme name of the Father, Son, and Holy Ghost! God in Three Persons, blessed Trinity!

AND IT IS SO!

Day 208

FORASMUCH as my kind and faithful Father has breathed breath into my lungs to arise to the light of another day to live, move and have my being (Acts 17: 28); and

WHEREAS, songs of praise and thanksgiving swell within my soul to God for the marvelous and wonderful things that He has done for, in, through and to me during my earthly pilgrimage; and

WHEREAS, I rejoice in the Lord today for His awesome and powerful presence in my life, and the wonder of it all is that the Father delights, has joy, and sings over me with rejoicing;

and

WHEREAS, Elohim is Here; I know it, bear witness to it, and have no greater joy than to proclaim that His presence in my life is what motivates and moves me to exalt, glorify, honor and magnify His precious name more and more.

I DECREE AND DECLARE this Day 208 that

- Elohim is Here; He is my delight and desire, my imminent judgement for sin is past, and ultimate deliverance is my song

- Elohim is Here; the hand of evil is cast down and out; reproach was a burden (Zeph. 3: 18); I am now redeemed, repaired and restored, and the righteous hand of God rests mightily upon me

- Elohim is Here; He has undone (handled roughly) every affliction that was upon me, and those driven out (Zeph. 3: 19) have returned to a regathering and a revival in the arms of sweet deliverance

- Elohim is Here; He is mighty in my midst, and the ways and works of Satan against me are nullified and void of effect upon me

- Elohim is Here; I am favored, flowering and fruitful, and the blessings and bounty of His hand enable me to be salty and savory in the lives of others in the global village

BE IT THEREFORE RESOLVED by me this day that

- I will shine as the noonday sun, and bring many to righteousness, and all the glory goes to Elohim

- I will stand steadfast and sure in the Omnipotence of Elohim, and all dominion, majesty and might belong to Him (Matt. 6: 13)

BY VIRTUE OF MY RIGHTEOUS STANDING WITH THE FATHER IN CHRIST, I DRIVE THESE PROPHETIC DECREES, DECLARATIONS, AND RESOLUTIONS AS MAINSTAYS AND STAKES IN THE GROUND; they are established and settled by the fruit of my mouth (Prov.13: 2; 18: 21); the Supreme Court of Glory grants them legislated assent; the Devil is powerless and pitiless, and can do nothing about them (Isa. 54: 17), and the light shines upon my ways, because Elohim is Here (Job 22: 28).

In the high, holy and honorable name of the Father, Son, and Holy Ghost! God in three Persons, Blessed Trinity!

AND IT IS SO!

Day 209

FORASMUCH as my compassionate and kind Father woke me up this morning, and started me on our way to living a free and full life of salvation in Him through Christ (Rom. 6:11); and

WHEREAS, I count it all joy to have the blessing of daily fellowship and intimacy with my Heavenly Father; of feasting on manna from Heaven, and enjoying a Beulah-Land experience with Elohim; and

WHEREAS, the significance of this moment is not wrapped up in who I am, but, WHOSE I am, and WHOM I serve and worship with a grateful and thankful heart: Elohim, Creator, God of gods; and

WHEREAS, Elohim is Here; He is mighty in my midst to deliver and save me from the oppressor, and there is no argument or question that His Almighty power is at work in my life in so many ways.

I DECREE AND DECLARE this Day 209 that

- yesterday's burden is just that - yesterday's (Zeph. 3: 18); I am now beautified and blessed from the bountiful supply of Elohim

- singing, shouting, gladness, and rejoicing are my weapons of spiritual destruction; and, like sharp arrows, they pierce the dark domain, and the enemy is cast out from me (Zeph. 3:15)

- my hands are not dropping, limp, or slack in battle; instead, the right hand of Elohim, who is majestic in power, graces and grips me to shatter the enemy (Ex. 15:6; 17:11, 12)

- Elohim is Here; sighing and sorrow are banished; there has been a spiritual seismic shaking and shifting, and I now enjoy a happy, joyful jubilee

- Elohim is Here; the barren bring forth, afflictions are undone, the dispersed by the hands of oppression are the gathered by the strong right arm of Elohim's power, and men shall speak well of me everywhere (Zeph. 3: 20), and for repentance, Elohim grants restoration and revival fully, finally, and forever.

BE IT THEREFORE RESOLVED by me this day that

- I will remain fearless in the fight for the faith because Elohim is Here

- I will ready myself with the weapons of my warfare, which are mighty through Elohim, to the pulling down of strongholds (2 Cor. 10: 4)

BY THE AUTHORITY OF ELOHIM, I DRIVE THESE PROPHETIC DECREES, DECLARATIONS, AND RESOLUTIONS AS ANCHORS AND STAKES IN THE GROUND; they are entrenched and established by the fruit of my lips (Prov. 13: 2;18: 21); they are granted Heavenly backing and benediction; the antagonisms of Satan against them are subject to rupture and ruin, and the light shines upon my ways (Job 22: 28). Elohim is Here!

In the ever-faithful, never-failing name of the Father, Son, and Holy Ghost! God in three Persons, blessed Trinity!

AMEN!

Day 210

FORASMUCH as I am blessed by my Sovereign Father to be alive today to enjoy the benefits and bestowments of His gracious hand extended to me; and

WHEREAS, I give joyous praise and thanksgiving to God for His abundant favor and kindness toward me today; I continue to feast on manna from Heaven; I enjoy fellowshipping with my Father daily, and I have been freshened by His power and presence in my midst; and

WHEREAS, I journey in the global village according to the dictates and direction of the Holy Ghost, who allows me to encounter and experience God in copious and glorious ways for spiritual stamina, strength, and supply, and I am not weary or worn out; instead, the oil of gladness and joy is upon me, and the refreshment I receive from God's hand fuels my appetite for more of Him; and

WHEREAS, Elohim is Here; He is mighty in my midst (Zeph. 3: 17); He is the center of my attraction, the core object of my affection, and the heart of my adulation.

I DECREE AND DECLARE this Day 210 that

- the Lord has cast my enemy out (Zeph. 3: 15); my worst days are behind me (Phil. 3: 13); today is my winning day (Rom. 8: 37), and my best days are ahead of me (Jer. 29: 11)

- Elohim is Here; He has mightily saved me (Zeph. 3: 15, 17), and the sanctifying, satisfying, and solidifying power of His Spirit living within me propels me to spiritual activation and occupation in the global village for His glory and honor

- I refuse to wallow in self-accusation and condemnation (Rom. 8: 1); instead, singing songs of Zion, shouting loud hosannas, and rejoicing with unspeakable joy to my Father (Zeph. 3: 14; 1 Pet. 1: 8) erupt from my spirit through the fruit of my lips into the atmosphere, and these weapons in my spiritual armory aggravate and agitate the dark domain into disarray and disorder

- Elohim is Here; He is mighty in the midst of my life; He has turned and reversed my captivity (Zeph. 3: 20), and the acclaim and praise of His name resounds and reverberates in the earth

- Elohim is Here; He is unassailable, unbeatable, unconquerable, and unstoppable, and through Him, I walk and war valiantly and victoriously for His righteous reign and Sovereign rule in the earth

BE IT THEREFORE RESOLVED by me this day that

- I remain wholly committed and devoted to the cause of the Kingdom of God - to proclaim the Gospel message of salvation through Jesus Christ to all

- I remain alert and attentive to the voice of the Spirit, and will not settle for carnal, cheap options that contaminate and corrupt the purity and truth of the glorious message of salvation to the world

BY THE ENABLEMENT OF THE HOLY GHOST, I ANCHOR THESE PROPHETIC DECREES, DECLARATIONS, AND RESOLUTIONS AS STAKES IN THE GROUND; they are firmly established by the power and warrant of my life-giving words (Prov. 13: 2; 18: 21); they are endorsed and energized by the open portals of Heaven; satanic resistance against them is pounded and pulverized by the power of Elohim, and the light shall shine upon my ways (Job 22: 28) because of Elohim!

In the endorsing and enduring name of the Father, Son, Holy Ghost! God in three Persons, blessed Trinity!

AND IT IS SO!

Day 211

FORASMUCH as my kind and loving Father has breathed His breath into my body today (Job 33: 4; Acts 17: 28), and by His grace, allowed me to see the dawn of a new day; and

WHEREAS, I arise today rejoicing with exceeding joy for the marvelous things that God has done for me, and the jubilation I have within is without doubt and question; and

WHEREAS, I can affirm and testify having experienced miraculous manifestations of God's glorious power in my life through spiritual breakthrough, deliverance, healing of body and spirit, triumph and victory; and

WHEREAS, my reality is wrapped up in as Psalmist's declaration: "When the Lord turned again the captivity of Zion, we were like them that dream, and our mouth was filled with laughter, and our tongues with singing" (126: 1, 2); and

WHEREAS, the sanctifying work of the Spirit continues in my life during my Christian journey; I remain on the Potter's wheel

(Jer. 18: 1-6), and am being "Processed to Perfection" by Him (Phil. 3: 12-14; Rom. 12: 1, 2).

I DECREE AND DECLARE this Day 211 that

- I do not pressure myself to expect sinless perfection in my life (Rom. 3: 23); mine is a life of process and progress (Rom. 7: 1-25), and today I choose to become more like Jesus

- I submit to the Process to Perfection, which is sanctification (Lev. 21: 8; 1 Thess. 4: 3), and lay my actions, thoughts and words on the altar (Rom. 12: 1) under subjection to the purifying work of the Spirit in me

- I will not rely upon what I hear, feel, or see; instead, like the caterpillar that turns into a butterfly, I will yield to the transforming power of Jesus who beautifies me from the inside out

- I push away and push back influences of evil that seek to seduce me to conform to corrupting and destroying standards for my life; instead, I passionately chase after the character that Christ wills for me

- I will not be overtaken or overrun by the challenges, conflicts and constraints I face in my life; instead, because I trust in God's ability to "perfect" what concerns me (Psa. 138 8; Rom. 8: 28), I surrender to being "Processed to Perfection".

BE IT THEREFORE RESOLVED by me this day that

- I remain surrendered to the beautifying and sanctifying work that being " Processed to Perfection" yields in my life

- I reject and resist the temptation to conform; rather, I remain malleable and moldable in the Potter's hand, who specializes in the process to perfection

BY VIRTUE OF MY POSITION OF SANCTIFICATION BY THE FATHER, I DRIVE THESE PROPHETIC DECREES, DECLARATIONS, AND RESOLUTIONS AS STAKES IN THE GROUND; by the fruit of my lips (Prov. 13: 2), they are established and settled; the holy Court of Heaven affirms and approves them; diabolical activities against them are blown of course by the wind of the Spirit, and returned to sender as rebuked and rejected, and the light shall shine upon my ways (Job 22: 28) as I am "Processed to Perfection".

In the processing-to-perfecting name of the Father, Son, and Holy Ghost! God in three Persons, blessed Trinity!

AND IT IS SO!

Day 212

FORASMUCH as it is my Sovereign Father's good pleasure to touch me with His tender hand of compassion, grace and mercy to arise from overnight rest to the dawning of a new day with life in Him (Acts 17: 28); and

WHEREAS, words are inadequate and insufficient to describe the gratitude, thanksgiving and praise that I have toward the Lord for empowering and enriching me on my Christian journey in the earth as His child; and

WHEREAS, my citizenship in Heaven (Phil. 3: 20); I fellowship in the Spirit (2 Cor. 13: 14), I am an heir of the Father, and a joint heir with the Son (Rom. 8: 17), and I worship God in spirit and in truth (Jn. 4: 23; Phil. 3: 3); and

WHEREAS, as clay in the hands of the Master Potter (Isa. 64: 8; Jer. 18: 1-6), and as the sanctifying work of the Holy Spirit on my inner man continues until the coming of the Lord Jesus (1 Thess. 5: 23), I am being "Processed to Perfection" (Phil. 3: 12-14; Rom. 12: 1, 2), and the possibilities and potential of the final, perfected product fills me with expectancy and hope in the Son.

I DECREE AND DECLARE this Day 212 that

- I will not take short cuts to perfection; they stunt and stymie the finished product; instead, I will stay on the Potter's wheel and become Processed to Perfection

- I will allow the Processor to fashion, refine and shape me, and not rebel or resist His handiwork as He completes a finished vessel that will bring Him glory and honor in the earth

- as flies in the ointment (Eccl. 10: 1) annoy, devalue and spoil it, I closely look within myself and take cautionary and corrective action so that being "Processed to Perfection" in me is not devalued or diminished

- demonic insinuations and suggestions have no part or place in me; I rebuff and rebuke the wiles and works of the evil one against me; being "Processed to Perfection" is and will be the Father's plan and pleasure to do so in me

- I lay the drama, pain and shame of my yesterday on the altar of sacrifice, and the fire thereon emblazons the signature of the Potter on me: "Processed to Perfection".

BE IT THEREFORE RESOLVED by me this day that

- I take joy and pleasure in being "Processed to Perfection" by the sanctifying power of God in my life

- I will constantly make progress in life through Christ, and being "Processed to Perfection" is my direction and ultimate destination

BY VIRTUE OF THE CONSECRATING WORK OF THE SPIRIT IN ME, I DRIVE THESE PROPHETIC

DECREES, DECLARATIONS, AND RESOLUTIONS AS STAKES IN THE GROUND; I speak their establishment by the fruit of my lips (Prov. 13: 2; 18: 21); the Master Potter of Heaven affirms and confirms the finished, perfected product; the evil one's devices against them are handcuffed and halted, and the light shines upon my ways (Job 22: 28). I am being "Processed to Perfection".

In the living and loving name of the Father, Son, and Holy Ghost! God in three Persons, blessed Trinity!

AND IT IS SO!

Day 213

FORASMUCH as it is by the Divine Providence and Sovereignty of God that I am alive and well today with a sound mind, and the activity of my limbs and senses; and

WHEREAS, I arise very driven and passionate about telling others about the Gospel of life and love found in Jesus alone (Jn. 3: 16, 17); and

WHEREAS, praise, prayer and worship, and the Word of God are the core and essential reasons why I have a sense of direction and purpose in my life; I am feasting from a limitless supply, I drink from the Fountain that never runs dry, I joyfully and jubilantly dwell in the presence of Jehovah lifting my hands and heart to Him who is worthy to be adored, glorified, honored, and magnified for the marvelous and wondrous manifestations of His power toward me; and

WHEREAS, I am being "Processed to Perfection" (Phil. 3: 12-14; Rom. 12: 1, 2), a journey of consecration and sanctification by the Holy Ghost in my inner man, the results of which yield fruit unto righteousness, and which will remain (Jn. 15: 16).

I DECREE AND DECLARE this Day 213 that

- I am not abandoned, despised, or rejected, as the devil will suggest (Jn. 8: 44); instead, God delights in me (Zeph. 3: 17), desires my ultimate good according to His plans for me (Jer. 29: 11), and lavishes the balm of care and love upon my life (Psa. 31: 7; Rom. 8: 35, 37-39)

- being "Processed to Perfection" is not without its levels of aches, pain, and tears (Psa. 42: 3); however, because God knows and sees the beautiful end of my story, I choose to stay in the process with Him (Psa. 66: 12)

- although I am being "Processed to Perfection", and will have to endure some things (Heb. 12: 8), I will still be found exalting, honoring, and lifting up the name of Jesus (Psa. 34: 1-3), and living to bring credit and value to the Kingdom of God in the earth

- I will stay encouraged in the process, and the Master Potter's safe and skillful hands will fashion and shape me to an honorable and pleasing vessel (Jer. 18: 4) - there will be glory and a glow after this

- I speak confidence, excitement, faith, gain, and hope to myself, and I cancel and silence every innuendo and voice of Satan who seeks to detract and distract me (Jn. 10: 10) from being "Processed to Perfection".

BE IT THEREFORE RESOLVED by me this day that

- I remain in the hands of the Master, whose wonders of skill and workmanship upon me yields a prized possession

- I remain a work in process and progress, and, as a living sacrifice, I will seek to be an acceptable and pleasing offering to God at all times

BY VIRTUE OF THE RIGHTEOUSNESS WITHIN ME BECAUSE OF JESUS CHRIST, I DRIVE THESE PROPHETIC DECREES, DECLARATIONS, AND RESOLUTIONS AS FOUNDATION STAKES IN THE GROUND; they are established by the fruit of my lips (Prov. 13: 2; 18: 21); they are stamped endorsed by the seal of Heaven; satanic devices set against them are subject to disruption and utter destruction, and the light shall shine upon my ways (Job 22: 28) as I. am "Processed to Perfection".

In the peerless, perfecting, and priceless name of the Father, Son, and Holy Ghost! God in three Persons, blessed Trinity!

AND IT IS SO!

Day 214

FORASMUCH as God, Creator, Sovereign Ruler, and Upholder of all things, has graciously caused me to arise today to enjoy and experience life and living in Him because of Jesus my Savior (Acts 17: 28); and

WHEREAS, this is a great day of celebration for me; I have the honor and privilege to seek the face of God during dark and difficult days in the earth; look at what the Lord has done (Psa. 118: 23); and

WHEREAS, God continues to anoint me with an audacious spirit, and He authorizes me with grace and power to pray and make a difference in the global village; and

WHEREAS, when I look back over my life, I would not have thought that God would raise me up as a radical, righteous Christian in the earth, and I seize every moment of opportunity to blaze spiritual frontiers and territories for the glory and honor of the Kingdom of God in the earth; and

WHEREAS, the Lord knew me before the foundation of the world, and in the High and Supreme Court of Heaven He called me for usefulness in the earth.

I DECREE AND DECLARE this Day 214 that

- I am who I am because of the Father, and I proclaim His greatness, power, glory, victory, and majesty; He is exalted as head above all (1 Chron. 29: 11), and He ONLY will receive service and worship from me (Deut. 6: 13; Lu. 4: 8)

- I celebrate who I am because of Jesus, the Son, and I proclaim His life-giving, life-transforming power in the earth, and the Father will draw men unto Him when His Son Jesus is lifted up (Jn. 12: 32)

- I celebrate because of the Holy Ghost; I am enabled, engaged, equipped, and empowered for end-time impact and soul-winning in the earth by His dynamic power

- I celebrate; my prayers disturb, disrupt, and disorient every demonic spirit from the dark domain

- I celebrate; the river of God's presence in my life runs deep with fertility and fruitfulness (Ezek. 37: 8-10); the Mantle will not be dropped by me (2 Ki. 2: 12-15); I launch into the deep from the shoreline to catch men (Lu. 5: 1-5); I tear the roof off for the manifestation of miracles (Mk. 2: 1-12), where it will undoubtedly be said, "Elohim is Here" (Zeph. 3: 14-20); I am being "Processed to Perfection" (Phil. 3: 12-14; Rom. 12: 1, 2)

- I celebrate; I will flow, go, grow, and overthrow, and the world will know to whom I belong

- I celebrate; I am well-able and stable, and I am refined and refreshed by the dainties from His table

BE IT THEREFORE RESOLVED by me this day that

- I choose to be known as a foot-stomping, hand-clapping, heart-swelling, neighbor-loving, celebrator-of-Jesus, whose nail-scarred handprints are all over me

- I remain a keeper of the covenant-relationship with my Father, who takes great delight in me, and rejoices with singing over my deliverance (Zeph. 3: 17)

BY REASON OF THE RIGHTEOUSNESS IN ME BECAUSE OF JESUS, I DRIVE THESE PROPHETIC DECREES, DECLARATIONS, AND RESOLUTIONS AS STAKES IN THE GROUND; they have the full backing of Heaven's Triune Order; Satan, his cohorts, and hordes of evil scamper and scatter because of the power of Jesus' blood, and the light shall shine upon my ways (Job 22: 28).

In the celebrated and commemorated name of the Father, Son, and Holy Ghost! God in three Persons, blessed Trinity!

AND IT IS SO!

Day 215

FORASMUCH as I am alive because of the gracious hand and sure mercies of my Heavenly Father to experience a day that will never come my way again with its challenges, changes, and choices; and

WHEREAS, I continue to joyfully celebrate and commemorate the blessings and bounty of God upon my life as a Christian in the earth; and

WHEREAS, as God continues to "Process me to Perfection", the possibilities of His mighty hand of Providence upon the sacrifice of my life (Rom. 12: 1, 2), and the sacrifices of praise by the fruit of my lips to His name (Heb. 13: 15) are endless; and

WHEREAS, as I faithfully journey on in the power of the Spirit, I am filled with anticipation, excitement and a holy expectancy, because the day of God's manifested glory and power in me is here, and I am being "Processed to Perfection" by Him (Phil. 3: 12-14; Rom. 12: 1, 2).

I DECREE AND DECLARE this Day 215 that

- by the eye of a fixed and focused faith in Jehovah God, sharp spiritual discernment and insight is heightened in me as He processes me to perfection (Heb. 5: 14)

- as I am being "Processed to Perfection", I surrender to the cleansing and sanctifying power of the Word spoken to me (Jn. 15: 3); the motivating impact to fulfill His will through me (Phil. 2: 13), and the quickening power of the Spirit that will cause me to be a change-agent and a difference-maker in the earth (2 Cor. 3: 6)

- being "Processed to Perfection" means obtaining the ultimate adornment of God's beauty and excellence in my life; therefore, I refuse to abort His processing to perfection in me, thereby causing a miscarriage of the finished vessel of honor God has planned for me to be in the earth (2 Tim. 2: 21)

- being "Processed to Perfection" also means enduring the threats and menaces of Satan against me, whose chief aim is to steal, kill, and destroy me (Jn. 10: 10), but his tactics and taunts are subject to the One processing me to perfection, and they shall not prevail (Isa. 54: 17)

- I will fervently pray (Jam. 5: 16) during the process, passionately praise Him (Psa. 86: 12) during the process, be the right person (Rom. 12: 1, 2) for Him during the process, and walk as He walked (1 Jn. 2: 6), and by His power, I will live my days in the earth according to His plans, promises and purposes (Jer. 29: 11)

BE IT THEREFORE RESOLVED by me this day that

- I remain under the mighty hand and help of Jehovah, whose delight is to complete, finish, and perfect that which concerns me (Psa. 138: 8)

- I will resist the temptation to quit the process when I get tested and tried, God has a safe processing plan for my perfection

BY VIRTUE OF MY DESIRE AND YEARNING TO STAY IN THE PROCESSING-TO-PERFECTION PLAN OF GOD, I HAMMER THESE PROPHETIC DECREES, DECLARATIONS, AND RESOLUTIONS AS STAKES IN THE GROUND; by the fruit of my lips, I speak their establishment and fulfillment (Prov. 13: 2; 18: 21); they are sanctioned and sealed by the Order of Heaven; the diabolical acts of the Devil against them are intercepted and incinerated in fire and brimstone, and the light shall shine upon my ways (Job 22: 28) because I remain committed to being "Processed to Perfection".

In the exalting, exciting, and exhilarating name of the Father, Son, and Holy Ghost! God in three Persons, blessed Trinity!

AND IT IS SO!

Day 216

FORASMUCH as it was by the faithful, merciful, and powerful hand and love of my Heavenly Father that death behaved itself throughout the night, and that I arose from rest to see another day with a sound mind, my senses, and the use of my limbs (Acts 17: 28); and

WHEREAS, I rejoice because of the wonder of God's hand upon my life, and for the honor of representing the King in the global village as a citizen of His Kingdom; and

WHEREAS, I am being "Processed to Perfection" (Phil. 3: 12-14; Rom. 12: 1, 2), a journey to completion, fulness, and total transformation by the sanctifying hand of the Master; and

WHEREAS, it is the Father's good pleasure and will that I am fully developed and entire, lacking nothing (Jam. 1: 4), and the process to that place of perfection in Him demands that I present my body as a living sacrifice that is pleasing and acceptable to Him (Rom. 12: 1).

I DECREE AND DECLARE this Day 216 that

- no sacrifice I make of myself on the altar of "Processing to Perfection" will fall to the ground in ruin, scrap, or waste; instead, the "Process" will yield a diadem (Isa. 62: 3), a jewel, a treasure in me that no one but God saw and still sees

- by being "Processed to Perfection", the cleansing and purifying work of the Holy Ghost will ignite a burning, fiery flame of passion and power within me, and the world will know by my living that I have been with Jesus (Acts 4: 13)

- I release myself from the bondage and enslavement of my past; being "Processed to Perfection" will peel, strip and wash away the dross and the dung of yesterday's hurt, pain, and torment, and the healing Balm of Gilead applied to my spirit lifts me from the ash and trash heap to beauty and radiance in Him (Isa. 61: 3)

- the Devil thought he had me captive and imprisoned by his evil, sinister seductions and suggestions (Jn. 8: 44), but the fowler's snare is broken, and I am escaped like a bird (Psa. 124: 7) to the processing place that perfects me

- the Lord will be exalted and extolled, lauded and lifted up, and, by "going through", I will receive the revelation that being harnessed, held, and helped by Him during "Processing to Perfection" produces anthems of psalms, and hymns and spiritual songs, singing and melody in my heart to the Lord (Eph. 5: 19).

BE IT THEREFORE RESOLVED by me this day that

- I determine to praise Him where I am going - to completion, healing, and wholeness through "Processing to Perfection"

- I remain focused on the finished article - a man/woman of God who will shine as the noon day sun, having been "Processed to Perfection", nothing broken, and nothing wasted

BY VIRTUE OF MY HEALED AND WHOLE STATE IN CHRIST, I DRIVE THESE PROPHETIC DECREES, DECLARATIONS, AND RESOLUTIONS AS ANCHORS AND STAKES IN THE GROUND; they are established and settled in the earth by the fruit of our lips (Prov. 13: 2; 18: 21); Heaven backs and blesses their fulfillment and fruitfulness; satanic traps and tricks set against them are consigned to the eternal flames of Hell fire, and the light shines upon my ways (Job 22: 28c) as I am being "Processed to Perfection".

In the amazing and astounding name of the Father, Son, and Holy Ghost! One God in three Persons, blessed Trinity!

AND IT IS SO!

Day 217

FORASMUCH as the steadfast care and compassion of my loving Heavenly Father were my blessings during the night, and they caused me to awaken from rest to the dawning of a day that I have never seen, nor will ever see again; and

WHEREAS, this is a day to joyfully proclaim the goodness of the Lord to the world; I have journeyed in the Spirit under His glorious power and presence as His representative in the earth; and

WHEREAS, my Father has positioned me to experience wave after wave of the demonstration of His Almighty power in my life, and then I have the honor of impacting others my God's enablement and grace; and

WHEREAS, as I rely totally upon God, He works with and through me, and I am being "Processed to Perfection" (Phil. 3:12-14; Rom. 12:1, 2), a holy place, a sanctified place, a place from which I can give witness to development and refinement to the place of completion as I give myself as a living sacrifice (Rom. 12: 1, 2),

I DECREE AND DECLARE this Day 217 that

- I lay my thoughts, actions, and words on the altar of sacrifice, and the purifying and sanctifying work of the Holy Spirit processes me into a product of value and worth in the earth for my King (Jam. 1: 4) - I am in no hurry to leave God's process upon my life; rather, I decisively, deliberately and determinately wait upon Him for His timing and perfecting, without a murmur (Isa. 64: 4)

- I will be creditable and dependable for the causes of the Kingdom in the earth; therefore, I will not avoid or shy away from the difficult and hard lessons and places that shape my character whilst being "Processed to Perfection" (2 Tim. 2: 3-5)

- being "Processed to Perfection" will open doors and opportunities for maximum Kingdom effectiveness for me in the global village, despite adversity and hostility from Satan (1 Cor. 16: 9)

- by my subjection, submission, and surrender to being "Processed to Perfection", I will give affirmation to the work and worth of the process - nothing I learn will fall to the ground in failure (Rom. 8: 28; Phil. 1: 6)

BE IT THEREFORE RESOLVED by me this day that

- I remain compliant to the commands of God upon me as He processes me to perfection

- I remain reliant upon the faithfulness of God during the process to perfection, knowing that He delights in the complete fulfillment of His plans and purposes in my life (Jer. 29: 11)

BY THE AUTHORITY OF THE GRACE THE FATHER GIVES ME, I DRIVE THESE PROPHETIC DECREES, DECLARATIONS, AND RESOLUTIONS AS STAKES IN THE GROUND; they are complete and established in the earth by the fruit of my lips (Prov. 13: 2; 18: 21); Heaven backs, blesses, and braces them; demonic antagonism against them is disarmed and dismembered, and the light shall shine upon my ways as God "Processes me to Perfection (Job 22 28).

In the strong and sturdy name of the Father, Son, and Holy Ghost! God in three Persons, blessed Trinity!

AND IT IS SO!

Day 218

FORASMUCH as this is the day which the Lord has made (Psa. 118: 24); He has raised me this new day with life because of Him (Acts 17: 28); and

WHEREAS, there is no better time like now to give glory, honor, majesty, praise, and thanksgiving to the Lord my God Most High, for the marvelous and wonderful things that He has done for me; and

WHEREAS, today marks the dawning of a new opportunities and privileges for me as God's child to be effective, impactful and influential for the King in the global village, and, as I remain on the crucible of God's fashioning, shaping, and sharpening, my encounter with Him exposes me to a dynamic of the Kingdom that makes me different and distinctive in the world - "The Power of the Anointing" (Luke 4: 18; Acts 2: 16-21); and

WHEREAS, "The Power of the Anointing" gives attention and attraction to Jesus Christ, who, by the power of the anointing, lived among men in the earth and impacted everyone everywhere He went, teaching, preaching the Gospel of the Kingdom, and healing all manner of sickness and all manner of disease among the people (Matt. 4: 23); and

WHEREAS, this is my mandate, ministry and mission in the earth, and God has graced and gifted me with "The Power of the Anointing" to effect change for the King in the global village.

I DECREE AND DECLARE this Day 218 that

- as "The Power of the Anointing", by and through the Holy Ghost (Acts 1: 8), is the difference-maker and dynamic promised to the Church by Jesus before He ascended to the Father (Acts 2: 39) , I avail and open myself to all the power He has made available to me (Lu.10: 19), so that, like Jesus my model, I can blaze a trail of Gospel impact in the earth (Lu. 4: 18)

- I subject and surrender myself to the molding and work of the Spirit in my inner man, and His purifying and sanctifying work will produce in me a vessel free of carnal debris, dregs, and dross (2 Tim. 2: 21)

- by "The Power of the Anointing", I rattle, shake, and startle the ways and wiles of the Devil, who busily seeks to devour (1 Pet. 5: 8), and his limited authority as the prince of the power of the air (Eph. 2: 2) will have no effect on the Gospel spanning the globe with power

- by "The Power of the Anointing", chaos and disorder overruns and overtakes every satanic assault and attack against me, and the anointing by which I function will quash all forms, religiosity, and systems designed to create apostasy and idolatry (2 Cor. 10: 5)

- "The Power of the Anointing" is the secret by which I will be known in the world, and this is that (Acts 2: 16) which will be demonstrated and manifested through God's sons, daughters, young men, old men, servants, and handmaidens (Acts 2: 17, 18), and the poor, the brokenhearted, the captives, the blind, and the bruised will experience encounters of the Holy Ghost-kind that will result in deliverance, healing, salvation, and total transformation for the glory of God (Lu. 4: 18).

BE IT THEREFORE RESOLVED by me this day that

- I will remain an uncommon child of God, with an uncommon anointing, that causes uncommon change in the earth

- I do not seek the affirmation, applause, or approval of man; I will perpetuate and proclaim the full Gospel of Jesus Christ in the earth by "The Power of the Anointing"

BY THE AUTHORITY THAT GOD'S ANOINTING UPON ME AFFORDS, I DRIVE THESE PROPHETIC DECREES, DECLARATIONS, AND RESOLUTIONS AS ANCHORS AND STAKES IN THE GROUND; I am persuaded that they are enlivened and established in the earth by the power of my tongue (Prov. 13: 2; 18: 21); the Eternal Triune Godhead grants them holy assent; the devil can do nothing to stop or stymie them, and the light shall shine upon my ways (Job 22: 28), which are graced by "The Power of the Anointing".

In the governing, guarding, and guiding name of the Father, Son, and Holy Ghost! Triune God, blessed Trinity!

AND IT IS SO!

Day 219

FORASMUCH as it was my Heavenly Father's good pleasure to allow my body the privilege of breathing, living, and moving on this new day (Acts 17: 28); and

WHEREAS, this is a great day to praise the Lord for His care, goodness, and kindness toward me, and to make mention that His name is exalted in the earth through me (Isa. 12: 4) is my greatest delight; and

WHEREAS, I am filled with excitement and joy to have the honor and joy of connecting with the Lord in private devotion for usefulness for Him in the global village; and

WHEREAS, God is moving by His Spirit and power in the earth; He is demonstrating His Almightiness through signs and wonders as He moves in my life, and the best is yet to come (Jer. 29: 11); and

WHEREAS, God has raised an army and a battalion of radical, relentless, and righteous soldiers in the global village, of which I am a part, and I am positioned for end-time Gospel impact, a recipient of "The Power of the Anointing" (Lu. 4: 18; Acts 2: 16-21).

I DECREE AND DECLARE this Day 219 that

- "The Power of the Anointing" raises the banner and the standard of the righteous causes of God in the global village, and by this power working in and through me, I boldly seize territory for the King and His Kingdom, and call forth the establishment of His prominence (Psa. 24: 1-3; 89: 11)

- I live today saturated, smeared and soaked in "The Power of the Anointing", and by this unction, when I associate with people, burdens will be lifted, and yokes destroyed by reason of the anointing (Isa. 10: 27)

- "The Power of the Anointing" abiding in, and activating through me, causes terror and torment to the designs and devices of the evil one, and his limited power in the air is subject to the dominion and rule of the Sovereign God, a man of war (Ex. 15: 3), whose dominion is further, higher, and mightier than the gods of the earth, who are but carved idols (Isa. 42: 8)

- "The Power of the Anointing" will break forth in every place where I function in the earth (Acts 2: 17, 18), and the unction of audacity and authority in the Holy Ghost will obstruct and obliterate principalities and the powers of darkness that attempt to erect strongholds of evil

- God Most High will be exalted, glorified, and magnified through me in the earth, and "The Power of the Anointing" is set upon me as it was in the days of the 1st Century Church - energized, organized, and mobilized by the impetus and impulse of the Holy Ghost.

BE IT THEREFORE RESOLVED by me this day that

- I remain radical, ready and refined by "The Power of the Anointing" to reach and reap a ripe harvest of souls for the King in the earth

- I remain dedicated, devoted and dutiful to the Master's call and commission, and "this is that" (Acts 2: 16), "The Power of the Anointing", which I embrace

BY VIRTUE OF MY AUTHORITY BECAUSE OF "THE POWER OF THE ANOINTING", I DRIVE THESE PROPHETIC DECREES, DECLARATIONS, AND RESOLUTIONS AS STAKES IN THE GROUND; I believe in them and their establishment in the earth; the Lord of the battle and the war endorses them; satanic schemes and systems set against them are a puff of wind, and the light shines upon my ways (Job 22: 28), because of "The Power of the Anointing".

In the indomitable, indestructible, and invincible name of the Father, Son, and Holy Ghost! Triune Godhead, blessed Trinity!

AND IT IS SO!

Day 220

FORASMUCH as God my loving Heavenly Father has touched me with His finger of love, breathed His breath into my body (Job 33: 4), and caused me to arise today to function and have life in Him (Acts 17: 28); and

WHEREAS, God has been good to me, and I am glad to enter into His presence of God for daily devotions, fellowship with Him, prayer to Him, to praise Him, and to feast on the Word of God; and

WHEREAS, as with the Israelites (Ex. 13: 21, 22), the cloud of God's glory and presence dwells powerfully in my life, and the impact, influence, and weight of the glory that He has manifested in me is sometimes beyond description and explanation (Rom.11: 33); and

WHEREAS, there are no options or substitutes to what I am experiencing in the Lord's presence; His glory in my life is the deep yearning of my heart, and by this, I am living and witnessing the impact of holy unction that Jesus spoke of in Luke 4: 18:   "The Spirit of the Lord is upon me..."; and

WHEREAS, this is no new phenomenon; rather, "this is that" (Acts 2: 16) which has engulfed me in unstoppable dimensions of power: "The Power of the Anointing", a baptism that defies the human intellect, and which is the outpouring of the Holy Spirit of God that Jesus promised to the 120 that gathered in the Upper Room (Acts 1: 8).

I DECREE AND DECLARE this Day 220 that

- I do not apologize for this place and position of power; I am authorized and emboldened by "The Power of the Anointing", and this end-time unction graces me to have effect and impact upon others in the global village for the glory of God

- I do not regret making myself available to "The Power of the Anointing"; I am anointed and appointed to live and walk in Holy Ghost power in the earth, so that yokes of bondage will be destroyed (Isa. 10: 27)

- "The Power of the Anointing" pushes back the dark and destructive ways and works of Satan, and his taunts and torments against me are barred and blocked from causing mayhem and upheaval in my life (Isa. 54: 17)

- by "The Power of the Anointing", I boldly speak healing to the broken heart that needs mending, deliverance to the imprisoned by sin, sight to the blind by the traps and tricks of the Devil, and the liberty to laugh, live and love again to the battered and bruised (Lu. 4: 18)

- it is "The Power of the Anointing" that will use me to command stormy seas to calm and peace in this lives of those with whom I associate, and the unction of the Spirit causes a holy respect and reverence for the Omnipotence and Sovereignty of God.

BE IT THEREFORE RESOLVED by me this day that

- I remain fully aware and cognizant of my utter dependance upon God in the earth, and to be immersed in "The Power of the Anointing" for maximum Kingdom effectiveness

- I continue to live by, and remain loyal to, the precepts and tenets of the Christian faith based on God's holy Word, to the complete rejection and renunciation of all other creeds, dogmas, and ideologies that advance and promote the causes of systems that are unfriendly to the grace that God gives

BY THE AUTHORITY OF "THE POWER OF THE ANOINTING", I DRIVE THESE PROPHETIC DECREES, DECLARATIONS, AND RESOLUTIONS AS STAKES IN THE GROUND; by the fruit of my lips, we speak their existence and establishment (Prov. 13: 2; 18: 21); they are supported by Heaven's limitless source and supply; demonic interference against them are subject to desolation and destruction, and the light shall shine upon my ways (Job 22: 28) because of "The Power of the Anointing".

In the Sovereign and Supreme name of the Father, Son, and Holy Ghost! God in three Persons, blessed Trinity!

AND IT IS SO!

Day 221

FORASMUCH as the angel of the Lord encamped about me throughout the night (Psa 34: 7), and He said "No" to death; and then, God touched me to arise from rest to see His goodness in the land of the living (Psa. 27: 13); and

WHEREAS, my soul magnifies the Lord, and my spirit rejoices in God my Savior (Lu. 1: 46, 47) for the wonder of it all - just to think that God loves me the way He does: unconditionally, unquestionably, and unreservedly (Rom. 5: 8; 8: 35; 2 Thess. 2: 16); and

WHEREAS, I am a very grateful and thankful child of God for the blessing and privilege to enjoy sweet fellowship with Him in His holy presence, where His glory and power is manifested in abundant measure; and

WHEREAS, it is delightful to encounter Him and grow in grace and in the knowledge of Jesus Christ 2 Pet. 3: 18); the impulse and momentum of the Holy Ghost sustains me and prompts me to live audaciously by His authority; and

WHEREAS, Luke 1: 48; Acts 1: 8; 2: 16-21 continues to be fulfilled in my life, and God has engulfed and immersed me in "The Power of the Anointing"!

I DECREE AND DECLARE this Day 221 that

- I am called by God (Rom. 8: 30), and function by faith under the validation and warrant of "The Power of the Anointing"; He has called me, and He equips me

- I am chosen by God (Jn. 15: 16); His assignment and purposes for me in the earth will be fulfilled, and "The Power of the Anointing" is my fire and fuel to fulfill the work of the King and His Kingdom (Jn. 14: 12)

- I am commissioned of God (Lu. 9: 2) in the nations of the world, or wherever God plants me; and by "The Power of the Anointing", bodies are healed, cancers disappear and dry up, disorders are brought into proper creative order, and everybody I reach will be affected and influenced by the anointing

- I live and walk in the confidence of my convictions; it is "The Power of the Anointing" that makes the difference in my life, and no traces of arrogance and haughtiness will infect the anointing that God has placed upon my life

- I am courageous, and have the mindset of a champion (Josh. 1: 6, 7, 9; Acts 4: 13), and by "The Power of the Anointing", the hordes of hell are shaken, and they shudder to the core by the bold, courageous, and daring unction upon me, and they are powerless to stop me (Acts 6: 10).

BE IT THEREFORE RESOLVED by me this day that

- I remain sober and vigilant in the battleground, for to whom much is given, much is required (Lu. 12: 48)

- I remain keenly aware and sensitive to the voice of the Spirit; it is ONLY by "The Power of the Anointing" will the causes of the King prevail in the earth

BY THE AUTHORITY OF MY KINGLY AND PRIESTLY POSITION WITH THE FATHER (Rev. 1: 6), I DRIVE THESE PROPHETIC DECREES, DECLARATIONS, AND RESOLUTIONS AS STAKES IN THE GROUND; they are established and have their existence by the fruit of my lips (Prov. 13: 2; 18: 21); Heaven's Court seals and signs their assent; the minions of Satan are mangled and mutilated by "The Power of the Anointing", and the light shines upon my ways (Job 22; 28). The anointing makes the difference (Isa. 10: 27).

In the vanquishing and vindicating name of the Father, Son, and Holy Ghost! Triune God head, blessed Trinity!

AND IT IS SO!

Day 222

FORASMUCH as the Lord's compassion, faithfulness, and tender mercies (Lam. 3: 22, 23) are mine this new day; I have my being in Him (Acts 17: 28); and

WHEREAS, I exalt and extol the Lord of glory for the great and marvelous things He has done for me; I enjoy sweet fellowship with my Heavenly Father, my faith is fortified, I fare and feast sumptuously from Heaven's bountiful supply, and His banner over me has been and is love (S. Sol. 2: 4); and

WHEREAS, I have high-fever, intense anticipation and expectation of what God will do in, to, and through me; and

WHEREAS, God has not failed to demonstrate and manifest His power in my life; the best is yet to come, and I align myself and come into agreement with the Holy Ghost, who emboldens and empowers me for Kingdom service in the earth; and

WHEREAS, "The Power of the Anointing" is upon me; this dynamic of the Holy Ghost is the firepower of my life, and by Him, and through Him, I go forth conquering (Rev. 6: 2).

I DECREE AND DECLARE this Day 222 that

- "The Power of the Anointing" graces me to weather storms that assail me, and rather than sink under the pressure of it all, Holy Ghost unction within me lifts me to the harbor and haven of safety (Psa. 107: 30)

- it is the Father's good pleasure and will to use me as a vessel of honor for His Kingdom in the earth (2 Cor. 4: 7; 2 Tim. 2: 21), therefore, by "The Power of the Anointing", I function by faith in accordance to the commands of the Lord, and I will not allow my usefulness for Him to be compromised, contaminated, or corrupted (Eccl. 10: 1) by anything or anyone, in any way, at anytime

- "The Power of the Anointing", resident within me, will attract opposition and resistance from evil and wicked spirits of the dark domain; however, the designs and devices of the Devil will not prevail or prosper against me (Isa. 54: 17), and my Sovereign King reigns over all (Ex. 15: 18; Psa. 47: 8; 93: 1; 146: 10)

- I am not faithless or fearful of anyone or anything; instead, "The Power of the Anointing" drapes and envelopes me with a spiritual backbone and boldness, and my utter dependence upon the Holy Ghost, and faith in God's ability to do anything (Eph. 3: 20), is the secret to my bravery

- God's Kingdom will flourish in the four corners of the earth (Dan. 7: 14), and as a king and priest with Him (Rev. 1: 6), I will exercise my rightful authority and dominion (Psa. 8: 6; Lu. 10: 19); and because of "The Power of the Anointing", reports of my will cause my enemies to tremble and be in anguish of me.

BE IT THEREFORE RESOLVED by me this day that

- I will not rest or relax my stance under God's holy order, and I remain placed and positioned for occupation in the earth to honor and glorify the King and His Kingdom

- I will not resort to carnal, fleshly means or methods in my service for the Master (Lu. 19: 13); instead, I employ all things that pertain to life and godliness given to me by the Father to fulfill His will (2 Pet. 1: 3)

BY THE AUTHORITY GIVEN TO ME BY THE HOLY GHOST, I DRIVE THESE PROPHETIC DECREES, DECLARATIONS, AND RESOLUTIONS AS PILLARS AND STAKES IN THE GROUND; they are established and set in the earth by the words I speak (Prov. 13: 2; 18: 21); Heaven's holy Court affirms and approves them; satanic resistance against them is pushed back, plundered and pulverized to dust, and the light shines upon my ways (Job 22: 28) as I function by "The Power of the Anointing".

In the Eminent and Eternal name of the Father, Son, and Holy Ghost! God in three Persons, blessed Trinity!

AND IT IS SO!

Day 223

FORASMUCH as my Sovereign God and Father extended compassion and grace to me today to arise to see a day that I have never seen before, and will never see again; and

WHEREAS, being alive to see the dawning of a new day signals and speaks that it is pregnant with possibilities and potential for me as a citizen of the Kingdom of God in the earth; and

WHEREAS, I joyfully and wholeheartedly embrace the mandate and mission to me from God through Jesus Christ my Savior, and by the power of the Holy Spirit, I have the privilege take the message of the Gospel to a world that is decaying and degenerating in sin; and

WHEREAS, because God has lifted me out of the mire of sin through salvation, and transformed me by the cleansing power of Jesus' blood, I do not see myself as a Christian existing and living in the earth in a bubble and a vacuum, merely going through the minutia, the motions and the mundane of church; and

WHEREAS, God has a better way for me as His disciple in the global village, and that is, to gladly herald the joyful sound of life in Christ Jesus - a call and commission to "Go into all the world, and preach the Gospel to every creature" (Mark 16: 15).

I DECREE AND DECLARE this Day 223 that

- I have a message of hope from the Lord; therefore, I rise from spiritual sleep and slumber (Prov. 24: 30-34), buckle up my shoes, dust myself off from church as usual, and I get started reaching people, and teaching and preaching to the lost the glorious message of the Gospel to the whosoever (Jn. 3: 16)

- I will not sit idly by and watch people degenerate in sin (Ezek. 33: 6, 7); I blow the trumpet of warning to lost souls that the "night is far spent, and the day is at hand to cast off the works of darkness and to put on the armor of light" (Rom. 13: 12)

- as a laborer in the Gospel vineyard, I set myself to keenly listen to the voice of the Spirit as He downloads the who/what/why/where/when strategy and vision for end-time proclamation of the Gospel of Jesus Christ in the earth

- I take fresh courage and strength, and a renewed energy and excitement in the Holy Ghost to maximize doors of opportunity (1 Cor. 6: 9) to spread the life-changing, life-transforming power of Jesus to all (Matt. 28: 19, 20)

- I push back all personal barriers and blockages that prevent me from heralding the joyful sound, and I choose to engage in my Gospel assignment for the King and the Kingdom at all times.

BE IT THEREFORE RESOLVED by me this day that

- as God gifts and graces me (Jn. 4: 34), I embrace the challenge from Jesus (Mark 16: 15) for maximum Kingdom effectiveness in the earth

- wanting to hear the Lord's "well done" (Matt. 25: 23), I accept my responsibility as a laborer for the King to populate Heaven and plunder hell by "occupying" until Jesus comes (Luke 19: 13)

BY THE AUTHORITY OF MY CALL FROM JESUS (Mark 16: 15), I DRIVE THESE DECREES, DECLARATIONS, AND RESOLUTIONS AS STAKES IN THE GROUND; by the fruit of my lips (Prov. 13: 2; 18: 21), they are established and settled; they have the blessing of the Triune Godhead of Heaven as their seal and security; the hordes and hounds of evil set against them are tied and tangled up in a mess, and the light shines upon my ways (Job 22: 28).

In the engaging and enlightening name of the Father, Son, and Holy Ghost! God in three Persons, blessed Trinity!

AND IT IS SO!

Day 224

FORASMUCH as it is of the Lord's mercies that I am not consumed, because His compassions fail not (Lam. 3: 22), and because of His great faithfulness (Lam. 3: 23) I am alive and well in the land of the living with my faculties intact (Acts 17: 28); and

WHEREAS, this is a great day for me to pay homage, and to give honor, glory and praise to my Sovereign Heavenly Father for the awesome demonstration of His Almighty power in my life; and

WHEREAS, I magnify, praise, and worship the God of my salvation, who has faithfully tabernacled with me during my Christian journey in the earth, and I passionately long and yearn for more and more of God's power and presence in my life; and

WHEREAS, the signs of the times are everywhere in the earth; men's hearts are failing them for fear (Luke 21: 26), the hour is late, lost souls of the world are at stake, and this is the hour to proclaim and pronounce to all that the rapture of the Church is imminent, and that men ought to be ready for the sound of the trumpet (1 Cor. 15: 52); and

WHEREAS, necessity is laid upon me to win the lost (Prov. 11: 30), and to call mankind to salvation through the preaching and proclamation of the Gospel, as Jesus commanded in the Scriptures (Mark 16: 15; 1 Cor. 9: 16), and the challenge and charge to the Jesus's Church in the earth is a serious one.

I DECREE AND DECLARE this Day 224 that

- I will not compromise, dilute, or water down the message of the Gospel of Jesus Christ in the global village to reach souls; rather, I determine to preach the whole counsel of God (Acts 20: 27) in unapologetic and uncompromising ways that promote the truth only found in Jesus (Jn. 14: 6)

- I abandon the acclamation and applause of man, reject the promotion of the flesh, and discard all forms of religiosity in the Lord's Church that will devalue and diminish the centrality of the name of Jesus Christ, the Leader, and Lord of His Church (Col. 1: 18)

- I will only listen to the voice of the Holy Spirit (Acts 15: 28a) for direction, instruction, and wisdom (Jam. 1: 5) for my God-ordained assignments in the earth, and I will only initiate those ministry functions that are saturated and soaked in the disciplines of fasting and prayer (Matt. 17: 21)

- I realign and reposition myself for complete submission to the Lord's way and will (Psa. 40: 8); any other way is conformity to the world (Rom. 12: 2a), idolatry, and an insult to the Lord of glory

- I will seek God's power and presence in my life; the anointing has primacy and priority.

BE IT THEREFORE RESOLVED by me this day that

- I maintain my standing as an authentic Christian in the earth; remaining loyal to the call and commission of the Lord to preach the Gospel to every creature (Mark 16: 15)

- I will endeavor to please the Lord my Head, and, as this means causing agitation and angst to the enemy of my soul, I will not faint, falter, or fear his evil agendas

BY VIRTUE OF MY STANDING IN CHRIST, I DRIVE THESE DECREES, DECLARATIONS, AND RESOLUTIONS AS STAKES IN THE GROUND; by the fruit of my lips (Prov. 13: 2; 18: 21), they have their enforcement and establishment; Heaven's high and holy Court sanctions and seals them; satanic resistance to them is arrested and annihilated by the blood of Jesus, and the light shall shine upon my ways (Job 22: 28).

In the empowering and establishing name of the Father, Son, and Holy Ghost! God in three Persons, blessed Trinity!

AND IT IS SO!

Day 225

FORASMUCH as it was my Heavenly Father's providence and pleasure to assign an angel to watch over me throughout the night (Psa. 34: 7), and to touch me with His finger of love to arise today with life and limbs (Acts 17: 28); and

WHEREAS, like Mary, "My soul doth magnify the Lord, and my spirit hath rejoiced in God my Savior' (Luke 1: 46, 47), and the Psalmist, who said, "My heart is inditing (overflows with) a good matter...my tongue is the pen of a ready writer" (45: 1); and

WHEREAS, I excitedly and exuberantly proclaim the goodness and graciousness of God toward me for the great thing He has done by touching and transforming my life; and

WHEREAS, the change that God has made in my life is such that I am on a quest to populate the Kingdom of Heaven during this age of grace, and to plunder and pulverize the dark domain of hell before the trumpet sounds (1 Thess. 4: 16), and God's chosen people gather in the air from the four corners of the earth (Matt. 24: 31-41; 1 Thess. 4: 17); and

WHEREAS, the imminence of the rapture of the Church from the earth challenges me to win souls from eternal loss and separation from God in hell (Ezek. 33: 6, 7; Prov. 11: 30; Mark 16: 15, 16).

I DECREE AND DECLARE this Day 225 that

- preaching, teaching, and reaching lost souls with the Gospel of Jesus Christ is my commission in the earth, and I bar and banish all other practices and platforms that will prevent the main thing from remaining the main thing

- I will not allow or employ optional means by which I function to win the lost, and I will not tinker or trifle with the absolutes of the Gospel: God is Sovereign all by Himself (Isa. 45: 5); Jesus' precious blood is still the only means of redemption of the soul (Eph. 1: 7; Heb. 9: 14); the Holy Ghost still manifests and moves in the earth in power (Acts 2: 1-16; 39), and the Word of God still works (Rom. 1: 16; 1 Pet. 1: 23)

- I lay my affections on the altar and leave them there, lest I bring accusation and offence to the purity of the Gospel of Jesus in the global village (2 Cor. 6: 3)

- I rebuke and reject ritualism and rules over relationship with Jesus in my life, and I renounce all impiety and religiosity from my life, and Christ, alone remains on the throne (1 Cor. 2: 2) as the crucified One

- the ancient hallmarks and landmarks of Bible authenticity and centrality will not be lost on how I function in the earth; they remain my firmly established, grounded, and rooted core values in all that I undertake for the King and the Kingdom

BE IT THEREFORE RESOLVED by me this day that

- I will remain biblically relevant and radically righteous in this anti-God world, and my relationship with the Savior graces me to impact the globe with the transforming power of the Gospel of Jesus Christ - I remain committed to being Christ's vessel in the earth, and through the indwelling and convicting power of the Spirit, lost souls are drawn to the Savior

BY VIRTUE OF MY AUTHORITY BY THE HOLY SPIRIT, I CEMENT AND DRIVE THESE DECREES, DECLARATIONS, AND RESOLUTIONS AS STAKES IN THE GROUND; by my words (Prov. 13: 2; 18: 21), they are emphatically established and enforceable; Heaven's holy order sanctions and seals them; demonic opposition to them fall flatly to the ground in failure and futility, having no effect upon them (Isa. 54: 17), and the light shines upon my ways (Job 22: 28c).

In the hallowed, high and holy name of the Father, Son, and Holy Ghost! God in three Persons, blessed Trinity!

AND IT IS SO!

Day 226

FORASMUCH as there is nothing that I have done, or could do, to earn or merit the privilege of being alive and well today; it is all because of God's grace and goodness toward me (Psa. 27: 13); and

WHEREAS, rivers of joy overflow the banks of my soul as I consider the wonder of God's love and mercy toward me, and the marvelous works of His hand in my life; and

WHEREAS, I am not short on acclamation and shouts of praise to God for the glory He has manifested in the earth (Hab. 2: 14), and His power in my life; and

WHEREAS, all that is left is time to live for, and declare, the Gospel of Jesus Christ to every creature, as Jesus commanded in Mark 16: 15; and

WHEREAS, given the danger and darkness in the earth because of the scourge of sin, necessity is laid upon me to win the lost.

I DECREE AND DECLARE this Day 226 that

- I will not reduce or relegate the centrality of the message of salvation through Jesus to a hit-and-miss function; I will fully engage and declare the whole counsel of God (Acts 20: 27) in this sin-cursed world

- I will not be diverted and drawn away from hearing the voice of the Spirit for ministry functioning during these end-times, and petitioning and seeking what seems good to the Holy Ghost for ministry effectiveness will have prime importance to me (Acts 15: 28)

- I will be an authentic Christian in the global village as I proclaim the Gospel of Jesus to the lost, being loving, caring, kind, and inclusive; no one I engage with will be shut out from experiencing the life-transforming power of the message (Jn. 3: 16, 17)

- I welcome doors of opportunity the Lord opens for me to reach the lost, and despite adversity and agitation from the forces of evil against me (1 Cor. 16: 9), I will labor tirelessly and unflinchingly for the King and His Kingdom (Luke 19: 13)

- God is my Commander-in-Chief, Jesus is my treasure within (2 Cor. 4: 7), the Holy Ghost is my constant companion (Jn. 16: 13), the Word of God is our Compass and Instruction Manual (Psa. 119: 105), and I have one mindset that prevails: I TRIUMPH and WIN!

BE IT THEREFORE RESOLVED by me this day that

- I remain fully committed and submitted to the ways and will of the Father, expecting to reap an abundant harvest of souls for the Kingdom (Luke 14: 23)

- I remain hidden in the Rock (Psa. 18: 2-12), the safest place to be for refuge and rest from the Devil and his devices

BY THE BOLDNESS THAT THE HOLY SPIRIT GIVES ME, I HAMMER THESE DECREES, DECLARATIONS AND RESOLUTIONS AS STAKES IN THE GROUND; by the power of the words that I speak (Prov. 13: 2; 18: 21), they are established and settled; The Triune Godhead of Heaven sanctions and seals them; Satan's weapons against them are disheveled, dismembered and utterly destroyed, and the light shines upon my ways (Job 22: 28c).

In the Precious and Pre-eminent name of the Father, Son, and Holy Ghost! God in three Persons, blessed Trinity!

AND IT IS SO!

Day 227

FORASMUCH as my Father's hand of protection and providence were my blessings throughout the night as I rested, and then He blessed me and breathed His breath (Job 33: 4) into my body so that I can be alive another day (Acts 17: 28); and

WHEREAS, God has been/is being/and will continue to be, good to me; I find no fault in Him; He's my good, good Father, all His ways are perfect (Psa. 18: 30), and, as the songwriter said, "If He keeps on blessing and blessing, I don't know what I'm going to do"; and

WHEREAS, I am a witness to the mighty and Sovereign works of the Lord in my life, and to encounter God every day during my Christian journey can sometimes be indescribable; His ways are past finding out (Rom. 11: 33); and

WHEREAS, I am enjoying rich spiritual delicacies at the Lord's table; His banner over me is love (SS 2: 4), and my desire is that others will taste and see that the Lord is good (Psa. 34: 8); and

WHEREAS, in my joy and jubilation, the stark reality is that countless numbers of mankind are perishing in the destructiveness of sin; therefore, it is necessary that I engage the harvest as Jesus commanded (Mk. 16: 15) - His return is imminent; the trumpet shall sound; eternity looms.

I DECREE AND DECLARE this Day 227 that

- in light of eternity and the imminence of the trumpet sound (1 Cor. 15: 52), I discard a lifestyle and mindset that hinders my witness for Christ, and live and walk in authentic, biblical righteousness and truth that will draw men to Jesus (Matt. 5: 16)

- the ancient landmarks set by my spiritual fathers/elders have eternal significance and worth (Prov. 22: 28); therefore, I will not relegate and substitute these spiritual pillars for what is cheap, valueless and unfriendly to grace

- like the sons of Issachar, I will acclimatize and acquaint myself with the times (1 Chron. 12: 32), and provide solid and sound godly wisdom to those in seats of authority in the land

- I will assume an all-hands-on-deck mindset in my quest to win the lost, and I refuse to sit in the grandstand warming the bench and doing nothing for the King and the Kingdom (Lu. 2: 49; Col. 3: 23)

- I will rethink, reorganize, realign, and reposition myself, and redeem the time for effective, impactful, influential engagement for Jesus in the earth, until all have heard the glorious, life-changing message of salvation through Him alone (Jn. 14: 6; Acts 4: 12)

BE IT THEREFORE RESOLVED by me this day that

- I remain dedicated and loyal to the tenets of biblical authenticity in the global village, and be the "epistle" Paul spoke of, "known and read of all men" (2 Cor. 3: 2)

- I ignore blogs and bulletins of anti-God sentiment in the earth, and remain steadfast and unmovable (1 Cor. 15: 58) as I obey Jesus' command to "Go", "preach" and "teach" the Gospel to every creature

BY VIRTUE OF MY PRIVILEGE TO LIVE BY THE IMPUTED RIGHTEOUSNESS OF GOD THROUGH CHRIST (Rom. 3: 22), I DRIVE THESE DECREES, DECLARATIONS, AND RESOLUTIONS AS STAKES IN THE GROUND; they are established and settled by the fruit of my lips (Prov. 13: 2; 18: 21); the Unified Godhead of Heaven backs, blesses, and gives benediction to them; the plans, plots and ploys of Satan against them boomerang back to sender, and the light shall shine upon my ways (Job 22: 28c).

In the impenetrable, impregnable name of the Father, Son, and Holy Ghost! God in three Persons, blessed Trinity!

AND IT IS SO!

Day 228

DEDICATED TO YOUNG PEOPLE

FORASMUCH as it was my gracious Father's good pleasure to touch me to arise again today from overnight rest to be in the land of the living breathing His fresh air (Job 33: 4), having the use of my limbs, and the blessing of a sound mind to go on with Him; and

WHEREAS, today is a great day to praise the Lord, and to give thanks at the remembrance of His holiness (Psa. 3-: 4); and

WHEREAS, I count it all joy that I have the desire and longing to praise and worship the Lord with psalms and hymns and spiritual songs, singing and making melody in my heart to Him (Eph. 5: 19); and

WHEREAS, today for me, the prime importance of Jesus' command to "Go into all the world, and preach the gospel to every creature" (Mk. 16: 15) compels and prompts me to service for Him in the global village; and

WHEREAS, there is a necessity to abandon every humanistic practice and program for Kingdom effectiveness, and a return to, and realignment with, the central and core values of biblical authenticity, fidelity, and truth to minister for the King in the global village.

I DECREE AND DECLARE this Day 228 that

- although approaches and methods may change to win young people to the Lord who are lost in sin, the message of salvation through Jesus alone will not, by any means, be hidden from them (Acts 4: 12)

- I will not deceive or delude young people for them to come to Christ; rather, I will be ruthlessly honest with them, and call sin for what it is (Rom. 6: 23), wrong for what it is, and live a life of credibility and integrity before them that models genuine Christianity (2 Cor. 6: 3)

- I will give room for the youth to bloom and blossom with their spiritual gifts for the benefit of ministry functioning, and provide avenues for their enlargement and expansion in service for the King and His Kingdom (2 Pet. 3: 18)

- I will provide space for grace to the youth, a "no condemnation zone" of unconditional acceptance, inclusion, and love so that they have a safe harbor and haven when they encounter the storms of life

- the mighty hand of God's goodness and grace rests upon the youth in body of Christ; they have the help of Heaven, and their lives have impact and meaning for Jesus

BE IT THEREFORE RESOLVED by me this day that

- I will remain true to the Bible in these days of decadence, decay and decline, and the power of the Holy Ghost braces and blesses all that I do for Him with demonstrations and manifestations that bring glory and honor to Jesus

- I will not regress or relent in my labor and service for the King in the earth; "the night is far spent, the day is at hand" (Rom. 13: 12-14); the Father's business demands haste (Lu. 2: 49).

BY VIRTUE OF THE WITNESS OF THE BLOOD OF JESUS, I BOLDLY DRIVE THESE PROPHETIC DECREES, DECLARATIONS, AND RESOLUTIONS AS STAKES IN THE GROUND; by the fruit of my lips (Prov. 13: 2; 18: 21), they are established and settled in the earth; the high and holy order of Heaven seals and stamps them as "done"; the hordes and hounds of hell back off from them in horror and terror, and I am confident that the light shall shine upon my ways (Job 22: 28c).

In the delightful, desirable and dependable name of the Father, Son, and Holy Ghost! God in three Persons, blessed Trinity!

AND IT IS SO!

Day 229

FORASMUCH as I am a recipient of the choice blessings and bountifulness of my Sovereign Heavenly Father, who has graciously allowed me to arise to see a brand new day, I am alive only because of Him (Acts 17: 28), I magnify and praise Him; and

WHEREAS, this is a great day to glorify, honor, laud, magnify, praise, and worship my King, who delights in having rescued me from the grip, power and stain of sin, and transformed and translated me into the Kingdom of His Son (Col.1: 13); and

WHEREAS, I am moved to ascribe all glory and honor to God for choosing me to be His child (Jn. 15: 16), and I magnify Him for manifesting His awesome power and presence in my life; and

WHEREAS, the truth is that I ambled along the path of life aimlessly and without direction, and instantaneously, and without notice or warning, the light of Jesus broke through, and the nightmare of my life became the song of the soul set free (Psa. 32: 7); and

WHEREAS, suddenly, based on Psa. 126; 137: 1-4; and Acts 2: 1-2, the Omnipotence of God moved, reversed, and turned my life around, and circumstances and situations of my life became aligned to the timing of His divine plans and purposes.

I DECREE AND DECLARE this Day 229 that

- life had me discarded, disqualified, dumped, and left for dead, and suddenly, help arrived, hope sprang alive in me, and I sing a song that even angels cannot – I am redeemed (Psa. 77: 15)

- our personal "and suddenly" is not contingent or dependent upon what someone does or does not do for me; it is the Lord's doing (Psa. 118: 23), and men will know and see that God signed and sealed my life for His glory

- I will resolutely and steadfastly fix and focus my affections upon the goodness and greatness of God (Col. 3: 2), and He will undoubtedly "suddenly" show up and demonstrate His power and providence

- I will sow seeds in fertile waters, and watch and weep and wait for the harvest; the Lord will work, and I will reap and return rejoicing with the sheaves (Psa. 126: 6)

- my "suddenly" will aggravate and antagonize my chief accuser, the Devil, and because this "suddenly" is the hand of the Lord, the actions and reactions of the Adversary to God's "and suddenly" in my life only serves to cement and secure God's ways, will, and work (Jer. 29: 11)

BE IT THEREFORE RESOLVED by me this day that

- my heart and spirit remains in rhythm and syncopation with the Holy Ghost, and I will remember Zion, even in a strange place (Psa. 137: 4)

- I will not forget to remember what the Lord has done for me, and even the heathen will speak of the great things He has done (Psa. 126: 2)

BY VIRTUE OF MY REDEMPTION STATUS IN CHRIST, I DRIVE THESE PROPHETIC DECREES, DECLARATIONS, AND RESOLUTIONS AS STAKES IN THE GROUND; they are established and settled by the words I speak (Prov. 13: 2; 18: 21); Heaven's high and holy order sanctions and secures them as "done"; the works of the dark domain against them are outnumbered and outwitted, and the light shall shine upon my ways (Job 22: 28c).

In the All-Sufficient and All-Supreme name of the Father, the Son, and the Holy Ghost! One God in three Persons, blessed Trinity!

AND IT IS SO!

Day 230

FORASMUCH as the angel of the Lord brooded over me during the night, and God, by His power, held death at bay from me, and by His finger of love, He raised me to behold the dawn of a new day with life and limbs (Acts 17: 28); and

WHEREAS, I exclaim and shout from the rooftop that God is good (1 Chr. 16: 34) - incomprehensibly good, inexplicably good, manifestly good, mysteriously good, praiseworthy good, mmm mmm good; and every time I talk about the Lord, I feel good; and

WHEREAS, with abundant joy and heartfelt thanksgiving, I laud and lavish praise to the Lord for the privilege by His grace to encounter intimate fellowship with Him every day, and to receive my daily bread from the His table (Matt. 6: 11); and

WHEREAS, I was not, but now am "in Christ"; I had not obtained mercy, but now have, and I enjoy the honor of being chosen and given entrance and access to my Fathers throne (1 Pet. 2: 9, 10); and

WHEREAS, God touched me, He turned me, and He tuned my heart to sing praises unto Him, all because of my "and suddenly" moment, when the Holy Ghost filled and took abode within me in glory and power.

I DECREE AND DECLARE this Day 230 that

- the "and suddenly" day of God's power and presence will permeate my surroundings in copious measures, and everyone I associate will be impacted by the torrential outpouring and rain of breakthrough, deliverance, healing, liberty, and salvation that the Holy Spirit brings (Isa. 59: 16; 61: 1-3);

- the "and suddenly" of God's high and holy arm will influence jobs and places of association and employment where I am to the degree and extent that fear and a holy reverence for God, and a revival of Holy Ghost proportions will blanket and envelope businesses and centers of enterprise and commerce for the glory of God (Prov. 14: 34);

- the "and suddenly" of God's hand of healing will touch the despised, diseased, and downcast, "and suddenly", they shall celebrate, shout and sing the high praises of God - Deliverer, Way Maker, and Miracle Worker (Isa.53: 5);

- as He fell and manifested His power in the First Century Church, I call forth the "and suddenly" of the Holy Ghost of God upon cell Bible study groups, congregations, and church denominations in the global village, and a tsunami of holy anointing will cause astonishment and awe as God moves and manifests His miraculous power in the earth by His Spirit (Hab. 2: 14);

- I intercept and interrupt every demonic plot set against the move of God in the earth, and I wield every weapon available to me in God's armor to pull down strongholds and principalities that seek to exalt themselves above the knowledge of God (2 Cor. 10: 4, 5).

BE IT THEREFORE RESOLVED by me this day that

- I remain encamped in God's "and suddenly" zone, availing myself to receive all that my Father has provided

- at no time, and under any circumstance, will I surrender to alternatives and substitutes to God's authentic glory and power

BY VIRTUE OF MY POSITION IN CHRIST (Eph. 2: 6), I DRIVE THESE PROPHETIC DECREES, DECLARATIONS, AND RESOLUTIONS AS STAKES IN THE GROUND; by the fruit of my lips, we establish, seal and set them (Prov. 13: 2; 18: 21); Heaven is pleased to affirm and approve them as "done"; demonic and diabolical schemes and systems against them are dead, doomed and dusted, and the light shall shine upon my ways (Job 22: 28c).

In the indivisible and invincible name of the Father, Son, and Holy Ghost! One God, three Persons; blessed Trinity!

AND IT IS SO!

Day 231

FORASMUCH as God's grace and kindness has been extended to me to be alive another day, and I enjoy the benefits of His Providence and Sovereignty; and

WHEREAS, I rejoice in the goodness of God in my life as I journey with Him as His child in the earth, and I praise Him for delivering me, healing me, liberating me, and saving and setting me free, by the power of His hand; and

WHEREAS, God continues to astound and amaze me for how He manifests Himself in my life; glory and honor are due to Him through the fruit of my lips through intense and intentional praise, prayer, and worship of Him (Heb 13: 15); and

WHEREAS, the quickening power of God is evident in my life; He specializes in things thought impossible, and He undoubtedly can do what no other power can do; I am witness to His amazing power; and

WHEREAS, according to Psalm 126; 137: 1-4; and Acts 2: 1-4, God is the God of the suddenly; "And Suddenly" sets Him apart and distinct from any and all others in terms of Divine and supernatural manifestations and power; let all the other gods fade away before Him!

I DECREE AND DECLARE this Day 231 that

- I set my gaze upon the "And Suddenly" of God, who alone can do anything but fail, and as I wait on Him to manifest His promised power and presence (Acts 2: 1), I engage in intense and intentional praise and worship of His holy name by the fruit of my lips (Heb. 13: 15)

- I will not engage in fighting back, settling scores, or seeking vengeance against those who oppose me (Deut. 32: 35; Rom. 12: 17-19); "And Suddenly", God reverses the effect and impact of my doubters and detractors upon me, and He causes them to be at peace with me (Prov. 16: 7)

- I will seek to personally know the voice of God, and when Satan appears to have me circled or cornered, "And Suddenly" God blocks enemy hostility (Isa. 54: 17), and He who sees in secret rewards me openly (Matt. 6: 4)

- the Holy Spirit dwells within me in power (Acts 1: 8; 2: 1-4); God's "And Suddenly" is a treasure worth having in perilous times, and I will not endorse or entertain anything in my life that is illegal or prohibited in the Spirit that will contaminate who I am in Him (2 Cor. 6: 15-17)

BE IT THEREFORE RESOLVED by me this day that

- God has turned my captivity (Psa. 126: 4), and singing unto the Lord remains my constant anthem, chief joy, and testimony

- I refuse to forget the holy solemnities of God (Jerusalem - Psa. 137: 5), and I long and yearn for the power and presence of God to overflow from and through me

BY THE AUTHORITY OF MY RIGHTEOUS STANDING WITH GOD IN CHRIST (Eph. 1: 3), I DRIVE THESE DECREES, DECLARATIONS, AND RESOLUTIONS AS STAKES AND TESTIMONIALS IN THE GROUND; they are established and settled in the earth by the words I speak (Prov. 13: 2; 18: 21); Heaven fully backs and blesses their establishment; satanic assaults against them are reduced to a puff of wind, and the light shall shine upon my ways (Job 22: 28). "AND SUDDENLY", God turns the fight into my favor!

In the indisputable and indivisible name of the Father, Son, and the Holy Ghost! God in three Persons, blessed Trinity!

AND IT IS SO!

Day 232

FORASMUCH as the compassions (Lam. 3: 22, 23), lovingkindness and tender mercies of my Heavenly Father have been freely given to me today to be alive and well, and because of Jesus, life now is sweet, and my joy is complete (Jn. 10: 10); and

WHEREAS, the unspeakable joy that fills and overflows the banks of my soul can sometimes be difficult to explain; therefore, continuous and unceasing eruptions of praise and thanksgiving to God gush forth from my heart through my mouth, and into the atmosphere (Heb. 13: 15) for all to see; and

WHEREAS, as I journey in the Spirit, I rejoice that God blocked Satan for me, cancelled his hostility against me, did it for, in, and through me, and by the Holy Ghost, He empowered me..." And Suddenly!"; and

WHEREAS, Psa. 126; 137: 1-4, and Acts 2: 1-4 cements my witness of God's visitation in my life, and His glorious power has guarded and guided me while the stormy seas rolled, and now, I am edified, enabled, encouraged, and equipped with timeless truths of how "Suddenly" God takes and turns my captivity (Psa. 126: 1), and as He leads me safely into the harbor and haven of rest (Psa. 107: 28-31), I joyfully sing a song of the Lord's deliverance (Psa. 126: 2).

I DECREE AND DECLARE this Day 232 that

- my journey is one of joy and jubilation; God took and turned my captivity and chaos into delight and deliverance (Psa. 126: 2)

- Zion calls me to a higher place of praise; "And Suddenly", we take my harp off the willow, and right in the strange land, I shout and sing songs of liberty and life (Psa. 137: 2) in Christ (Eph. 1: 3)

- I am fully ablaze with Pentecostal firepower (Acts 2: 4); "And Suddenly", my critics are amazed, astonished, and in awe at the fertility and fruitfulness of God in my life

- the "And Suddenly" of God in my life is beyond the reach of diabolical duress of the Devil against me, and I will walk with a pep in my step, my head is held high, I will weep no more, but reap the harvest of sheaves, and return with rejoicing (Psa. 126: 6)

BE IT THEREFORE RESOLVED by me this day that

- I remember the great things the Lord has done for me (Psa. 126: 3), and I refuse to harbor wailing and woe in my spirit

- I remember that I am a beneficiary of God's "And Suddenly"; therefore, I laugh, live and love unconditionally

WITH THE CONFIDENCE I HAVE IN GOD'S "AND SUDDENLY" IN ME, I DRIVE THESE DECREES, DECLARATIONS, AND RESOLUTIONS AS PILLARS

AND STAKES IN THE GROUND; they are established and settled in the earth by the fruit of my mouth (Prov. 13: 2; 18: 21); Heaven's high and holy court affirms and confirms their establishment; satanic bombardments against them boomerang back to the sender, and the light shines upon my ways (Job 22: 28). The Lord turned it..." And Suddenly"!

In the transforming and triumphant name of the Father, the Son, and the Holy Ghost! God in three Persons, blessed Trinity!

AND IT IS SO!

Day 233

A DECLARATION FOR YOUNG PEOPLE

FORASMUCH as the faithfulness of my loving Heavenly Father has been shown to me one more day; the angel of the Lord encamped round about me throughout the night (Psa. 34: 7); then, by God's hand of Omnipotence, He woke me up this morning to a day full of promises and prospects in Him (Jer. 29: 11); and

WHEREAS, today I am ecstatic and joyful about the manifestations of God's grace and supernatural power in my life; He has undoubtedly touched and transformed my life and living; and

WHEREAS, God at times has moved instantaneously on my behalf, and the immediate turnaround for good seemed like a dream, as the psalmist declared in Psalm 126, and my lamenting has turned to laughter and singing (Psa. 126: 2); and

WHEREAS, what God is doing in the global village speaks to whom He is - the God of immediacy AND SUDDENLY (Acts 2: 1-4), who has no equal or rival, nor has He ever taken counsel from anyone, at any time, about anything, anywhere (Rom. 11: 34; Eph. 1: 11).

I DECREE AND DECLARE this Day 233 that

- God will manifest Himself in the Present Next Generation, the youth, AND SUDDENLY, like David who tended sheep, they will take down Goliath (1 Sam. 17: 49)

- this is their season; they are favored by the unmerited grace of God, AND SUDDENLY, like Ruth who worked the field, they own it (Ruth 4: 9-12)

- theirs is the God of the unthinkable turnaround; life in Lodebar had them limp, losing and lost (2 Sam. 9: 4, 5), AND SUDDENLY, like Mephibosheth, they feast from their seat on the king's meat at the king's table (2 Sam. 9: 13)

- they will not bow their knees to the anti-God systems around them, but will stand true to the One and ONLY living God; this may land them in the fiery furnace like the Hebrew boys, AND SUDDENLY, God, who controls the thermostat, will turn the heat off (Dan. 3: 25)

BE IT THEREFORE RESOLVED by me this day that

- the youth will remember the days of sowing and weeping, AND SUDDENLY, they are reaping, returning, and rejoicing (Psa. 126: 6)

- the youth will not forget the great things God has done for them; He took them, touched them, transformed and turned them...AND SUDDENLY!

BY THE AUTHORITY OF MY BLESSINGS IN HEAVENLY PLACES IN CHRIST (Eph. 1: 3), I DRIVE THESE DECREES, DECLARATIONS, AND

RESOLUTIONS AS SOLID STAKES IN THE GROUND; they are established and settled in the earth by the words that I speak (Prov. 13: 2; 18: 21); the witness of Heaven says "Yes" to them; satanic resistance against them is rebuffed and reduced to ruin, and the light shall shine upon their ways (Job 22: 28). AND SUDDENLY... God triggered a tremendous turnaround!

In the undaunted, undefeated, and undeniably powerful name of the Father, Son, and Holy Ghost! One God, three Persons! Blessed Trinity!

AND IT IS SO!

Day 234

FORASMUCH it is the Father's good pleasure and will to allow me by His compassions and mercies to arise to a brand new day with life and fulness of joy in Him (Acts 17: 28); and

WHEREAS, yesterday is gone, and will never be again, and tomorrow may never be mine; therefore, because I only have today, I take every opportunity to honor, praise and worship my Heavenly Father, who is greatly to be praised (Psa. 145: 3); and

WHEREAS, I am full of unspeakable gladness and joy today for the unsearchable goodness and greatness of God to me as I journey in this earth as His child; and

WHEREAS, the excitement I have is because when I think of the goodness of Jesus, and all He has done for me; my soul cries out and shouts HALLELUJAH!; thank God for saving me (Psa. 126: 1)!

I DECREE AND DECLARE this Day 234 that

- I will not walk and wallow in misery and murmuring; that is the mire I was in yesterday; AND SUDDENLY the Savior appeared, He paid the price of my ransom and redemption (Col. 1: 14)...and I AM SAVED!

- I will not be lulled and lured into spiritual apathy and lethargy; I AM SAVED; Jesus is alive in me; He's my sanctifier, my satisfier, and my source (1 Thess. 2: 13)

- I confidently proclaim the secret of my strength, weakness, weariness, and wretchedness had sway over me; AND SUDDENLY, God's grace and mercy said "No"; AND SUDDENLY, singing and shouts of joy rang out..." I AM SAVED", and I know that I am

- this is my season of the Supernatural in my life; AND SUDDENLY, Holy Ghost power takes dominance, precedence and preeminence over the weak and beggarly elements of life, and miracles, signs and wonders manifest in me according to God's will (Heb. 2: 4)

BE IT THEREFORE RESOLVED by me this day that

- I remain a vessel unto honor (2 Tim. 2: 21) wherein the treasure dwells (2 Cor. 4: 7); there's no more wallowing in the mire (2 Pet. 2: 20-22)

- I rest myself in the safe harbor and haven of salvation in Christ (Psa. 107: 29, 30; Acts 4: 12), and will take no chance of getting lost

BY VIRTUE OF MY BLOOD-CLEANSING AND WASHING BY CHRIST (Eph. 1: 7), I DRIVE THESE DECREES, DECLARATIONS, AND RESOLUTIONS AS STAKES IN THE GROUND; they are established and settled by the fruit of my lips (Prov. 13: 2; 18: 21); Heaven is all too pleased to affirm and approved them; the wind of the Sprit blows all satanic systems against them off course and into chaos and confusion, and the light shall shine upon my ways (Job 22: 28). I am no longer a slave! I AM SAVED!

In the unfailing, unfathomable, unforgettable name of the Father, the Son, and the Holy Ghost! God in three Persons, blessed Trinity!

AND IT IS SO!

Day 235

FORASMUCH as my Sovereign Father cared for and watched over me throughout the night as I slept safely in Him; then, He breathed His air (Job 33: 4) into my body and granted me the blessing and privilege of life (Acts 17: 28); and

WHEREAS, it is truly amazing that God continues to superintend over my life; His providential care of me as one of His children is simply astonishing and awesome; what a mighty God I serve!; and

WHEREAS, God is a going and a moving God; He specializes in things thought impossible and unthinkable; there is no searching of His understanding (Isa. 40: 28), and His power has no boundaries or limits; and

WHEREAS, He is the God of the "And Suddenly", and Psalm 126; 137: 1-4, and Acts 2: 1-4 demonstrate and speak distinctly to the awesome ability of God to move instantaneously, suddenly and without notice or warning, in circumstances and situations on behalf of His chosen people in the earth..."when the Lord turned again the captivity of Zion" (Psa. 126: 1a); and

WHEREAS, when the Omnipotent God acts, He does so after the counsel of His own will (Eph. 1: 11); "And Suddenly", I AM DELIVERED praise His name becomes the speech and the song that erupts from the heart of the delivered one.

I DECREE AND DECLARE this Day 235 that

- I was held captive by Satan and sin - that's my past; "I Am Delivered" is now the anthem of my soul; no more chains hold me

- my soul rests safely and securely in the Father's great work of deliverance in me, and satanic backlash, residue and stains of the past have no authority over me (Isa. 54: 17)

- I do not have amnesia, my brain is not idle, nor am I deluded; multiplied sadness, sighing, and sorrow are memories of my yesterday (Isa. 51: 11); "I Am Delivered" is not a figment of my imagination, but a song of emancipation and freedom from captivity and enslavement permeates the atmosphere of my life, and gushes forth with unspeakable and unstoppable joy from my lips (Psa. 150: 1, 2)

- my present distress and duress do not define or describe my end; "And Suddenly", sorrow becomes my sowing, and rejoicing will be my reaping, and in the bleak face of danger, waving crops of the harvest invite me to a golden harvest (Psa. 126: 6).

BE IT THEREFORE RESOLVED by me this day that

- I embrace the toil of sowing precious seed, knowing that my reaping time is coming by and by (Psa. 126: 6)

- I remain persuaded that God has better and greater things for me, and shouts and songs of deliverance from captivity fully dominate my life and living

BY THE AUTHORITY OF MY GOD-GIVEN DELIVERANCE AND LIBERTY, I DRIVE THESE PROPHETIC DECREES, DECLARATIONS, AND RESOLUTIONS AS MARKERS AND STAKES IN THE GROUND; they are established and set in the earth by the words of my mouth (Prov. 13: 2; 18: 21); Heaven fully legislates and legitimizes them; Satan's hordes set against them are smothered and stifled, and the light shall shine upon my ways (Job 22: 28). I AM DELIVERED! I have met the Man from Galilee! I am free!

In the bondage-breaking, shackle-releasing name of the Father, Son, and Holy Ghost! God in three Persons, blessed Trinity!

AND IT IS SO!

Day 236

FORASMUCH as the safe and strong hand of my Heavenly Father kept me from danger, disaster, and death throughout the night, and He has blessed me to arise today with a sound mind and life in Him (Acts 17: 28); and

WHEREAS, I am highly favored and blessed by God to continue my journey of joy with the Lord in the global village; I am a beneficiary of the abundant bestowments of His providential care; and

WHEREAS, praise and thanksgiving resound and rise unto my King for the amazing manifestations of His power and presence in my life, and God is never short of surprises of grace and sudden demonstrations of breakthrough and victory for me; and

WHEREAS, "And Suddenly", based on Psalms 126; 137: 1-4; and Acts 2: 1-4, has me contemplating the unequalled and unrivaled nature of how immediately, quickly and suddenly God moves (Acts 2: 1), and the impact and results are astonishing and astounding (Acts 2: 12).

I DECREE AND DECLARE this Day 236 that

- this "And Suddenly" of God causes my spirit to soar, and my mouth erupts with intense praise and worship to God with shouts of "I AM FILLED"; the banks of my soul overflow with gratitude and thanksgiving for the amazing and marvelous things He has done for me (Psa. 118: 23)

- "I AM FILLED" with power; the dynamic enablement of the promised Holy Spirit who lives in me, and who guides me into all truth (Jn. 16: 13) as a Kingdom citizen in the earth armed with the King's mandate and mission (Rev. 1: 6)

- "I AM FILLED"; my speech has changed; I no longer speak of the mire, the misery, and the muck of my yesterday (Psa. 40: 2); instead, my tongue is now the pen of a ready writer (Psa. 45: 1), and my testimony loudly echoes overcoming triumph and victory every day and everywhere I go (Rev. 12: 11)

- "I AM FILLED"; Holy Ghost power has taken me, touched me, turned me, and transformed me, I, the nobody, will tell everybody about Somebody who can favor and fill anybody

BE IT THEREFORE RESOLVED by me this day that

- I remain postured to receive the continuous infilling and overflowing of the power and presence of the Holy Ghost in my life (Eph. 5: 18, 19)

- I remain a filled and going child of God who sow in tears, knowing that I will reap and return with rejoicing, bringing the sheaves (the harvest of souls) with me (Psa. 126: 6)

BY VIRTUE OF THE RESILIENCE AND TOUGHNESS OF THE HOLY GHOST WHO LIVES IN ME, I DRIVE THESE DECREES, DECLARATIONS, AND RESOLUTIONS AS ANCHORS AND STAKES IN THE

GROUND; by the fruit of my mouth, they are enforced and established (Prov. 13: 2; 18: 21); Heaven is pleased to sanction and seal them; the designs and devices of the dark domain set against them are busted, destroyed, and dusted, and the light shall shine upon my ways (Job 22: 28).

I AM FILLED WITH GOD's FAVOR, FERTILITY AND FIRE!

In the highly Exalted, Holy and Excellent, name of the Father, the Son, and the Holy Ghost! One God in three Persons, blessed Trinity!

AND IT IS SO!

Day 237

FORASMUCH as my Heavenly Father has lavished His unfailing love upon me with the blessing to arise from rest throughout the night with breath in my body (Job 33: 4), and the added blessing of eternal life in Christ (Eph. 1: 3b); and

WHEREAS, right now is as best a time as ever to praise the Lord, and to proclaim His greatness and power as the Sovereign God of all, who is above all, and through all, and in all (Eph. 4: 6); and

WHEREAS, today I joyfully and jubilantly offer thanksgiving and worship unto God by the fruit of my lips (Heb. 13: 15) for the great, marvelous, and wonderful works of His hand in and upon my life; and

WHEREAS, God is the God of "And Suddenly" (Acts 2: 1-4), and I make a bold announcement for the world to hear, know, and see: "I AM REVIVED!"

I DECREE AND DECLARE this Day 237 that

- "I AM REVIVED"; distinctly alive, and will not die accidentally or prematurely, but I will declare the works of the risen, reviving Lord in me until He promotes me to glory, or the trumpet sound announces the rapture of the Church (Psa. 118: 17)

- "I AM REVIVED"; "RE" meaning again and again and again, and my repetition of "I AM REVIVED" loudly echoes and reverberates in the corridors of my spirit; "And Suddenly" joy (Phil. 4: 4), singing (Psa. 126: 2), and worship (Jn. 4: 24) pierces and reverses my negative circumstances and situations

- "I AM REVIVED"; the breath and wind of the Holy Ghost has resuscitated my inner man, and the flame and fire of revival resurrects every dead thing in me that God has planned and purposed to be activated and fully functional in the Kingdom (Jer 29: 11)

- "I AM REVIVED"; and every plot, quandary, and reviling of the Devil against me is subject to death; he cannot and will not prevail against the power and quickening of the Spirit who lives in me (Isa. 54: 17)

BE IT THEREFORE RESOLVED by me this day that

- triumph and victory in Zion is my anthem and song, and I remain saturated, soaked and steeped with the refreshing aroma and fragrance of revival that the Spirit brings

- I will activate, live, preach, teach, and think "I AM REVIVED" until others come forth and are loosed from the bands, chains and shackles of death to live again

BY VIRTUE OF MY REVIVAL AND RESURRECTION, I DRIVE THESE DECREES, DECLARATIONS, AND RESOLUTIONS AS TESTIMONIAL STAKES IN THE

GROUND; they are established and settled in the earth by the life in the power of my words (Prov. 18: 21); the Triune Godhead of Heaven is pleased to affirm and approve their establishment; the hordes and hounds of hell designed to derail them are handcuffed and hauled off to the prison of death and destruction, and the light shall shine upon my ways (Job 22: 28). My space has been invaded by mercy and grace! I AM REVIVED!

In the redeeming, resurrecting, and reviving name of the Father, the Son, and the Holy Ghost! God in three Persons, blessed Trinity!

AND IT IS SO!

Day 238

FORASMUCH as "it is a good thing to give thanks unto the Lord, and to sing praises unto His name, the Most High" (Psa. 92: 1), on this brand new day, full-term pregnant with promises and prospects because of Jesus, thanksgiving and worship to the Most High are the expressions of my heart; and

WHEREAS, I reflect with awe and wonder upon the might and power that God has demonstrated and manifested in my life on so many occasions; and

WHEREAS, the immediate and sudden deliverance and turning of captivity by God evoked a song in the Old Testament (Psa. 126: 1, 2), and the immediate and sudden descent of the Holy Ghost upon the 120 disciples in the Upper Room that prompted supernatural wonders of speech in the New Testament, depict how deliberate and intentional God is when He manifests "And Suddenly" moments for His children in the earth; and

WHEREAS, I recall and remember how barren, battered, broken, and bruised I was from the traumas and troubles of life, when God invaded my space with His "And Suddenly", and now my song from that nightmare is "I AM HEALED"!

I DECREE AND DECLARE this Day 238 that

- "I AM HEALED" testifies to the new place and season I am in, no longer broken and bruised, but mended and made whole, nothing wanting, and nothing wasted (Jn. 5: 1-14)

- "I AM HEALED", not only from bodily infirmity, but also from spiritual affliction; we will NOT stay where weak and beggarly elements abound, but will abide in the complete and total wholeness that God's "And Suddenly" brought to our lives

- "I AM HEALED", and the same power that broke the malady off my life suddenly ushers forth the manifestation and miracle needed by others in Jesus' name!

- "I AM HEALED"; completely, totally, and without question, in soul, spirit, and body (Ex. 15: 26; Isa. 53: 5; Jer. 30: 17), and every lie and lure of Satan that speaks (Jn. 8: 44) to the contrary I refuse, reject and resist in Jesus' name!

BE IT THEREFORE RESOLVED by me this day that

- I remain at rest in the promise that healing is my bread (Matt. 15: 22-29); "And Suddenly"!

- my faith in God's supernatural ability to do exceeding, abundantly, above all (Eph. 3: 20) will not wane, weaken, or wilt - God turned it for me!

"I AM HEALED"; THEREFORE, I DRIVE THESE DECREES, DECLARATIONS, AND RESOLUTIONS AS IMMOVABLE STAKES IN THE GROUND; they are established and settled by the fruit of my mouth (Prov. 13: 2; 18: 21); the Unified Godhead of Heaven is pleased to grace and grant them holy assent; the suddenly of the Spirit of God smothers and sweeps away all satanic interferences set against them, and the light shall shine upon my ways (Job 22 28).

God blocked it, God turned it, and He did it for me! I AM HEALED!

In the All-Powerful, Only-Wise name of the Father, Son, and Holy Ghost! God in three Persons, blessed Trinity!

AND IT IS SO!

Day 239

FORASMUCH as the faithfulness and providential care of our Heavenly Father is the reason why I am alive and well today, and His blessings upon me evoke a deep desire within to live for and serve Him acceptably with reverence and godly fear (Heb. 12: 28) in the earth; and

WHEREAS, I rejoice with exceeding joy for the marvelous and miraculous acts of His hand upon my life, and praise, thanksgiving and worship erupts from my heart and into the atmosphere (Heb. 13: 15); and

WHEREAS, I am moved by God to march militantly on in the earth, conquering and to conquer (Rev. 6: 2); deliverance is my song, healing is in my hands, everlasting joy, and gladness in my heart (2 Tim. 2: 4); and

WHEREAS, the bondage-breaking, chain-destroying, mountain-moving God, who can do anything but fail, has pierced and penetrated the captivity of my life; I was harassed and hassled by the adversary, the Devil, and God's power has chased the intruder away, and I now shout aloud from the housetop, "I AM CHANGED"... "And Suddenly"!

I DECREE AND DECLARE this Day 239 that

- God's "And Suddenly" has shifted the atmosphere of my life; the wind of the Spirit has blown into my being, and the firepower of Heaven has altered and moved me for good (Acts 2: 1-4)

- "I AM CHANGED"; bondage is broken, captivity has turned (Psa. 126: 1), chains snapped off, and demise and depression were preludes to my deliverance (Isa. 61: 1)

- "I AM CHANGED"; "And Suddenly", the power of God intercepts, interrupts, and intrudes upon the insurrections and satanic schemes and systems designed to derail and destroy me (Isa. 54: 17);

- "I AM CHANGED"; praise is now my weapon of choice in warfare (Eph. 6: 18), Holy Ghost power pushes back the darkness (Zech. 4: 6), and the Word of God promotes and prompts an inner blaze within me (Jer. 20: 9; Heb. 4: 12)

BE IT THEREFORE RESOLVED by me this day that

- I will not miss the season of power and purpose that God has orchestrated and ordained for me (Jer. 1: 5; 29: 11)

- I will unapologetically proclaim the good news that drew me to a suddenly "I-AM-CHANGED" encounter with God (Luke 14: 23; Acts 9: 4-20)

BY VIRTUE OF THE SUDDEN "I AM CHANGED" BY GOD UPON MY LIFE, I DRIVE THESE PROPHETIC DECREES, DECLARATIONS, AND RESOLUTIONS AS IMMOVABLE STAKES IN THE GROUND; they have their establishment by the fruit and power of my words (Prov. 13: 2; 18: 21); Heaven fully backs and braces them as secure and settled; the angst and antagonism of anti-Christ devices set against them are ruptured and ruined, and the light shall shine upon my ways (Job 22: 28).

In the Devil-chasing, yoke-destroying name of the Father, Son, and Holy Ghost! God in three Persons, blessed Trinity!

AND IT IS SO!

Day 240

FORASMUCH as my gracious, kind, and loving Father has breathed breath into my body one more time (Job 33: 4); He woke me up this morning, and allowed me the privilege of life because of Him (Acts 17: 28); and

WHEREAS, I only have this day and time to lift my heart, hands and voice unto God in thanksgiving and thunderous applause for the awesome, marvelous, and mighty things He has done for me; and

WHEREAS, in Christ dwells all the fulness of the Godhead bodily (Col. 2: 9), and since God has blessed me with all spiritual blessings in heavenly places in Christ (Eph. 1: 3); and

WHEREAS my cup runneth over with joy, I find it easy to pray, and to sing every day, for my cup runneth over with joy, which is unspeakable and full of glory (1 Pet. 1: 8b); and

WHEREAS, the reason for the inexplicable joy and jubilation of my heart is that God has invaded my space, and, "When God

Invades Your Space", He blesses ALL that I have, according to 1 Chron. 13: 14.

I DECREE AND DECLARE this Day 240 that

- God saw and searched me out; saved and sanctified my life, and the invasion of salvation in Christ has filled me to the overflow, and I am not the same (2 Cor. 5: 17)

- there has been a God-invasion of my space; I did not get what I deserved (mercy - Eph. 2: 4, 5)), and got what I did not deserve (grace - 1 Cor. 15: 10), the life-altering and soul-transforming blessings of being in Christ (Eph. 1: 3)

- like Obed-Edom, and all that pertained to his house, the bestowments of God's blessings and bountifulness drape and drench everything and everyone connected to me, and the glory and goodness of God's hand permeates my space

- God has invaded my space, and anthems, hymns, and songs of praise, thanksgiving and worship erupt from within me (Heb. 13: 15), and they pierce and pervade the atmosphere of my life to the extent that astonishment and awe overcomes those with whom I connect

BE IT THEREFORE RESOLVED by me this day that

- I will announce, proclaim, speak, and testify to the masses that the Person and work of Christ has invaded my space, and reversed all that the devil thought he had done to me

- I will remain in right standing with God and His righteousness imputed into me because of Christ (2 Cor. 5: 21)

BY VIRTUE OF MY ADOPTION, SONSHIP, KINGLY, AND PRIESTLY POSITION WITH GOD IN CHRIST, I

DRIVE THESE DECREES, DECLARATIONS, AND RESOLUTIONS AS ANCHORS AND STAKES IN THE GROUND; they have their establishment and settlement by the words I speak (Prov. 13: 2); the Triune Godhead of Heaven signs, seals, and stamps them as "done"; the hordes and hosts of hell tremble in terror because of them, and the light does shine upon my ways (Job 22: 28). God has invaded my space with mercy and grace!

In the all-consuming, all-invading name of the Father, Son, and Holy Ghost! God in three Persons, blessed Trinity!

AND IT IS SO!

Printed in Great Britain
by Amazon

43598550R00219